C. L. R. James
and Revolutionary Marxism

C. L. R. James
and Revolutionary Marxism

Selected Writings of C. L. R. James
1939–1949

Edited by
Scott McLemee
and Paul Le Blanc

Haymarket Books
Chicago, Illinois

Originally published in 1994 by Humanities Press International, Inc.

This edition published in 2018 by
Haymarket Books
P.O. Box 180165
Chicago, IL 60618
www.haymarketbooks.org

ISBN: 978-1-60846-864-5

Trade distribution:
In the US, Consortium Book Sales and Distribution, www.cbsd.com
In Canada, Publishers Group Canada, www.pgcbooks.ca
In the UK, Turnaround Publisher Services, www.turnaround-uk.com
All other countries, Ingram Publisher Services International,
IPS_Intlsales@ingramcontent.com

This book was published with the generous support of
Lannan Foundation and Wallace Action Fund.

Cover design by Rachel Cohen.

Library of Congress Cataloging-in-Publication data is available.

Entered into digital printing February, 2021.

Contents

Acknowledgments

Since my first encounter with C. L. R. James's work in 1988, I have been encouraged and assisted by a number of his friends and associates. Research into the development of James's thinking and activity has in itself been extremely rewarding as an investment of energy. But no less gratifying is the sense of community, even at times of collective effort, that has accompanied the process. In preparing this volume alone, I have incurred debts of gratitude to several people. It is with pleasure that I acknowledge if not repay them now.

Marty Glaberman—"an unreconstructed Johnsonite, there aren't too many around any more," as he once put it—provided me with innumerable source materials from his papers at Wayne State University. He also shared otherwise impossible-to-get pamphlets, anecdotes, and responses to questions I had despaired of ever having answered. Selwyn Cudjoe encouraged me to write for *The C. L. R. James Journal*, where I first sketched some of the ideas presented in my Afterword. Kent Worcester, a fellow toiler in the fields of primary Jamesian research, was audience to some of my more esoteric speculations, discoveries, and wild guesses; his forthcoming book on James promises to be a standard reference on James's politics.

To Paul Buhle I owe a good deal more than the gratitude that develops with a close friendship. His work as interpreter and publicist of James has no equal. Besides publishing the first anthology of James's writings, editing the first collection of essays about him, and writing the first book-length study of James's life and work, Buhle has been tireless and undaunted as James's advocate among historians and activists in the United States. No one else has been so constant a source of encouragement in my own research—and I suppose everything I write on James is informed (at levels overt and subtextual) by a kind of "anxiety of influence" from our dialogue.

Finally, Paul Le Blanc: I wish his Introduction had been available in 1988, for it is precisely what I most wanted to read at the start of my research. I greatly appreciate his invitation to work on this book. Trotsky somewhere points out that patience is a very great revolutionary virtue. Throughout our collaboration, I have gathered much evidence that Comrade Le Blanc is, in this respect, a paragon.

SCOTT MCLEMEE

When I first conceived of this book of C. L. R. James's "Trotskyist" essays, I naturally turned to Paul Buhle, hoping for advice and encouragement. He offered generous portions of each, for which I am immensely grateful. I especially appreciate his considerable efforts in making me, and so many others, more aware of the importance of James. One of Paul's most valuable suggestions was that I get to know a young "Jamesian scholar" named Scott McLemee. The basic shape of this volume was in place before we decided to be co-editors—but then Scott's energy, ideas, and immense labors made this very much his book as well; our intellectual partnership in this effort has added greatly to my own understanding of James and his contributions to Marxism. The late George Breitman has influenced me in innumerable ways. His writings on black nationalism, Marxist theory, and the history of American Trotskyism have been decisive for my own intellectual development. It was through Breitman's work that I first became aware of C. L. R. James. Dorothy Breitman, Frank Lovell, Sarah Lovell, and Evelyn Sell were able to give me a personal sense of James and his political context in the period covered in this volume. I also want to thank Carol McAllister, whose feminist, anthropological, and revolutionary insights have profoundly influenced my thinking over the past decade, and who has been my best friend. Finally, the staff of Humanities Press deserves thanks, especially our capable production editor, Cindy Kaufman-Nixon, and the ever-patient Keith Ashfield.

PAUL LE BLANC

* * *

Portions of the essay by Charles van Gelderen first appeared in the British journal *Socialist Outlook*.

The essay by Martin Glaberman first appeared in *New Politics*, Vol. 2, No. 4 (new series), Winter 1990.

Essays by John Bracey and (in an earlier version) Paul Buhle first appeared in *Urgent Tasks*, No. 12, Summer 1981.

The following articles by James first appeared in *New International* under the name of J. R. Johnson: "Revolution and the Negro" (December 1939); "Native Son and Revolution" (May 1940); "Trotsky's Place in History" (September 1940); "Imperialism in Africa" (June 1941); "To and From the Finland Station" (June 1941); "In the American Tradition" (November 1943); "In the International Tradition" (January 1944); and "The American People in 'One World'" (July 1944).

The following articles by James first appeared in *Fourth International* under the name of J. Meyer: "The Revolutionary Answer to the Negro Problem in the United States" (December 1948); and "Stalinism and Negro History" (November 1948 and December 1948).

Introduction and Afterword were written especially for this volume.

Preface to the 2018 Edition

We are pleased that this collection we co-edited in 1994 is now available in a new edition through Haymarket Books. Now more than ever, it is important for activists to have easy access to the contributions that C. L. R. James made to the task of understanding the world in which we live and to the struggle for human liberation.

James has enjoyed—for a number of decades—a considerable esteem globally among activists and intellectuals, particularly in the United States, Europe, Africa, and the Caribbean. His influence is arguably felt more widely now than was the case at any time during his life. He is best known for his magnificent history of the Haitian Revolution, entitled *The Black Jacobins* (first published in 1938 and reprinted often since then), and for pioneering contributions in the theorization of the black liberation struggle in the United States, but many other facets of his work have also attracted attention.[1]

James's contributions are an essential source for those in any way concerned with the relevance or application of Marxism in the United States and beyond. The writings in this selection—first gathered and published more than two decades ago—were composed when he was seen as one of the most important intellectual figures in the small but vibrant revolutionary socialist movement associated with the perspectives of Leon Trotsky. Between 1939 and 1953 he was a leading member of the Socialist Workers Party, then of Max Shachtman's Workers Party, and—before his final break from the Trotskyist movement—back for a brief time in the Socialist Workers Party. During most of that time, he was also a leader of what was known as the Johnson-Forest Tendency, working in close collaboration with Rae Spiegel, better known as Raya Dunayevskaya (he was Johnson, she was Forest), and others. The Johnson-Forest Tendency focused particularly on the application of Hegel's philosophy and Marx's early Economic and Philosophical Manuscripts to questions of revolutionary analysis and strategy—providing innovative approaches to questions of popular culture and popular insurgencies, notions of what might now be called "intersectionality," and the conceptualization of the USSR as a "state capitalist" formation.

James's interests and thought went far beyond any specific organizational and ideological boundaries, and consequently his writings, lectures, and the rich conversations he had with innumerable groups of people and individuals in the course of his life had genuine impact in diverse quarters. "Everyone produces his/her own James," commented one of his closest comrades and most thoughtful interpreters, Martin Glaberman. "People have, over the years, taken from him what they found useful and imputed to him what they felt necessary."[2] This is not surprising, given the quality and breadth of his thought. Yet the driving force in this thought—aside from James's own dynamic personality and passion—was, from the early 1930s until the day he died, a commitment to the global triumph of a working-class majority, the creation of a society of the free and equal, and a commitment to helping further the processes that might make this so.

We hope that readers of the essays gathered here will feel the challenge of James's ideas as we did, and be stirred to engage with his other writings as well. Each of us—as Glaberman's words suggest—can make good and creative use of what James offers us as we seek to understand and change the world.

PAUL LE BLANC AND SCOTT MCLEMEE
NOVEMBER 2017

Notes

1. James's major books include: *The Black Jacobins: Toussaint L'Overture and the San Domingo Revolution* (New York: Vintage Books, 1989); *World Revolution 1917–1936: The Rise and Fall of the Communist International* (London: Martin Secker & Warburg, 1936); *American Civilization*, ed. Anna Grimshaw and Keith Hart (Oxford: Blackwell Publishers, 1993); *Mariners, Renegades, and Castaways: The Story of Herman Melville and the World We Live In* (Hanover, NH: University Press of New England, 2001); *Modern Politics* (Oakland, CA: PM Press, 2013); *Nkrumah and the Ghana Revolution* (London: Allison Busby, 1982). Also important are materials gathered in Scott McLemee, ed., *C. L. R. James on "The Negro Question"* (Jackson: University Press of Mississippi, 1996).

Among the studies of his life and ideas are: Paul Buhle, *C. L. R. James: The Artist as Revolutionary* (London and New York: Verso Books, 1988); Kent Worcester, *C. L. R. James, A Political Biography* (Albany: State University Press of New York, 1996); Aldon Lynn Nielson, *C. L. R. James: A Critical Introduction* (Jackson: University Press of Mississippi, 1997); Frank Rosengarten, *Urbane Revolutionary: C. L. R. James and the Struggle for a New Society* (Jackson: University Press of Mississippi, 2008). Collections of essays on him worth consulting include: Paget Henry and Paul Buhle, eds., *C. L. R. James's Caribbean* (Durham, NC: Duke University Press, 1992); Selwyn R. Cudjoe and William E. Cain, eds., *C. L. R. James: His Intellectual Legacies* (Amherst: University of Massachusetts Press, 1995); and Grant Farred, ed., *Rethinking C. L. R. James* (Oxford: Blackwell Publishers, 1996). Special mention should be made of an incredibly rich account—Constance Webb, *Not Without Love: Memoirs* (Lebanon, NH: University Press of New England, 2003).

2. Martin Glaberman, introduction to *Marxism for Our Times: C. L. R. James on Revolutionary Organization*, ed. Martin Glaberman (Jackson: University Press of Mississippi, 1999), xxv.

Introduction

C. L. R. James and Revolutionary Marxism

Cyril Lionel Robert James (1901–1989) is generally acknowledged to have been one of the most original Marxist thinkers to emerge from the Western hemisphere, yet essential aspects of his identity came from the other side of the Atlantic, from Europe and Africa. As he explained to his friend John Bracey: "I am a Black European, that is my training and my outlook."[1] He offered penetrating analyses on the interrelationships of class, race, and gender, and his discussions of colonialism and the anti-colonial revolution could be brilliant. But C. L. R. James also embraced the heritage of the Enlightenment and the French Revolution, the working-class and socialist movements of Europe and North America, the Bolshevism of Lenin and Trotsky which transformed Russia and promised to liberate the world from all oppression.

An essential aspect of James's method is to make links between seemingly diverse realities, sometimes to take something that is commonly perceived as being marginal and to insist that it is central. This is done in a manner that profoundly alters (rather than displaces) the traditionally "central" categories. Perhaps the most widely acknowledged example is his pioneering discussion of "the Negro question" in the 1930s and 1940s, which illuminated the realities of race and class and politics, contributing to a new understanding of the role of African Americans in the struggles of the U.S. working class.[2] The attentive reader will find that such a methodological approach generates innumerable fruitful challenges, which will help to move one's thinking forward on a variety of issues.

This is hardly the first anthology of James's writings to be published. The very first was a special issue of *Radical America* in July–August 1970, "The C. L. R. James Anthology," a sampling of articles and excerpts edited by the New Left historian and theorist Paul Buhle. The next three—*The Future in the Present, Spheres of Existence,* and *At the Rendevous of Victory*—supplement one another, constituting a three-volume "selected works." They have much to offer, especially when read in conjunction with Paul Buhle's boldly New Left biography, *C. L. R. James: The Artist as Revolutionary.* A fifth anthology, *The C. L. R. James Reader,* edited by Anna Grimshaw, has

1

appeared shortly before the present volume.[3] With the exception of one essay ("The Revolutionary Answer to the Negro Problem in the United States"), none of the material in this book has appeared in the other volumes that have been published.

The other collections seek to provide a sampling of James's writings from the 1930s to the 1970s and 1980s—giving greater attention to James's cultural criticism, as well as to Caribbean nationalist and Pan-Africanist contributions. By contrast, this one offers a concentrated selection of writings from his "Trotskyist" period in the 1930s and 1940s. A follow-up volume will be a new Humanities Press edition of James's 1960 classic *Modern Politics*. (Our original intention had been to include here these wonderful 1960 lectures, delivered in his native Trinidad.) James's experience and evolution in his earlier Trotskyist period heavily flavor the interpretation of Western civilization that he presents in *Modern Politics*. While some James enthusiasts are inclined to give the Trotskyist aspect of James's career short shrift, the continuities as well as the discontinuities between the "early" and the "mature" James are quite illuminating.[4] More important, these passionate and critical-minded writings have much to offer readers even four and five decades after they were written.

In the present introductory essay, an exploration of James's relationship with Trotskyism will be combined with a partial and critical evaluation of certain aspects of his thought, with special emphasis (particularly in the notes) on his complex and shifting views about the question of revolutionary organization.

JAMES AND THE TROTSKYIST MOVEMENT

Some of James's most enduring contributions to Marxism were made when he was part of the Trotskyist movement, a revolutionary political current that had arisen within the larger world Communist movement in the late 1920s. Fighting for the conceptions which had animated the original Russian Bolsheviks led by Lenin and Trotsky, those drawn to Trotskyism opposed the rise of the bureaucratic tyranny which dominated the Soviet Union and world communism under the later leadership of Joseph Stalin. Lenin had died before the struggle against Stalinism fully unfolded, but Trotsky became the symbol of an intransigent alternative—a democratic and internationalist communism—which attracted relatively small groups of workers and intellectuals in many lands.

"Trotsky's life from the death of Lenin onwards was devoted to a practical and theoretical struggle to free the international workers' movement from bureaucratic domination so that it could resume a successful overthrow of capitalism on a world scale," Perry Anderson has observed, adding that "the tradition descended from Trotsky . . . provides one of the central elements for any renaissance of revolutionary Marxism on an international scale." Contrasting it to the politically passive yet academically prestigious "Western Marxism," Anderson noted that "this other tradition—persecuted, reviled, isolated, divided—will have to be studied in all the diversity of its underground channels and streams. It may surprise future historians with its resources."[5]

"I became a Marxist through the influence of two books I read," James once told an interviewer. "One was Trotsky's *History of the Russian Revolution* and the other was *The Decline of the West* by Oswald Spengler." Yet it was more than simply reading books that propelled him into a revolutionary trajectory; there was, of course, his own intimate experience with imperialism and racism as an inhabitant of the British colonial preserve in the West Indies, and also his early contact with the working-class and revolutionary movements upon coming to England as a young journalist. "I joined the Trotskyist movement," he explained to several listeners in 1986, "and I learned Marxism in the Trotskyist movement."[6] The Trotskyist organizations with which James was associated in the United States and Britain never had more than one or two thousand members at any one time, and the distinctive political tendency which he led—from the Johnson-Forest Tendency to the Facing Reality group—never numbered more than a hundred adherents. Yet their analyses and political activities had a far greater weight, sometimes influencing tens or hundreds of thousands and in some ways even more.

James came to the Trotskyist movement very much as an independent thinker, with a substantial store of previous knowledge and insights. His book *World Revolution* was a critical history and analysis of the Communist International, greatly influenced by the "Left Opposition" perspectives associated with Leon Trotsky, yet by no means uncritical of Trotsky. James's intellectual and political qualities were highly valued by Trotsky, who stressed that "it is very important to convince James that his criticisms are not considered by any one of us as an item of hostility or an obstacle to friendly collaboration in the future." While complaining of a "formalistic" and one-sided quality in the book's analysis of Stalinism, Trotsky accepted some of James's criticisms of his own earlier positions, asserting that "not only Bukharin, but I and all of us at various times wrote absurd things, I will grant you that."[7]

World Revolution is a popular history of high quality and holds up well more than half a century after publication, demonstrating the breadth and depth that were to become a hallmark of James's work. The first chapter on Marxism stresses what E. J. Hobsbawm later termed the central importance of the "dual revolution"—the French Revolution and the Industrial

Revolution—in the formation of the "scientific socialism" of Marx and Engels; it highlights Marxism's internationalism and class analysis, concluding with a discussion of political tactics that indicates a continuity from the call for "permanent revolution" by Marx to the theory of permanent revolution developed by Trotsky. In the chapter on Lenin we are treated to a thought-provoking confrontation of Lenin's libertarian goals as outlined in *State and Revolution* with the failure to realize those goals in post-1917 Russia. Throughout, James demonstrates the utter incompatibility of the bureaucratic and authoritarian qualities of Stalinism with the revolutionary, democratic, scientific, and humanistic qualities of Marxism.

In 1938 James moved to the United States to contribute to the work of the newly formed Socialist Workers party (SWP). This organization was led by James P. Cannon and Max Shachtman, prominent veterans of American communism and, since 1928, among the foremost representatives of the international current associated with Trotsky's ideas. Frank Lovell has offered this description of James's entry into the U.S. revolutionary movement:

> When C. L. R. James came to this country from Britain, where he was a leader of the Trotskyist movement, he was welcomed into the Socialist Workers Party and given leadership responsibilities.
>
> James was an impressive speaker with his British accent and his poise. He was a tall, handsome Black man, originally from the British West Indies. He spoke without notes, standing aside from the podium on the speakers platform. It was as if he were a great actor delivering a famous oration.
>
> At his first appearance he shared the platform with Shachtman and Cannon in the Irving Plaza meeting hall where Trotskyist meetings were often held. Shachtman was the first speaker and was not brief. James came on next and even though his talk was longer than Shachtman's, he completely captivated the audience and received a big ovation.
>
> Cannon was the last speaker. Although he was the national secretary of the party and had been announced for a major speech, Jim had no intention of standing on his dignity or trying to hold the audience so late at night in order to have his turn. He put aside his notes, congratulated James on his speaking ability and welcomed him to the Socialist Workers Party.[8]

Among James's most substantial contributions was his assistance in making the SWP aware of the centrality of "the Negro question" to the class struggle and to any genuinely revolutionary perspective in the United States. The classic essay reprinted here, "Revolution and the Negro," which first appeared in the SWP's theoretical journal *New International*, is one of the first and one of the finest efforts to relate the experience of

African peoples and revolutionaries to the perspectives and development of Marxism. At the same time he made a genuine contribution to Marxist theory which was reflected in resolutions written for the SWP in 1939.

"The American Negroes, for centuries the most oppressed section of American society and the most discriminated against, are potentially the most revolutionary elements of the population," James explained in one resolution. "They are designated by their whole historical past to be, under adequate leadership, the very vanguard of the proletarian revolution." He added that "the broad perspectives of [Trotsky's theory of] the permanent revolution will remain only a fiction" unless revolutionary socialists could find their way to the African-American masses. A second resolution noted that African Americans might feel moved, on the basis of their own historic oppression, to advance "the demand for the establishment and administration of a Negro state." He explained that "in a revolutionary crisis, as they begin to shake off the state coercion and ideological domination of American bourgeois society, their first step may well be to demand the control, both actual and symbolical, of their own destiny."[9]

Rejecting schematic definitions having to do with whether blacks in the United States constitute "a nation," James pointed out that "the raising or support of the slogan by the masses of Negroes will be the best and only proof required." Under such circumstances, revolutionary socialists should support the demand, the realization of which could constitute a "step forward to the eventual integration of the American Negroes into the United Socialist States of America." James added: "The advocacy of the *right* of self-determination does not mean advancing the *slogan* of self-determination. Self-determination for Negroes means that Negroes themselves must determine their own future."[10]

He also observed that

> . . . the awakening political consciousness of the Negro not unnaturally takes the form of independent action uncontrolled by whites. The Negroes have long felt, and more than ever feel today the urge to create their own organizations under their own leaders and thus assert, not only in theory but in action, their claim to complete equality with other American citizens. Such a desire is legitimate and must be vigorously supported even when it takes the form of a rather aggressive chauvinism.

James's next point is of particular interest: "Black chauvinism in America today is merely the natural excess of the desire for equality and is essentially progressive while white American chauvinism, the expression of racial domination, is essentially reactionary."[11]

This general orientation was a creative application to U.S. realities of Lenin's position on oppressed nationalities, an orientation which James elaborated in dynamic interaction with Trotsky. It was so advanced for its time that the SWP proved incapable of fully assimilating it. James was by no means the only black leader in the Socialist Workers party. Ernest Rice McKinney—a black social worker, journalist, and trade union organizer— had been prominent in the U.S. Trotskyist movement since 1935 and held a different, integrationist-assimilationist position. This position had been advanced in an SWP resolution a year earlier, which simply expressed the party's aim "to convince the white workers on the one hand, the workers of the Negro and other oppressed groups . . . on the other, that their interests are the same," and that "the complete equality of the Negroes and all other races" boiled down to the elimination of "every form of race discrimina- tion" combined with "the complete abolition of capitalism." Even James soon felt compelled to raise a public criticism of "an overstatement" of the importance of African Americans in his 1939 resolution—instead of being "the very vanguard of the proletarian revolution," they could not be more than "*in* the very vanguard." In any event, a split in the SWP in 1940 (which took James as well as McKinney out of the organization) contrib- uted to the insights and perspectives of the 1939 resolutions remaining unimplemented.[12]

The position which James had advanced, however, exercised a residual influence which could be seen in the SWP's recruitment of a layer of militant black workers in the mid-1940s (which may have contributed to James's own 1947 return to the party). In the 1960s James's position also established a basis for understanding the rising tide of militant struggles and nationalist consciousness in the black community. While these new developments proved to be unexpected by and utterly confusing to many observers, Trotskyist analyst George Breitman was able to draw on the earlier perspec- tives to provide a revolutionary Marxist explanation. Especially important was Breitman's ability to highlight, document, and help popularize the profoundly revolutionary meaning of the ideas and example of Malcolm X—which would have been impossible without the kind of analysis pioneered by James twenty-five years before.[13]

At the same time, it is clear from materials in this volume that James by no means confined himself to "the Negro question." His approach to the world around him was comprehensive, multifaceted, and penetrating. As a revolutionary internationalist, he concerned himself with revolutionary events in Europe, Asia, Latin America, Africa—and with the real struggles of working people and the oppressed in the United States. James partici- pated in the founding of the world network of revolutionary socialist organizations formally established by Trotsky and his co-thinkers in 1938, the Fourth International, and he served as part of its international executive committee from 1938 to 1940.

In 1939–1940 James was part of the wing of the Trotskyist movement led by Max Shachtman that split away from the Socialist Workers party. Despite the brutal purge trials of the 1930s and the Nazi-Soviet Pact of 1939, Trotsky had maintained that the Soviet Union continued to be a workers' state—that some of the gains won by the workers during the Russian Revolution survived and should be defended not only from the bureaucratic dictatorship of Stalin but also, in event of any military conflicts, from any capitalist country. Shachtman argued that the Soviet Union had ceased to be a workers' state, that in the event of a war between the Soviet Union and capitalist countries revolutionary socialists should remain neutral, opposing both combatants. According to Shachtman, the Soviet Union had become a new form of class society—which he termed "bureaucratic collectivist"—that was no less oppressive and exploitative than capitalism.

James and a grouping of co-thinkers agreed with Shachtman in part, but they asserted that the Soviet Union had, in fact, evolved into what they called "state capitalism." The old "private-property capitalism" was disintegrating from its own contradictions, being superseded by a system falsely claiming to be socialist. Yet "the gigantic bureaucratic mechanism in Russia confronts the individual worker with economic and political consequences [that are not] other than those of capitalism," James argued. The growing power of the working class—promising to dissolve the alienating dynamics of bourgeois society—could only be subdued by the use of state terror and "totalitarian savagery" represented by the Stalinist bureaucracy. Two representatives of the more "orthodox" Trotskyist perspective were later to explain the SWP majority's criticism of this perspective:

> By . . . designating Stalinism as the typical development toward which the whole world is heading in default of the victorious proletarian revolution [James and his co-thinkers] actually endow this transitory bureaucratic formation with a social and economic foundation of its own and with both an historical necessity and future.

It seemed to James and those sharing his views that they had much more in common with the orientation of Max Shachtman, though this would soon prove to have been an illusion.[14]

At first James assumed a prominent position in the newly formed Workers party led by Shachtman. The Workers party (WP) had taken control of the SWP's prestigious theoretical magazine, *New International*, and James remained as one of its important contributors, along with a significant layer of intellectuals and writers who accompanied Shachtman. The polemics between the two components of the fractured movement were fierce. From the SWP, in its new magazine *Fourth International*, Joseph Hansen expressed special indignation over James's critical appreciation of Trotsky contained in this volume. (James penned the article under his party name, J. R. Johnson.) "Johnson praises Trotsky's brilliance as a theoretican," Hansen complained, "only in order to lay down an authoritative basis for making Trotsky out a gullible and pathetic fool in practical politics, and therefore in the politics of the last faction struggle in which Trotsky engaged and in which Johnson bitterly opposed Trotsky." Hansen's extensive defense of Trotsky contained the severe judgment that "Johnson's views of politics are the views of a petty-bourgeois intellectual drawing back from politics."[15]

In fact, Hansen himself would soon conclude that the judgment was too severe. Within a few years James had become alienated from Shachtman's leadership of the Workers party and developed a more positive appreciation of the SWP. A grouping around James and Raya Dunayevskaya (whose party name was F. Forest), known as the Johnson-Forest Tendency, favored the reunification of the two groups. In the opinion of such SWP leaders as James P. Cannon, there were significant elements in the Workers party "struggling valiantly against the revisionist, retrogressionist current [of Shachtman], especially the Johnsonite faction . . . [who hold a] rather false position, in our opinion, on the Russian question, but on all other questions are very close to us and the Fourth International."[16]

James's contributions to the 1943 and 1944 issues of *New International* that are reproduced here suggest why Cannon might have been so favorably impressed. "In the American Tradition: The Working-Class Movement in Perspective" focuses our attention on the indigenous militant traditions of the U.S. working class, yet James also places these traditions in an international context, with a comparative look at the British working class. The conclusions of this article reflect a revolutionary optimism about the U.S. class struggle which coincides with the line of the 1946 SWP document written by Cannon, "The American Theses," published with an important speech of his in the pamphlet *The Coming American Revolution.*

The Johnson-Forest Tendency felt that "the speech of Cannon with its programmatic reorientation and integration of revolutionary perspectives at home marks the coming of age of American Bolshevism." The tendency similarly lauded Cannon's earlier work, *The Struggle for a Proletarian Party,* as "an outstanding contribution to American Bolshevism," although this was the major work of the SWP majority in the 1940 split. In fact, the Johnson-Forest group (blaming themselves no less than Shachtman) termed the split "an unpardonable error," an "unprincipled split" for which the minority was responsible: "the existing documents of both the Majority and the Minority in 1940 prove that there was not the slightest basis for the charge being made today that the Minority of 1940 had been bureaucratically mishandled by the Cannon-led Majority." They became severely critical, in fact, of the Workers party under Shachtman's leadership—"the 'all-inclusive party,' concerned only with sects, grouplets, and shades of opinion, . . . concerned not with the party as an instrument of struggle for the proletariat but for the protection, as they say officially and unofficially, 'of the ideological life' of minorities." The result: "Behind all the anarchistic freedom of speech, the one solid political reality is Shachtman's response at a given moment to the political and organizational pressures by which he decides the political line for today." The political line resulting from this method was a pessimistic view of the political backwardness of American workers and of the consequently poor possibilities for socialist revolution, a perspective characterized by "economic determinism masquerading as Marxism, the preoccupation with 'honest leadership,' the belief in the passivity of the masses under the control of leadership," whereas—in the view of the Johnson-Forest Tendency—"the proletariat is not in any sense of the word 'backward.' . . . It is ready for revolution today as never before."[17]

James's outlook infuses the essay "In the International Tradition," reprinted here, which provides a comparative analysis of the contemporary European and U.S. labor movements, and at the same time highlights the importance of the revolutionary Marxist party and the possibility of a mass U.S. labor party. "The American People in 'One World'" similarly concludes: "In the contradictions and barbarism of world economy we see the soil from which, at whatever remove, and through whatever corruption without or within, must ultimately arise the Fourth International."

The revolutionary optimism of James and his closest comrades by no means represented an inability to engage in critical reflection. Over the next few years, in fact, all wings of the Trotskyist movement seriously attempted to come to grips with the failure of working-class revolution to materialize in Stalinist Russia and the capitalist West, although a revolutionary upsurge had been forecast by Trotsky as the probable outcome of World War II. The Johnson-Forest group welcomed "the process of re-evaluation [that] is taking place," but expressed dismay that the Shachtmanite majority in the Workers party had "revised the whole Marxist-Leninist-Trotskyist strategy in the light of the Russian degeneration." They were also critical, however, of "the official Fourth International [which], under the blows of the 'delayed' revolution, has continued to seek theoretical stability in the 'progressive character' of the degenerated workers' state." Their polemic titled "The Invading Socialist Society" was especially critical of Ernest Mandel—the dynamic, young Belgian who was a leading theoretician of the "official Fourth International"—whose party name at the time was Germain. Mandel advanced an analysis (based on Trotsky's old position) contradicting their own view that the Soviet Union had become "a vast state-capitalist trust." Yet, as they put it, "we join with Germain in holding off Shachtman and the other guerrillas in order to face him with the origins and consequences of his utterly false political position." The group's hope was that a reunification of the Workers party with the SWP would provide a framework for the clarification of these different positions. They were especially optimistic because "the SWP has a proletarian base which has accumulated years of experience and knowledge."[18]

Shachtman torpedoed unity negotiations in 1947. James later wrote of the Johnson-Forest Tendency that "precisely our serious attitude to the fundamentals of Marxism led us to leave the happy-go-lucky improvisations of the Workers Party, and in 1948, to return to the Socialist Workers Party."[19] Welcomed back into the ranks of the mainstream Trotskyists, James once again played an important role there, helping to orient the party in its black liberation work, and contributing major articles to the organization's magazine (using the pen name J. Meyer). Of special importance were his writings in the SWP magazine *Fourth International*, gathered in this volume, on the history and contemporary situation of African Americans.

At the same time, James and his co-thinkers gave eloquent expression to the revolutionary Marxist insight that working-class democracy was essential to the very conception of socialism. As he and others of the Johnson-Forest group asserted:

> The struggle for socialism is the struggle for proletarian democracy. Proletarian democracy is not the crown of socialism. It is its basis. Proletarian democracy is not the result of socialism. Socialism is the result of proletarian democracy. To the degree that the proletariat mobilizes itself and the great masses of the people, the socialist revolution is advanced. The proletariat mobilizes itself as a self-acting force through its own committees, unions, parties and other organizations.[20]

None of the members of the Socialist Workers party disagreed with this outlook; nor would they necessarily discount the Johnson-Forest insistence that "it is the task of the Fourth International to drive as clear a line between bourgeois nationalization [of the economy] and proletarian nationalization as the revolutionary Third International drove between bourgeois democracy and proletarian democracy." But the SWP majority was not in agreement with the corollary drawn by the Johnson-Forest Tendency: "The Russian proletariat in particular and the world proletariat in general must make no distinction whatever between Russian state capitalism and American imperialism as the enemies of the proletariat and the chief torturers and oppressors and deceivers of hundreds of millions of workers and peasants." No less critical of the vicious bureaucratic suppression of working-class democracy under Stalin, the SWP majority *did* make a sharp distinction between the nationalized planned economy in the Soviet Union (which should be defended) and the advanced forms of capitalism as they existed in the United States.[21]

The Johnson-Forest Tendency continued to advance its perspectives through democratic debate within the SWP. In a 1950 SWP internal discussion James and his co-thinkers explained to their comrades:

> All tendencies inside world Trotskyism, sharp as the differences may be, have been united in adherence to the fundamental theory of permanent revolution; in maintaining the traditions of Bolshevism; in irreconcilable opposition to all other tendencies [the reformist Social Democrats, the Stalinists, the adherents of "pure and simple" trade unionism or "business unionism," etc.] in the labor movement. The ideas put forward by "Johnson-Forest" originate in that common heritage and have no other purpose than to bind us together in the achievement of our aims.[22]

Yet the Johnson-Forest adherents also sharply differentiated themselves from the majority in the SWP. They noted that most of the contending currents in the Fourth International were sincerely attempting to apply Trotsky's perspective to new realities, "interpreting and bringing up to date the basic ideas of Trotsky." They pointed out: "We are not doing that. Our position is that the chaos in the International is due to the fact that Trotsky's method of analysis and system of ideas are wrong, and that the chaos in the International will continue to grow until a new system is substituted for the present one."[23] What was essential, they insisted, was to comprehend that the rise of "state capitalism" in the Soviet Union meant that world capitalism as a whole had entered a new phase—implying, as well, a new phase in the struggle of the working class.

The Johnson-Forest Tendency remained a loyal and energetic component of the SWP until 1951. Among those whom its adherents helped recruit to the party was Evelyn Sell, a young student activist whose wide-ranging interests, including art and theater as well as politics, made James's own expansive approach to reality especially appealing to her. Many years later she recalled James's truly impressive intellectual and personal—in fact, charismatic—qualities, asserting that "he was really a beautiful human being." She also found the members of Johnson's political tendency to be politically and intellectually impressive—and yet she came to view the group, as she wrote in 1976, as a

> . . . cult in the party [which] regarded Jimmy Johnson [as James was known by many party members] as a sort of god. At his signal, all of the Johnsonites in the party suddenly dropped their membership in 1951—without a political debate, without any explanation. Johnson, as it turned out, had a personal gripe with the party leadership, and he simply pulled out all his followers.

James himself remembered:

> They were expecting that we would come in [to the SWP], thinking that
> the people who were with the Johnson-Forest tendency, having joined
> their party, not because of me but because we had a clear doctrinal
> statement, would join them [ideologically], but we went on and trained
> them in that way [to remain loyal to the Johnson-Forest perspective]. Not
> one of them left [the Johnson-Forest group], and Cannon and company
> were very disappointed.

This is slightly overstated, since some tendency members (such as Art Fox,
Edie Fox, Steve Zeluck, and Barbara Zeluck) disagreed with the new split
and remained in the SWP until the mid-1960s. Sell herself, although becoming a leading SWP member in Detroit during the 1950s and 1960s, continued to adhere to the Johnson-Forest "state capitalism" perspective for
several years more. Yet the Johnson-Forest departure made little political
sense to her. The same was true for SWP leader James P. Cannon:

> The Johnsonites were the personal cultist followers of Johnson as a
> Messiah; and when he finally gave them the signal to jump out of this
> party for reasons known only to himself, but allegedly because of some
> personal grievance that he imagined, of which they had no knowledge
> and of which they had just heard about, they all left the party at the same
> hour, Eastern Standard Time.[24]

THE BREAK WITH THE TROTSKYIST MOVEMENT

There appear to have been substantial political differences between the
Johnson-Forest Tendency and the SWP majority which were brought to the
fore by the eruption of the Korean War. As early as 1948, James had
identified the expansion of the Stalinist-led world Communist movement
as an essentially imperialist phenomenon: "The Stalinists are overrunning
China. They aim at Burma, Korea, the Malay States, Indonesia, Indochina
and then India." The position of Cannon and the SWP majority was
different: "The Korean affair is part of the colonial struggle against American imperialism. . . . We have to support all these movements regardless of
the fact that they are led by Stalinism at the present stage—insurrectionary
movements in the Philippines, Indochina, China itself, Korea."[25]

By this time, the Johnson-Forest Tendency saw the SWP and the Fourth
International as being in the process of capitulating to Stalinism. Oddly, the
tendency found proof of this in the majority's positive attitude toward the
Yugoslav Communists under Tito, who *broke* with the Soviet dictator. But
Tito's regime was seen by Johnson-Forest as simply a variant of Stalinism.
They asserted:

Basically the world situation today is that there are two great masses of capital competing for world mastery, the U.S.A. and the U.S.S.R. Each of these has its own labor bureaucracy: the one, the Social-Democracy, the other, Stalinism. Revolutionary politics must oppose *both* from the basis of the revolutionary proletariat or be continually drawn in one direction or another.

The practical working out of this generalization could be found, they believed, in the politics of the SWP as well as the Workers party (the latter having given critical support to such figures as United Auto Workers president Walter Reuther, essentially a Social Democrat): "neither the SWP nor the WP sees the proletarian revolution in the U.S. as a realistic possibility. Hence each capitulates to the labor bureaucracy, the one in the form of Reutherism and the other in the form of Stalinism."[26]

Even at the very end, the Johnson-Forest group was willing to acknowledge: "The SWP cadre was able to establish itself as a propaganda group on the basis of the general ideas of Trotsky and the solid, in fact, genuinely Bolshevik character of the cadres it took over from the [1940] split, particularly those from Minneapolis." More than this, there was still a residual admiration for James P. Cannon: "Cannon's *Coming American Revolution* was the high point of the SWP. It came after the tremendous strikes of 1945–46. We hailed it." But disappointment soon followed:

> We soon found out that *The Coming American Revolution* had been taken by the membership and some leaders literally as a promise and as a reward for "sacrifices" of which they are so painfully conscious. . . . They had the mental attitude of children who had been promised candy and had been disappointed. They were told to be patient and be good children and the candy would come some day.[27]

By 1948 it was clear to most SWP members that the postwar proletarian upsurge was not materializing into a revolutionary socialist tidal wave. Some were initially attracted to the Progressive party campaign led by Henry Wallace, a left-liberal electoral effort calling for New Deal–type social reforms and a reversal of the U.S. cold war foreign policy—a campaign which was strongly supported by the Communist party and the handful of trade unions influenced by it. Cannon "pulled the leadership back" from its attraction to the Progressive party; the Johnson-Forestites approvingly noted: "In driving through an irreconcilable class line Cannon served to consolidate the leadership into a solid cadre."[28] Unfortunately, they believed, he failed to provide such guidance when the European leaders of the Fourth International, led by Michel Pablo, began to adapt to Stalinism:

Cannon was impotent to meet the enemy *within* Trotskyism as he had met the challenge of Wallaceism because of his incapacity to fight Stalinism as a *class* enemy. The result was that Pablo, the Secretary of the Fourth International, was entirely uninhibited in his exposition of the monstrous conception that the regimes in Eastern Europe, though "transitional," would last for centuries, and would remain one of the "roads to socialism."[29]

The Johnson-Forest group felt that the capitulation was due not only to Cannon's deficiencies as a Marxist theorist, but also to his loss of faith in the U.S. working class:

> In essence here is what Cannon said: The analysis of the American scene [that was contained in *The Coming American Revolution*] is wrong. We must not be dreamers and underestimate the truth, the truth being that the hysteria and red-baiting [of the McCarthy period] has overwhelmed the American proletariat. In fact, said Cannon with upraised fist, the American proletariat is backward, bourgeoisified.[30]

While this general critique of the SWP seems a theoretically coherent package, the realities were somewhat less tidy. For example, Cannon's position was more nuanced than he was given credit for. As he explained it in 1952 in a response to Art Fox (a former Johnson-Forest adherent who remained in the SWP):

> We have eleven years of unchanged prosperity. For us that is an episode, comrades. Why do we say it is an episode? Because we took the advice of Comrade [Murray] Weiss and we studied Comrade Marx, and we think in historic terms and we know that it is not only an episode but that it is going to change and must change as a result of the contradictions of the capitalist system itself. But how does it impress the ordinary worker? All he knows is that for eleven years he has been working more or less steadily and enjoying better wages and living conditions than he knew before. Do you mean to say that has not had a conservatizing effect on his psychology? I don't think you read it correctly if you say it hasn't.[31]

In fact, this described an important part of the reality of the U.S. working class. The pressure of that reality would soon be felt even more keenly by the Johnson-Forest group itself.

More than this, the confident assumption that "Pablo has captured Cannon politically" proved to be short-sighted. First of all, James's view that by 1951 "the Fourth International no longer had any historic reason for existence independent of the Stalinists" has not been borne out by history, given the Fourth International's continued existence (and Stalinism's final collapse) four decades later; indeed, by the early 1960s Pablo was no longer a force within the Fourth International. But even by 1952–1953, after the exit of the Johnson-Forest Tendency, a fierce debate flared up within the SWP and the Fourth International as a whole, in which Cannon himself led a battle against the "Pabloism" that the Johnson-Forest Tendency had claimed Cannon was incapable of opposing.[32]

While these political premises for the Johnson-Forest split from the SWP seem problematical in retrospect, other reasons the tendency members offered for leaving the SWP help to shed light on the realities leading to their break.

Ironically, given their rejection of left-wing "vanguardism," James and his co-thinkers had a remarkably *vanguardist* approach to the SWP, an organization that they saw as being "completely uneducated in Marxism." Before entering the SWP,

> . . . we [of the Johnson-Forest Tendency had] mapped out the tasks with regard to Americanization and Internationalization, Americanization and the Problems of Modern Culture, Americanization and Historical Materialism, Americanization and Labor, Americanization and Marxian Economics, Americanization and Dialectical Materialism. We knew that either the SWP would see this clearly, do this work and take these steps, or it would be totally lost.[33]

The Johnson-Forest group had, after all, produced an independent and serious study of the U.S. working class (*The American Worker*), had independently translated and analyzed some of Marx's early manuscripts, had developed a considerable amount of material on Hegel's philosophy, the Soviet economy, etc. — giving them an intense sense of their own mission in revitalizing, perhaps even rescuing, American Trotskyism. Of course, it turned out that many in the SWP majority felt that they themselves also knew something about Marxism and were not inclined to become students of James and his co-thinkers.

The Johnson-Forest comrades "contributed more than their share of the daily grind of party work. At mobilizations [for SWP events and political interventions, sales of party literature, etc.] they attended out of all proportion to their numbers." This was a means to gain authority in the party in order to advance the Marxist education of the SWP membership:

> Through all this our tendency maintained an iron discipline and reserve. We used infinite patience, forbearance and finesse to make relations easy. We watched our behavior and our language, were prolific in smiles and sparing in frowns. We did our best to help them. . . . [F]rom the start we accepted our limitations cheerfully. . . . We tried to help them without offending them, looking always for ways and means [in articles, resolutions, leaflets] to add a Workers and Farmers Government here, or a revolutionary position there, to push the party along.

The strain of all this shows in the revealing outburst: "But these simpletons . . . could not understand us." A deep bitterness comes through in the comment that the organization's leadership could not

> . . . dream that we were anything more than some well-meaning, naive intellectuals who somehow wanted to cling on to them, to save our own souls. . . . [T]hey were unable to see how well-armed we were in every theoretical sphere, that . . . we could be as calm as we were only because we knew that we were armed for all eventualities. This blindness on their part is a conclusive sign of the thick conceit and insensitivity which overcomes a leadership when it sits in its own little bailiwick, out of all contact with the dynamics of the revolutionary process and certain that 700 can defeat 70.[34]

(These numbers apparently refer to the respective sizes of the SWP and the Johnson-Forest Tendency.)

The turning point came in 1950, after the Johnson-Forest Tendency submitted to the SWP's internal discussion *State Capitalism and World Revolution*, which constituted a sharp challenge to the traditional Trotskyist perspectives of the SWP, followed by the tendency's opposition to the alleged "switch from anti-Stalinism to pro-Stalinism" represented by the critical support given to the Yugoslav Communist party. (Or as James put it, "The Socialist Workers Party and the Fourth International . . . capitulated completely to the totalitarian counter-revolutionary bureaucracy of Tito.")[35]

Almost like a natural law, it is the case that many members of a small revolutionary group, feeling the intensifying hostile pressures of the larger society, will react to serious internal dissent as an almost life-or-death threat. But it appears that the Johnson-Forest Tendency was ill prepared for such a reaction to its challenge. "The result was a new insight into the process of degeneration," according to the split document of the tendency. "The party turned on us with bared fangs." In the SWP branches in several cities, members of the majority hurled charges about politically "irreconcilable" differences. Referring to "the hysteria, the red eyes and the shaking fists," the split document noted that "the political flip-flop and the organizational hooliganism deeply affected the [Johnson-Forest] tendency." It was not the case that the Cannon leadership was intolerant of oppositionists, however. "We satisfied ourselves that the central leadership was not at the back of this." In fact, in some ways there was *too much* tolerance: "the same endless discussion of ideological differences, the same willingness to agree to disagree—all these climaxed the retrogressionist politics of the WP. These are now present in full force in the SWP. And, as always, this is called democracy."[36] Within a very strained and difficult political atmosphere in the larger society, and with the disappointment of the revolutionary hopes of the mid-1940s, Johnson-Forest adherents felt suffocated within a small revolutionary party in which a sense of comradeship had broken down. The desire to split became irresistible. "As we understood ourselves and where we were, the cry became unanimous [within the Johnson-Forest Tendency]: 'Let us get out of here at once. It is a political gas chamber. . . . All our principled politics have meant nothing to them. They cannot learn. We have not lost by it. But we want not a single second more of it.'" This desire to leave the SWP was heightened by the belief that great things were possible outside of this organization. There were radical and rebellious "native proletarians, white and Negro, men and women," who "are seeking primarily a revolutionary socialist organization in which they will gain the knowledge, the understanding, the discipline and the associations, which will fortify and develop them in their instinctive hostility to bourgeois society." There was a vision of an exciting educational atmosphere and an exhilarating sense of comradeliness among these yet-to-be recruited workers who "want the revolutionary education which will enable them to win over the dozens of workers and others among whom they live and whom they know want only what they themselves are seeking in order to build the party. . . . They are serious about building the party for a new way of life."[37]

This was seen as constituting a break from the Trotskyist movement altogether. "After twenty-three years of development of Cannonite and Shachtmanite Trotskyism," one Johnson-Forest spokesperson asserted, "there was not a soul in either party who could preserve the *revolutionary aims* of Leon Trotsky." As James explained:

> Everywhere that we were, few though we were in numbers, and for the last ten years functioning in the straightjacket of the politics, first of the Workers Party and then of the Socialist Workers Party, our members always found themselves closest in theory and practice to the rank and file workers. . . . This is the direction toward which our ten years has prepared us. Our break with the SWP now frees us to make this social milieu the basis of our whole existence. This is the revolutionary politics of Marx and Lenin. More than ever it is today the only revolutionary politics.

The new group took on a decentralized-sounding name, Correspondence Publishing Committees, and was devoted to producing a weekly (then semi-monthly and finally monthly) workers' newspaper, *Correspondence*, plus a series of pamphlets.[38]

Deported from the United States at the height of the "McCarthyite" anti-Communist hysteria in 1953, James was not able to hold the new organization together. One aspect of the problem certainly involved the consciousness of the American working class, which did not fully correspond to the expectations reflected in the 1951 split documents. The Johnson-Forest organization consequently failed to grow in the manner hoped for, and disappointed hopes brought new tensions to the surface, and new splits. In 1955, the culmination of differences which had emerged in 1953 caused Raya Dunayevskaya (Forest) and others to launch their own *News and Letters* committees of "Marxist-Humanists."[39]

By 1961 another significant fragment of James's supporters, led by James Boggs and Grace Lee Boggs, felt compelled to argue—in a far more extreme way than Cannon ever dreamed of doing—that the bulk of the U.S. working class was indeed "backward and bourgeoisified." They asserted that changes in technology and economic organization were creating a reality qualitatively different from that of Marx's time:

> Today the working class is so dispersed and transformed by the very nature of the changes in production that it is almost impossible to select out any single bloc of workers as working class in the old sense. . . . The working class is growing, as Marx predicted, but it is not the old working class which the radicals persist in believing will create the revolution and establish control over production. That old working class is a vanishing herd.

In what was to be a hallmark of 1960s radicalism, the Boggses and others looked to revolutions from the "third world"—not the working class—as the force that would bring an end to the capitalist system. James responded:

> The world around us is in social torment precisely because of the abandonment of the idea that the proletariat is the only part of society which can give the impetus to the reorganization of society. . . . To the realization of that truth humanity must come or perish. . . . To those who, having for years accepted it, are now determined to depart from it, we are enemies, outspoken and relentless.

This left a small fragment adhering to James's orientation, led by Martin Glaberman, which dissolved in 1970.[40]

James and his followers never seemed to question whether their break from Trotskyism was theoretically, politically, or historically necessary. The question poses itself, nonetheless: to what extent was the sharp differentiation of James's current from the Trotskyist movement a reflection of personal tensions and political frustrations brought to the fore by what was for revolutionary socialists an extremely difficult political climate? James and his co-thinkers posed major challenges for Marxists to confront regarding the interrelationship of philosophy, economics, history, and political action, and they made some significant theoretical contributions (including the first English translation of Marx's *Economic and Philosophical Manuscripts of 1844*). They also offered important insights into problems and weaknesses that cropped up in the organized Trotskyist movement, and displayed a special sensitivity toward the need to confront the oppression of African Americans and women—in society at large, but also within the labor and revolutionary socialist movements. In addition, they raised provocative questions about the understanding of the relationship between a revolutionary vanguard on the one hand and the masses of workers and oppressed people on the other.

All of these contributions can be harmonized with the broad revolutionary Marxist tradition identified with Trotskyism. But James and others felt compelled, finally, to carry out a theoretical break from essential components of the Trotskyist tradition. In the following section of this Introduction, and in the notes, we touch on certain aspects of this theoretical break. But the organization of this particular anthology reflects a belief that the essential and most fruitful contributions of C. L. R. James constitute an enrichment rather than a negation of the broader revolutionary tradition in which his political thought took form.

Many left-wing intellectuals of the 1930s and 1940s broke away from the political movements with which they had identified. Unlike most of these, however, James neither de-radicalized nor lost touch with the realities around him. As his 1960 classic *Modern Politics* demonstrates, he remained true to essential aspects of the revolutionary Marxism that had animated him when he had been a leading Trotskyist, utilizing this Marxism to grapple with new realities and advance fresh insights. In fact, there is a remarkable continuity between his Trotskyist and "post-Trotskyist" phases, and the contributions from each period offer much of interest to the present-day reader.

READING JAMES

As is the case with any serious writer, C. L. R. James should be read both sympathetically and critically: sympathetically because he has much to say that will not be understood unless he is taken seriously, given the benefit of the doubt, and listened to in such a manner that the logic of his argument is allowed to unfold; critically because the logic of his argument, once allowed to unfold, should be wrestled with and the texts confronted by contexts— our own but also his (i.e., examining the ways in which his ideas make sense now, and the ways in which they made sense *then*).

James was politically active, of course, in various settings—the Caribbean, Britain, the United States—and carried within himself diverse cultural traditions and experiences that often yielded incredibly rich insights. At times, one aspect or assertion of James seems to conflict with another—and one is reminded of a writer he respected, Walt Whitman, who commented: "Do I contradict myself? Very well, then, I contradict myself. I am vast. I contain multitudes."

A discussion of "contradiction" in James's thinking would hardly have disturbed this revolutionary dialectician. It is, after all, a central category in the thought of Hegel and Marx. Alleged contradictions in James's thought can also be said to reflect the contradictions in life itself, which must be expressed theoretically in order to grasp the dynamics of social change. Of course, not all contradictions are necessarily dialectical, nor are they necessarily profound in a positive sense. Each reader will have to decide what seems reasonable and what does not.

For example, one will find in James's various writings a thoroughgoing adherence to the ideas of Lenin, including his perspectives on the revolutionary party. A case in point is James's scornful 1943 demolition of Sidney Hook's classic critique of Lenin in *The Hero in History*, constituting an uncompromising defense against Hook of historical Bolshevism. Noting that Lenin and the Bolsheviks had "assimilated the lessons of the numerous generations sacrificed in the ceaseless efforts to overthrow Czarism," James approvingly quoted Lenin's insistence on the need for creating a revolutionary organization in *Where to Begin*: "[I]t would be too late to start building such an organization in the midst of uprisings and outbreaks"; and, "before our very eyes, broad masses of the urban workers and the 'common people' rushed into battle, but the revolutionaries lacked a staff of leaders and organizers." While accepting the validity of Lenin's organizational perspective, James insisted on a dialectical interaction:

> The proletariat as a whole, at all critical moments, followed the Bolsheviks. More important than this, however, is the fact that the Russian proletariat taught and disciplined Lenin and the Bolsheviks not only indirectly but directly. Basically, the organization of the party paralleled the organization of the proletariat. . . . The proletariat created the soviets. The Bolsheviks learned to understand the vitality and creative power of the proletariat in revolution. . . . The proletariat repeatedly led the Bolsheviks and gave Lenin courage and wisdom. Between 1890 and 1921 the interrelation between leader, party, class and nation was indivisible. . . . With the proletariat or against it, that is the future of every modern nation. What was the secret of Lenin's greatness is that he saw this so clearly because this choice was the inescapable product of the whole past of Russia.

James never repudiated any of this, yet in his later writings we find a blunt rejection of the Leninist party (which is moderated, however, in *Modern Politics* where—in addition to calling the Bolshevik party "the greatest political party the world has ever known"—he asserted that at least in the less industrialized "third world" countries the Leninist party has "continuing validity").[41] It is worth considering the explanation of one of his closest collaborators, Martin Glaberman:

> I don't think C. L. R.'s positions are contradictory so much as historical. He accepted the reality of historical change in the nature of the proletarian party. The Second International was not the First International and the Bolshevik Party was not the Second International. He believed that the validity of the Leninist type of vanguard party ended with the World War I period, so that his rejection of it for today was not necessarily a critique of Leninism (although he did have some differences). In addition, he was talking about a proletarian party, the nature of which would change with the development of capitalism and, therefore, of the working class. Basically, he accepted the idea that the *modern* proletariat was organized by the process of production itself and the vanguard party had become a brake on revolutionary developments. But when you deal with the underdeveloped third world countries, there is no proletariat organized by modern means of production. So that, when considering what are necessary peasant/national and not proletarian/socialist revolutions, the discussion of the nature of revolutionary parties takes on a different character.[42]

This seems a reasonable line of thought, yet new contradictions are suggested. For example, Lenin's party in Russia was based on the working class, not the peasantry. Also, why would the changes in advanced industrial countries since World War I eliminate the need for a revolutionary vanguard party within the working class? After all, as James (and Glaberman) would be the first to insist, workers don't think with a single mind, nor do *all* workers have the same level of understanding, consciousness, and commitment, let alone a level sufficient to develop a coordinated organizational network and plan of action necessary to bring about a revolution. Those who *are* prepared to do such things are a minority of the population and of the working class—a revolutionary vanguard. Revolutionary upsurges may be spontaneous, but they are generally prepared by a considerable amount of prior educational and organizational effort. More than that, it is questionable whether revolutionary *victories* can be "spontaneous," even among the most literate and conscious workers of the most advanced industrial society.

James and his co-thinkers have helped to document profoundly revolutionary insights among "ordinary" working people as well as the reality of periodic revolutionary upsurges of the working people in many countries. The fact remains that the *absence* of a revolutionary vanguard party (i.e., a genuinely revolutionary—not reformist—group that has a mass following) has seemed to prevent the possibility of a radical upsurge of workers successfully culminating in the working class coming to power. In fact, the reformist orientations of social democratic (Second Internationalist) and Stalinist (Third Internationalist) currents in the working-class movements of Spain and France in the 1930s, and in France and Italy in the 1940s during periods of radicalization and insurgency among the workers—to cite only a few examples—derailed revolutionary possibilities. These are realities which, again, James and his co-thinkers have helped to document.[43] There still seems to be a contradictory quality, then, in James's thought on the question of the revolutionary party.

A second contradiction sometimes arises in his treatment (or various treatments) of Leon Trotsky, from whose perspectives he broke partially in 1940 and more fully by the end of the decade. Trotsky's theory of permanent revolution was part of the theoretical bedrock of James's great history *The Black Jacobins* as well as his classic *World Revolution*, yet it is also a target of his major philosophical polemic *Notes on Dialectics* (1948), where he proclaims that "Trotsky's theory of permanent revolution was precisely lacking in . . . life, spirit, color, content," and that it "drove Trotsky *always* towards the Mensheviks [i.e., moderate socialists] and against Leninism."[44]

In *Modern Politics*, however, he seems to drop his criticism of permanent revolution, respectfully polemicizing against his former teacher on different grounds. In fact, at various points James restates key elements of the theory: 1) the "bourgeois-democratic" struggles can triumphantly advance only if they spill over into proletarian revolution, for true democracy can only be won by the majority of working people establishing their own political power; 2) working-class political power necessarily generates ongoing conflicts and transitions in the economy, society, and culture in innumerable ways leading in the direction of a socialist transformation; and 3) socialism can only be realized on a global basis, making revolutionary internationalism a practical necessity. In 1986 he commented that "in the Trotskyist movement we were against on the Russian question but in agreement on other issues," adding: "Trotsky died in 1940. I am positive if he had been alive he would have seen what we were talking about."[45]

One astute commentator, Alan Wald, has suggested that it is wrong to follow some of James's admirers in uncritically counterposing him to "the broader left movement from which he emerged and of which he remained a part, even if in an adversarial stance on many issues." Instead, Wald urges, we will more fruitfully see "the contribution and legacy of James . . . in an integrated view of a left movement of many countervailing tendencies and perspectives."[46] Many of James's most provocative insights are embedded in his "contradictions," but these cannot be adequately appreciated apart from a serious-minded understanding of the ideas that he is sometimes criticizing.

Not all of James's contradictions are necessarily guaranteed to be fruitful. A principled opponent of bourgeois reformism, James nonetheless (in *Modern Politics*) praised Franklin D. Roosevelt—the bourgeois reformer par excellence—as "the greatest political leader in the United States of the twentieth century." He further asserted: "Mr. Roosevelt and his wife together have a place in American history and in the minds of the American people that will never be forgotten." These seem odd comments for a revolutionary Marxist to make, and it is by no means clear how they fit in with other aspects of James's thought. He suggests that in the 1940s the liberal Democrat Roosevelt and the liberal Republican Wendell Willkie might have broken with conservatives and reactionaries in their own parties, joining together to create a new social reform party containing "the advanced elements, proletarians and liberals," and that this would in effect become a mass labor party.[47]

This analysis anticipated the approach of U.S. Social Democrats Norman Thomas and Michael Harrington, and especially civil rights strategist Bayard Rustin, who several years later put forward a so-called coalition politics perspective of working to transform the Democratic party from the inside with a liberal–labor–civil rights alliance. Rustin's orientation was scornfully rejected by the militant wing of the black liberation movement, in favor of grass-roots organizing, mass action, and political independence from all capitalist politicians. It was these independent-minded radical militants, however, with whom James unambiguously identified. Paul Buhle has characterized James's formulation in *Modern Politics* as "a passing phrase, made once only, and in deep contradiction to James's other work."[48]

Once again, it might be possible to indicate a more positive way of explaining, if not quite resolving, this contradiction between James's traditional support for working-class independence from pro-capitalist parties and his apparent "softness" toward the pro-capitalist Democratic party. Paul Berman has suggested: "He was too attached to the flesh-and-blood events of the world around him to cling to musty old doctrine. James used his respect for working people to argue, for instance, that the allegiance of American workers to the Democratic Party is not altogether stupid." Related to this, too, is James's rejection of Lenin's views on organization. The point has been made most sharply (perhaps too sharply) by another left-wing West Indian who chose to live in the United States, Lloyd D'Aguilar: "As the title of one of their many pamphlets implies, the new situation was an *Invading Socialist Society* which was imperceptibly overtaking capitalism. The masses were demonstrating their own capacity for organization." The creation of the great industrial unions through militant struggles in the 1930s and 1940s was a reflection of this capacity, in James's opinion, and the leadership of revolutionary Marxists was no longer necessary. "All that was required was an organization of propagandists to spread the 'word.' The masses would decide what political form the New Society would take. Anything else would result in the new 'counter-revolution.'" What this boiled down to, according to D'Aguilar, was that "there was no longer any need for revolution."[49]

This is misleading. "We do not make the revolution to achieve the socialist society," James proclaimed at the end of the 1960s. "The socialist society makes the revolution." This meant that in the here-and-now activists must work for "the transformation of the bourgeois institutions into socialist institutions, the unleashing of the strength of the working class first of all." Just as capitalism had evolved within feudal society for centuries before culminating in a series of bourgeois-democratic revolutions, so socialism was gestating within capitalist society. "Today there is no period of transition from one regime to another," James wrote—in contrast to the classical Trotskyist view.

> The establishment of the socialist regime, the power of the working class and those substantial elements in the nation who are ready to go with it, that is not something which one must look for to be achieved in the future. That is absolutely now, not only for the socialist society but to maintain the ordinary necessities of life and to defend the elementary rights of all society.[50]

There is an undeniable spontaneist element in James's thought in his "post-Trotskyist" period. "Vanguard Party, Social Democratic Party, Trade Union Leadership, all are bourgeois institutions," he scoffed. "The very structure of modern society prepares the working class and sections of society to undertake immediately the creation of socialist institutions." Yet it was not clear, from what James wrote, what role revolutionary Marxists should play in this process: "What are the new socialist institutions? Marxists do not know, nobody knows. The working class and the general mass of the population are creating them in action. Marxists are to be aware of that and to let the working class know that they alone can create the new institutions."[51]

This constitutes a shift away from important elements in James's own approach of many years. Back in 1947, he and his collaborators—still considering themselves Trotskyists, and one year before James's theoretical break with the notion of a Leninist party—attempted to define their political project:

> If the Johnson-Forest tendency has been able to make any contributions to Bolshevism, it has been because for it the study of the Hegelian dialectic in its Marxist form, of Marxian economics, and of the method of

the great Marxist revolutionaries is nothing more than intellectual preparation and the purging of bourgeois ideas in order to be able to understand and interpret and organize the instinctive drive and revolutionary instincts of the rank and file proletarian and the petty bourgeois but idealistic and eager youth.[52]

This recognition that, given the nature of capitalism, the working class is imbued with "revolutionary instincts" (which are consequently not *taught* by revolutionary intellectuals or organizers) did not mean a rejection of an organization of revolutionaries. In fact, there was a need for such an organization that would be capable of understanding, interpreting, and organizing "the instinctive drive" of the workers and the oppressed. But this is nothing if not a revolutionary vanguard organization.

The notion that what is "instinctive" will flower without "vanguardist" involvement, however, eliminates the reason for the party-building efforts that have been a centerpiece of the Leninist-Trotskyist orientation. In fact, James seems to have been of two minds about this, and the result has been poignant ambiguities in his later writings on the role of conscious Marxists. In the conclusion of his 1968–1971 commentary, "The Way Out—World Revolution," James elaborated on this theme:

> We must point out the stages of the Marxist movement. Marx put forward the basic ideas in *The Communist Manifesto* after profound studies in philosophy, and revolutionary history, and the watching of a movement of the workers in some insignificant part of France. Then followed the Commune in 1871. It was the Commune in 1871 which gave to Lenin and the Bolsheviks indications as to be able to understand what took place in 1905. 1905 was the dress rehearsal for 1917. We have to be able first for our own benefit to understand what has taken place between 1917 and 1968. *We need not go preaching this to the working class, but Marxists have to be quite clear as to the stage of development so as to be able to recognize, welcome, and intensify the advances that are taking place instinctively in the nation and in the world at large.* This work has to be done. The greatest mistake would be not to do it at all. *Equally mischievous would be the idea that it can be done apart from the concrete struggles that are taking place everywhere.* The World Revolution has entered in what could be a decisive and final stage. [Emphasis added][53]

It is difficult to understand James's meaning here, even though his intentions are obviously in harmony with the most uncompromising revolutionary activism. In the passages that we have emphasized it seems that he wants Marxists to *do* something—but precisely what remains unclear. They apparently should have nothing to do with developing a revolutionary vanguard organization, or a (social democratic) labor party, or a left-wing leadership in trade unions. There is instead a need to *understand* things, first of all for "our" (i.e., Marxist intellectuals') benefit. But this is not supposed to be a preliminary step for "preaching" anything to the working class, which in its own way is doing what needs to be done. Nor is it clear whether the working class *needs* to be aware that it is, without any clear consciousness of the fact, bringing about socialism within the womb of capitalism. The role of Marxists is to "welcome" the advances taking place—but also to "intensify" these advances in ways and through structures that James doesn't discuss.

These ambiguities and silences—despite (or in part because of) the sweepingly romantic and utopian qualities of James's revolutionary vision—leave the would-be revolutionary activist at an impasse. The practical consequence seems to correspond to the abandonment of revolutionary socialism to which Lloyd D'Aguilar points.

The stubborn fact remains, however, that James never renounced his lifelong commitment to revolutionary socialism. Elements of James's perspective may lead in directions that contradict the deeply radical impulses of the old revolutionary himself. Nonetheless, the sweep of James's vision in *Modern Politics*, and in his other writings, is breathtaking. The depth of his analysis can sometimes be profound. One should not see him as a god whose judgments are to be worshipped, but as a comrade from whom one can learn (sometimes even as one is challenging him and clarifying a disagreement). Even though the man himself passed away before the final decade of the twentieth century could begin, his thinking remains incredibly vibrant as we approach the problems of our own time and the promise of the century to come.

It may be appropriate to conclude with an indication of what constitutes James's strengths as a revolutionary thinker. Some of these have already been mentioned at the beginning of this essay. There is his great intellectual breadth, which is evidenced in the quality of his Marxism, reflecting a serious concern with philosophy, history, economics, culture, and practical political work. There is also his capacity to see things that aren't quite "there" yet, but that are in the process of coming into being. Related to this are his capacity to identify fruitful connections between seemingly disparate phenomena and his consequent ability to take what is "peripheral" and show that it is, in fact, central to an adequate understanding of politics and society. In addition, there is the deep humanism that is essential to revolutionary Marxism but that James makes very much his own, which opens to us a crucial insight: socialism is not something that is simply thought up by brilliant intellectuals—it is an integral part of the reality around us. Essential elements of it (setting labels and theoretical systems aside) can be found in the thinking, the perceptions, the values, the desires, the everyday life activities, the many ongoing struggles of human beings who are part of the working-class majority.

PAUL LE BLANC

Notes

I would like to thank Paul Buhle for urging me to write a more substantial essay than I initially did. Helpful in getting a sense of James were discussions with: Dorothea Breitman, Frank Lovell, Sarah Lovell, Evelyn Sell, and Charlie van Gelderen. Claire Cohen and Carol McAllister contributed to my appreciation for some of James's contributions. Scott McLemee provided valuable source material and suggestions.

1. John Bracey, "Nello," *Urgent Tasks*, Summer 1981, p. 125. This issue of *Urgent Tasks* was a special issue, edited by Paul Buhle, entitled "C. L. R. James: His Life and Work," with valuable discussions by dozens of political activists and left-wing scholars.
2. In addition to material presented in the second part of this volume, see George Breitman, ed., *Leon Trotsky on Black Nationalism and Self-Determination* (New York: Pathfinder Press, 1972), containing transcripts of James's extensive discussions with Leon Trotsky on this question. Also see Robert L. Allen, *Reluctant Reformers: Racism and Social Reform Movements in the United States* (Garden City, NY: Anchor Books, 1975), pp. 238–43, and Fred Stanton, ed., *Fighting Racism in World War II: C. L. R. James, George Breitman, Edgar Keemer, and Others* (New York: Monad Press, 1980).
3. The bibliographical details on the other editions of C. L. R. James's selected writings are as follows: *The Future in the Present* (London: Allison & Busby, 1977); *Spheres of Existence* (London: Allison & Busby, 1980); *At the Rendezvous of Victory* (London: Allison & Busby, 1984); Anna Grimshaw, ed., *C. L. R. James Reader* (London: Basil Blackwell, 1992). The stimulating intellectual biography by Paul Buhle, *C. L. R. James: The Artist as Revolutionary* (London: Verso, 1988), makes no pretense at being definitive or "balanced," but it is an indispensable source. Also of interest is Cedric J. Robinson's extensive discussion of James in *Black Marxism: The Making of the Black Radical Tradition* (London: Zed Press, 1983), pp. 349–415. Among the serious evaluations of James's place in Marxist thought are Harry Cleaver, *Reading Capital Politically* (Austin: University of Texas Press, 1979), pp. 45–49, 59–60, and Alex Callinicos, *Trotskyism* (Minneapolis: University of Minnesota Press, 1990), pp. 61–66. Among the best work on James are essays by Kent Worcester, such as *C. L. R. James and the American Century* (Puerto Rico: Inter-American University of Puerto Rico, CISCLA Working Paper No. 12, 1984) and "C. L. R. James and the Gospel of American Modernity," *Socialism and Democracy*, Nos. 1–17, 1992.
4. This point is persuasively made by an old friend of James from the British Trotskyist movement, Charlie van Gelderen, in a review of Buhle's book in *Socialist Outlook*, No. 14, April 1989, p. 30.

On the Trotskyist movement, see: Pierre Frank, *The Fourth International: The Long March of the Trotskyists* (London: Ink Links, 1979); Tom Barrett, ed., *Fifty Years of the Fourth International* (New York: Fourth Internationalist Tendency, 1990); James P. Cannon, *History of American Trotskyism* (New York: Pathfinder Press, 1972); George Breitman, ed., *The Founding of the Socialist Workers Party, Minutes and Resolutions 1938–39* (New York: Monad Press, 1982); and Paul Le Blanc, *Trotskyism in America: The First Fifty Years* (New York: Fourth Internationalist Tendency, 1987). An important and massive source, received after the completion of this essay, is Robert J. Alexander, *International Trotskyism, 1929–1985: A Documented Analysis of the Movement* (Durham: Duke University Press, 1991).

For a discussion of James's political evolution in and out of the Trotskyist movement over a fifty-year period, see the account by one of his closest comrades—Martin Glaberman, "C. L. R. James: A Recollection," *New Politics*, Vol. 2, No. 4 (new series), Winter 1990, pp. 78–84.

5. Perry Anderson, *Considerations on Western Marxism* (London: Verso, 1979), pp. 96, 98, 100.

6. MARHO: The Radical Historians Organization, ed., *Visions of History* (New York: Pantheon Books, 1983), p. 270; Al Richardson, Clarence Chrysitom, and Anna Grimshaw, *C. L. R. James and British Trotskyism: An Interview* (London: Socialist Platform, 1987), p. 2.

7. Naomi Allen and George Breitman, eds., *Writings of Leon Trotsky, 1937–38* (New York: Pathfinder Press, 1976), p. 329; Naomi Allen and George Breitman, eds., *Writings of Leon Trotsky, 1938–39* (New York: Pathfinder Press, 1974), pp. 260–66; C. L. R. James, *World Revolution 1917–1936: The Rise and Fall of the Communist International* (New York: Pioneer Publishers, 1937).

8. Frank Lovell in Les Evans, ed., *James P. Cannon as We Knew Him* (New York: Pathfinder Press, 1976), pp. 138–39.

9. George Breitman, ed., *The Founding of the Socialist Workers Party, Minutes and Resolutions 1938–39*, pp. 357, 354, 355.

10. Ibid., pp. 355, 356.

11. Ibid., pp. 358–59.

12. Ibid., pp. 202, 357. For general discussions of Marxist perspectives on the national question, see: V. I. Lenin, *The Right of Nations to Self-Determination, Selected Writings* (New York: International Publishers, 1951); Horace B. Davis, *Nationalism and Socialism, Marxist and Labor Theories of Nationalism to 1917* (New York: Monthly Review Press, 1967); Michael Löwy, "Marxism and the National Question," in Robin Blackburn, ed., *Revolution and Class Struggle, A Reader in Marxist Politics* (Glasgow: Fontana, 1977). Also see materials cited in Note 2 above.

Ernest Rice McKinney's party name was David Coolidge. He played a major role in the breakaway from the SWP led by Max Shachtman, the Workers party. In the Workers party in 1945 he helped to defeat James's perspective on black self-organization. See Milton Fisk, *Socialism from Below in the United States: The Origins of the International Socialist Organization* (Cleveland: Hera Press, 1977), pp. 18–19.

13. Among the important contributions by George Breitman are the following: *Marxism and the Negro Struggle* (New York: Merit Publishers, 1965); *How a Minority Can Change Society: The Real Potential of the Afro-American Struggle* (New York: Merit Publishers, 1965); *Malcolm X Speaks* (New York: Grove Press, 1966); *The Last Year of Malcolm X* (New York: Schocken Books, 1968);

"The National Question and Black Liberation in the United States," in Ernest Mandel, ed., *Fifty Years of World Revolution, An International Symposium* (New York: Pathfinder Press, 1971). Some useful information can be found in Naomi Allen and Sarah Lovell, eds., *A Tribute to George Breitman: Writer, Organizer, Revolutionary* (New York: Fourth Internationalist Tendency, 1987).

14. C. L. R. James, "After Ten Years," in *Spheres of Existence*, p. 65; C. L. R. James, F. Forest (Raya Dunayevskaya), and Ria Stone (Grace Lee), *The Invading Socialist Society* (Detroit: Bewick Editions, 1972), pp. 25, 26; William F. Warde (George Novack) and John G. Wright (Joseph Vanzler), "Marxist Method and Ideas and the Method and Ideas of Johnson-Forest," *Discussion Bulletin* (Socialist Workers Party), No. 7, April 1951, p. 19. One of the first expressions of James's analysis is J. R. Johnson, "Resolution on the Russian Question," in *Workers Party of USA, The Russian Question, Resolutions of the 1941 Convention of the Character of the Russian State* (New York, 1941?). For a survey of Trotskyist and "post-Trotskyist" analyses on the nature of the USSR (including James's), see Paul Bellis, *Marxism and the U.S.S.R.: The Theory of Proletarian Dictatorship and the Marxist Analysis of Soviet Society* (Atlantic Highlands, NJ: Humanities Press, 1979). I would like to thank Scott McLemee for helping to guide me through some of the complexities of James's thought on "state-capitalism."

15. Joseph Hansen, "Trotsky's Last Battle against the Revisionists," *Fourth International*, November 1940, reprinted in *Leon Trotsky, The Man and His Work, Reminiscences and Appreciations* (New York: Merit Publishers, 1969), pp. 27, 28. As of late 1991 there is not a full history of the Workers party and the later (decreasingly revolutionary) organizations led by Shachtman, but see: Stan Weir, "Requiem for Max Shachtman," *Radical America*, Vol. 7, No. 1, 1973; Paul Buhle, ed., *The Legacy of the Workers Party, 1940–1949: Recollections and Reflections*, mimeographed (New York: Tamiment Institute/Ben Josephson Library, 1985); Hal Draper, ed., *Introduction to Independent Socialism* (Berkeley: Independent Socialist Press, 1963); Maurice Isserman, *If I Had a Hammer: The Death of the Old Left and the Birth of the New Left* (New York: Basic Books, 1987), pp. 37–75; and the monograph by Milton Fisk, *Socialism from Below in the United States*, cited in Note 12 above. Also see Harvey Swados's fictional account, *Standing Fast* (Garden City, NY: Doubleday and Co., 1970). A late memoir of interest is Tim Wohlforth, "The Shachtmanites: Socialism in the 1950s," *Against the Current*, No. 14, May–June 1988, pp. 28–35, and "Socialist Politics after Hungary '56," *Against the Current*, No. 15, July–August 1988, pp. 39–44. Essential for an understanding of important intellectual currents in and around the Trotskyist and ex-Trotskyist organizations is Alan Wald's *The New York Intellectuals: The Rise and Fall of the Anti-Stalinist Left from the 1930s to the 1980s* (Chapel Hill, NC: University of North Carolina Press, 1987).

16. James P. Cannon, *The Struggle for Socialism in the "American Century," Writings and Speeches, 1945–47*, ed. by Les Evans (New York: Pathfinder Press, 1977), p. 335. Also see Cannon's "Theses on the American Revolution," pp. 256–71, and his reports on pp. 272–81 and 289–318. These indicate an optimism and approach coinciding, in important ways, with aspects of James's approach.

17. J. R. Johnson, F. Forest, and Martin Harvey (Martin Glaberman), *Trotskyism in the United States, 1940–47, Balance Sheet, The Workers Party and the Johnson-Forest Tendency*, August 1947, pp. 24, 25, 20, 17, 2, 16, 18, 27. A leading Shachtmanite of this period, the future founder and editor of the moderate socialist journal *Dissent*, Irving Howe, defended the notion that "the

workers at the moment are politically backward" in somewhat pragmatic-pedantic terms (a "hard-headed" Leninism with an elitist twist), and his explanation provides insight into the thought patterns among the Workers party majority against which the Johnson-Forest Tendency reacted:

> The main task of our party is to recognize the facts and to proceed from them to try to make its program accepted by the working class. . . . The recent militancy of the American workers [in the post–World War II strike wave] gives us enough cause for confidence in their future, *provided* we of the revolutionary movement learn to make contact with them and persuade them of our views. . . . Johnson's resolution is a product of fantasy churned with half-digested quotations; ours is a sober and concrete estimate of the situation we face and the tasks it imposes on us. (Irving Howe, "On Comrade Johnson's American Resolution—Or Soviets in the Sky," *Bulletin of the Workers Party*, Vol. 1, No. 9, March 28, 1946, p. 32)

It would seem that it was precisely this kind of interpretation of Leninism—which was hardly Howe's alone—that caused Johnson-Forest adherents finally to conclude "the age of the vanguard party is over." A typical critique by Martin Glaberman (in the 1969 Facing Reality pamphlet *Theory and Practice*) is instructive:

> That means, specifically, that because we have all these very fine ideas, etc., it does not thereby become our function to lead all these masses, that without this leadership they are lost, they don't even understand what they're doing. That's a lot of nonsense and anybody who thinks that there's any truth in that is in real difficulty. And the basic reason that the Old Left in the United States is in such constant difficulty is that they have no other conception of how to function. (pp. 11–12)

18. *Theory and Practice*, p. 20; James et al., *The Invading Socialist Society*, pp. 1, 4, 57.
19. *The Invading Socialist Society*, p. 1.
20. Ibid., p. 4.
21. Ibid., p. 57. This insight was by no means the sole property of the Johnson-Forest Tendency, of course. For similar statements made in 1942, 1952, and 1957 by one of the central leaders of the SWP see: James P. Cannon, *Socialism on Trial* (New York: Pathfinder Press, 1973), p. 36; Cannon, *America's Road to Socialism* (New York: Pathfinder Press, 1976), pp. 78–80, 94–96; Cannon, "Socialism and Democracy," in *Speeches for Socialism* (New York: Pathfinder Press, 1970), pp. 345–61.
22. C. L. R. James, Raya Dunayevskaya, and Grace Lee, *State Capitalism and World Revolution* (Chicago: Charles H. Kerr Publishing Co., 1986), p. 2. And yet for the friendly historian there is a troubling fly in the ointment here, an indication that the authors of this 1950 statement were not being completely honest. The so-called Nevada Document, later published as *Notes on Dialectics*, had been written by James in the three-month period between the tendency's leaving the Workers party and its entry into the SWP; it was then very secretly circulated among his adherents in 1948. The document challenged key aspects of this "common heritage," specifically the Leninist party and Trotsky's theory of permanent revolution. Reading it at the time, remembers Martin Glaberman, was "a fantastic experience," although "those of us who read it in 1948 were only dimly aware of where this was going." (I am quoting from Glaberman's manuscript "The Marxism of C. L. R. James," p. 8; also valuable is his

"C. L. R. James: The American Years," the text of a talk given April 20, 1991, at a Wellesley College conference on James, typed manuscript, p. 4.)

In a 1968 account by Glaberman (on p. 6 of his *Theory and Practice*), the secrecy is justified because, it is asserted, there would have been "immediate expulsion [from the SWP] for the ideas that were so radical to the Trotskyists." Yet the facts don't seem to justify this view. What may have been at stake was not the Johnson-Forest group's right to remain in the SWP, but rather its credibility with the SWP majority. By 1951 it is clear that most of the political differences had been figured out and were being polemicized against by the SWP majority, with no accompanying call for expulsion.

Instead, two prominent SWP polemicists concluded their critique of *State Capitalism and World Revolution* with the following relatively mild comments:

> Without realizing it, the Johnson-Forest comrades are gripped by a twofold contradiction: between their will to be revolutionists and their incorrect method and conclusions; and between their theoretical outlook and the objective realities of the class struggle. This is a basic weakness and an ever-present source of crisis for them. The only way to resolve this contradiction is to bring their revolutionary aspirations and devotion into harmony with social reality and the tasks of the class struggle. (Warde and Wright, "Marxist Method and Ideas and the Method and Ideas of Johnson-Forest," p. 26)

That the Johnson-Forest Tendency was being less than open about its actual perspectives is also suggested in its document written to explain the exit from the SWP: "At an immense expenditure of labor, tact and diplomacy, and using Trotsky as a smokescreen, we maneuvered them [i.e., the SWP] as far as we dared along the Marxist road" (F. Forest et al., *The Balance Sheet Completed: Ten Years of American Trotskyism*, August 1951, p. 16).

23. *State Capitalism and World Revolution*, p. 3.
24. Telephone interview with Evelyn Sell, January 29, 1991; Evelyn Sell, "Organizational Norms of the Socialist Workers Party (December 1976)," in Sell, *Organizational Principles and Practices* (New York: Fourth Internationalist Tendency, 1987), p. 24; *C. L. R. James and British Trotskyism: An Interview*, p. 15; James P. Cannon, *Speeches to the Party* (New York: Pathfinder Press, 1973), p. 185.
25. C. L. R. James, *Notes on Dialectics* (London: Allison & Busby, 1980), p. 226; Cannon, *Speeches to the Party*, pp. 112, 113. A 1962 account by Glaberman suggests that, on some level, the split may also have been part of a more conscious development. Briefly recounting the tendency's history of "patiently and carefully" studying Marxism and social reality during a ten-year gestation period "in the Trotskyist movement," he noted: "In 1951 we felt ourselves equipped to go directly to the American working class and the American public, and we formed an independent organization with the purpose of publishing a newspaper, *Correspondence*" ("An Introductory Preface," in J. R. Johnson [C. L. R. James], *Marxism and the Intellectuals* [Detroit: Facing Reality Publishing Committee, 1962], pp. 1–2).
26. F. Forest et al., *The Balance Sheet Completed: Ten Years of American Trotskyism*, August 1951, p. 4.
27. Ibid., pp. 21, 12, 13. This document contains a devastating (although factionally slanted) picture of internal life of the SWP in this difficult period. One of the more interesting criticisms—noting the fact that there was a substantial

recruitment but rapid loss of African-American workers in the 1940s—discusses an insensitivity of many white SWP comrades to the complexities of race and racism, stressing the need to create "the basis for harmonious relations between whites and Negroes under the pressure of bourgeois race prejudice which will increasingly be felt in the party as it draws into its ranks not intellectuals, but rank and file workers, both white and Negro" (p. 25). Another criticism involves the failure of even many female SWP members to confront and overcome "a sense of the same masculine domination which they had in bourgeois society," the women comrades being given to understand "that it was their revolutionary duty to work in offices or to stay at home in order to sustain their men either in unions or as party functionaries." The Johnson-Forest comrades found that many were responsive to their own approach: "Our women startled them by refusing to be mere appendages to men and going into the plant themselves. The SWP [majority] women followed suit. This at least was one good example which the SWP in Detroit followed" (p. 26).

While many of these criticisms were fundamentally in harmony with the underlying revolutionary perspectives of the SWP, aspects of the discussion of the party's internal life involved something more far-reaching. There was, first of all, what was becoming a recurring critique of vanguardist "elitism":

> The leading cadre sees itself very literally as leaders. The revolution will put the cadre, vastly extended, of course, but still the cadre, into power. The masses will make the revolution under their guidance. Then they will plan and organize, above all they will plan. They are honest, devoted, sincere; and the proof is their readiness to sacrifice. Their tasks therefore are two: 1) to maintain principled politics, i.e., politics which do not capitulate to the bourgeoisie; and 2) to prepare themselves and the party to get hold of unions and other organizations in preparation for the revolution. (p. 21)

Yet all of this earnest commitment and sense of revolutionary self-sacrifice— the Johnson-Forest comrades argued—was running up against increasing disappointment over the failure to persuade the working class to follow its leadership. "In line with this we noticed also the readiness with which the women cadres, and particularly the wives of the leaders, burst into tears at any moment. From the top to bottom of the party they swam in maudlin self-pity." The failure to win a mass following among the workers (thanks to what the Johnson-Forest Tendency saw as a pretentious and narrow-minded vanguardism) resulted, allegedly, in a capitulation to Stalinism, "but the abdication expressed itself in the bitterness against 'renegades,' the constant reminders of the great sacrifices which the 'renegades' could not and would not endure, and the ready tears." The self-image of Johnson-Forest adherents, in stark contrast, was as "vigorous, confident, without a trace of scepticism about the proletariat," and they "found it difficult to establish more than formal relations with many of these people" in the SWP majority (p. 33).

28. *Report and Discussion on Break with S.W.P.* (1951), p. 11.
29. Ibid., p. 11.
30. Ibid., p. 12.
31. Cannon, *Speeches to the Party*, p. 47.
32. *Report and Discussion*, pp. 21, 8. For a summary account of the fierce struggle against "Pabloism" in the SWP and Fourth International, see Cliff Conner, Les Evans, and Tom Kerry, *Towards a History of the Fourth International. Part I: Three Contributions on Postwar Developments* (New York: Education for Socialists,

Socialist Workers Party, June 1973). A documentary record can be found in Fred Feldman, ed., *Towards a History of the Fourth International. Part 3: Struggle in the Fourth International, International Committee Documents 1951–1954*, 4 vols. (New York: Education for Socialists, Socialist Workers Party, published by Pathfinder Press, March 1974).

33. *The Balance Sheet Completed*, pp. 15, 13.
34. Ibid., pp. 16, 18, 17. Those who were the nicest were in some ways the most exasperating. "At best they had a tolerant indulgence for 'Johnson-Forest' comrades with their unqualified relief in a revolution by the American proletariat," the split document complained (p. 33).
35. *Report and Discussion*, p. 8.
36. *The Balance Sheet Completed*, pp. 18, 4.
37. Ibid., pp. 35, 21. Even so, they felt compelled to write in the split document: "we must make clear that *all* the leaders and *all* the members of the SWP are not degenerate. It would be ridiculous to say that. There are in the leadership and far more, in the party, good comrades with whom we have worked satisfactorily and whom we would be sorry to leave behind" (p. 35).
38. *Report and Discussion*, pp. 10, 5.
39. On aspects of the background resulting in the break-up of the Johnson-Forest group, see Raya Dunayevskaya and Olga Domanski, *1953 as "A New Divide within Marxism"* (Chicago: News and Letters, 1989), Raya Dunayevskaya, *The Philosophic Moment of Marxist-Humanism* (Chicago: News and Letters, 1989), and Raya Dunayevska, *Twenty-five Years of Marxist-Humanism in the U.S.* (Detroit: News and Letters, 1980), pp. 1–4.

For an interesting and sympathetic portrait of Dunayevskaya, see Richard Greeman, "Raya Dunayevskaya: Thinker, Fighter, Revolutionary," *Against the Current*, Nos. 12–13, January–February and March–April 1988, pp. 55–56. An impressive tribute and sympathetic analysis by feminist writer and theorist Adrienne Rich can be found as a foreword in Raya Dunayevskaya, *Rosa Luxemburg, Women's Liberation, and Marx's Philosophy of Revolution*, 2nd ed. (Urbana, IL: University of Illinois Press, 1991), pp. xi–xx. In his 1986 interview with Al Richardson and others, published as *C. L. R. James and British Trotskyism*, James warmly recalled that Dunayevskaya (also known as Freddie Forest and as Rae Spiegel) had played a central role in his life. "She had a tremendous influence on me," James said. "If it hadn't been for Raya Dunayevskaya I would have come back to Britain. . . . We finally split in 1955, but as a role in my history, for staying in the United States (and I am glad I did) she did it and that should be said" (p. 7).
40. James Boggs, "The American Revolution: Pages from a Negro Worker's Notebook," *Monthly Review*, July–August 1963, pp. 15, 16; J. R. Johnson (C. L. R. James), *Marxism and the Intellectuals* (Detroit: Facing Reality Publishing Committee, 1962), p. 25. Also see James Boggs and Grace Lee Boggs, "A Critical Reminiscence," *Urgent Tasks*, Summer 1981, pp. 86–87. Boggs and Lee continued to evolve in a direction taking them a considerable distance from James's outlook, despite some residual commonalities. For example, in their interesting popularization *Revolution and Evolution in the Twentieth Century* (New York: Monthly Review Press, 1974) there is a strong tendency—due to their "third-worldist" adaptation to and idealization of Maoism—to soft-pedal any critique of Stalinism, and even to adapt to aspects of its authoritarian and elitist orientation. Although James Boggs and Grace Lee Boggs appeared at the time to represent

a tendency more in touch with contemporary realities than James, later developments in China, as well as the collapse of Stalinism in the late 1980s and early
1990s, suggest that this was illusory; a case can be made that their pessimistic
perspectives on workers were also one-sided. Diverse and informative analyses
of the U.S. working class in the years following World War II can be found in
the following: Art Preis, *Labor's Giant Step: Twenty Years of the CIO* (New
York: Pathfinder Press, 1972), pp. 257–520; Thomas R. Brooks, *Toil and
Trouble: A History of American Labor*, 2nd ed. (New York: Dell Publishing Co.,
1971), pp. 223–378; analyses by Martin Glaberman and George P. Rawick,
among others, in Mary M. Robischon, Bruce C. Levine, and Martin Glaberman, eds., *Work and Society* (Detroit: Wayne State University, 1977), pp.
193–347; James R. Green, *The World of the Worker: Labor in Twentieth-Century
America* (New York: Hill and Wang, 1980), pp. 174–248. Also see Don Fitz and
David Roediger, eds., *Within the Shell of the Old: Essays on Workers' Self-
Organization. A Salute to George Rawick* (Chicago: Charles H. Kerr Publishing
Co., 1990).

41. A. A. B. (C. L. R. James), "Philosophy of History and Necessity," *New
International*, October 1943, pp. 275, 276; C. L. R. James, *Modern Politics*
(Trinidad: P.M.N. Publishing Company, 1960), pp. 40, 65. A "universalist"
view on the Leninist party, more in harmony with James's 1943 formulations, is
offered in Paul Le Blanc, *Lenin and the Revolutionary Party* (Atlantic Highlands,
NJ: Humanities Press, 1990). Further exploration of these themes can be found
in Paul Le Blanc, ed., *Revolutionary Principles and Working-Class Democracy* (New
York: Fourth Internationalist Tendency, 1992), especially my essay "Leninism
in the United States and the Decline of the Socialist Workers Party," pp. 7–72.

42. Martin Glaberman, letter to author, January 14, 1991. The historical argument
on the alleged validity of a vanguard party for "backward Russia" but not
industrialized countries badly obscures the essence of James's (and Glaberman's)
thinking on the organization question. This is suggested by a careful reading of
Glaberman's interesting discussion, *Theory and Practice* (Detroit: Facing Reality,
1969), endorsed in a preface by James as correctly showing "the relation between the basic ideas and principles of Marxism and the concrete activity of a
small organization," expressing "what we have learned through thirty years of
study and struggle" (p. 2).

Here Glaberman argues it is necessary to see that "the age of the vanguard
party" is over, warning that otherwise "you begin to think of the Marxist party
as the party that has to organize everybody and win everybody over, because
unless you know what we know, you're wrong, which is nonsense." At the
same time, he insists on the need "for a Marxist organization, although it is not
the vanguard party of the past" (pp. 11, 13, 14).

The purpose and nature of this Marxist organization is "to develop and apply
theory as a living thing to continually understand the world in which we live, to
make it available to the broadest number of people, people who are functioning
in all sorts of ways in the concrete struggle for liberation. . . . It has to have
within itself, and base itself on, representative sections of the society and
participants in all the concrete struggles" (p. 14).

Glaberman's elaborations merit attention:

> It becomes absolutely necessary that, for your organization to live as a
> Marxist organization, and to make its contribution to the totality of the
> struggle, you have to have as members and participants in the constant

revision of your theory and ideas people who are taking part in the concrete struggles as participants, contributing what they have. If they have qualities of leadership, they become leaders. If they have qualities of mimeograph machine operators, they become mimeograph machine operators. If they have qualities of carriers of picket signs or walkers of picket lines, fine! The point is there is no imposition; there is a free exchange of personnel and experience and then the organization is able to learn from the movement. And unless it learns from the movement, it cannot develop its own theory and therefore contribute in turn to the movement.

He concludes: "Hopefully a Marxist organization can build itself up to the strength, the capacity, not only to carry out its own specific functions, but so that it can be a participant in all the significant movements and organizations that are existing in the society in which we live" (p. 15).

This seems like a revolutionary vanguard organization, not entirely different from the 1951 description of a Leninist party by two SWP members: "It studies, feels, absorbs the needs, the interests and the tasks of all the oppressed; invests them with the most conscious and rounded expression; and acts as the pole of attraction for the most energetic, courageous and intelligent elements in the workers' ranks" (Warde and Wright, p. 23). It can also be argued that the general approach outlined by Glaberman and endorsed by James—far more than the arrogant elitism they attribute to "the vanguard party"—is consistent with the theory and practice of Lenin and the Bolsheviks in "backward" Russia, especially in the period of 1905 through 1917. (See *Lenin and the Revolutionary Party*, cited in Note 41.)

43. On the actual consciousness of working people, and on the failure of the reformist leaderships, in addition to works already cited by James, see Martin Glaberman, *Wartime Strikes: The Struggle against the No-Strike Pledge in the UAW during World War II* (Detroit: Bewick Editions, 1980), and an earlier 1947 study by Paul Romano and Ria Stone, *The American Worker* (Detroit: Bewick Editions, 1972). Of interest, too, are the four essays collected in Martin Glaberman, *The Working Class and Social Change* (Toronto: New Hogtown Press, 1975).

The derailing of potentially revolutionary working-class insurgencies has also been discussed in various scholarly works, such as: Pierre Broué and Emile Temime, *The Revolution and the Spanish Civil War* (Cambridge, MA: MIT Press, 1970), especially Broué's contribution on pp. 31–318; E. H. Carr, *Twilight of the Comintern, 1930–1935* (New York: Pantheon Books, 1982), pp. 159–207; E. H. Carr, *The Comintern and the Spanish Civil War* (New York: Pantheon Books, 1984); Fernando Claudin, *The Communist Movement: From Comintern to Cominform*, 2 vols. (New York: Monthly Review Press, 1975), pp. 166–242, 316–70.

If one assumes that working people are or can be a revolutionary force, then one must be able to develop a coherent explanation for the failure of working-class revolution under most circumstances. Two Leninist critics of the Johnson-Forest Tendency made the essential point in 1951:

If these defeats resulted not from the crisis of leadership but from some other cause, including "the crisis of self-mobilization" [by the working class], . . . then the main obstacle to the march of the socialist revolution since 1914 has been not the opportunist and treacherous policies of the Social Democratic, Stalinist, Anarchist, centrist, trade-unionist leaderships, but some organic inadequacy of the working masses themselves. (Warde and Wright, p. 23)

Also worth considering are the reflections of Achin Vanaik, a critical-minded Indian Marxist, "In Defence of Leninism," *Economic and Political Weekly*, September 13, 1986, pp. 1635–42, who argues for the applicability for a Leninist-type party both in "advanced" countries such as Britain as well as in his native India.

44. James, *Notes on Dialectics*, p. 128. More than James, his former comrade and co-leader of the old Johnson-Forest Tendency, Raya Dunayevskaya, made the rejection of Trotsky's theory of permanent revolution a centerpiece of her own distinctive orientation, particularly after her political split from James; see Raya Dunayevskaya, *Philosophy and Revolution* (New York: Columbia University Press, 1989), pp. 128–50. For a positive discussion of Trotsky's theory, see Michael Löwy, *The Politics of Combined and Uneven Development: The Theory of Permanent Revolution* (London: Verso, 1981).

45. *C. L. R. James and British Trotskyism: An Interview*, p. 10.

46. Alan Wald, "From Margin to Center," *Monthly Review*, June 1990, p. 54. This essay is reprinted in Alan Wald, *The Responsibility of Intellectuals: Selected Essays on Marxist Traditions in Cultural Commitment* (Atlantic Highlands, NJ: Humanities Press, 1992), pp. 67–72. For a rich and invaluable survey of this broader Left to which Wald refers, see Mari Jo Buhle, Paul Buhle, and Dan Georgakas, eds., *Encyclopedia of the American Left* (New York: Garland Publishing Co., 1990).

47. *Modern Politics*, pp. 46, 47.

48. See Bayard Rustin, "From Protest to Politics," *Commentary*, February 1965, pp. 25–31, and "Black Power or Coalition Politics?" *Commentary*, September 1966, pp. 35–40; both can be found in *Down the Line: The Collected Writings of Bayard Rustin* (Chicago: Quadrangle Books, 1971), pp. 111–22, 154–65.

The background of Rustin's orientation—which intersected with that of the rightward-moving Shachtmanites—is discussed in Maurice Isserman, *If I Had a Hammer*, cited in Note 15, and Michael Harrington, *Fragments of the Century: A Social Autobiography* (New York: E. P. Dutton & Co., 1973). For a penetrating critique (by a former Shachtmanite who did not move to the right), see Julius Jacobson, "Coalitionism: From Protest to Politicking," *New Politics*, Vol. 5, No. 4 (old series), Fall 1966, pp. 47–65, reprinted in Burton H. Hall, ed., *Autocracy and Insurgency in Organized Labor* (New Brunswick, NJ: Transaction Books, 1972), pp. 324–45.

The more radical circles among whom James had influence are discussed in a fascinating memoir by Dan Georgakas, "Young Detroit Radicals, 1955–1965," *Urgent Tasks*, Summer 1981, pp. 89–94; also see Dan Georgakas and Marvin Survin, *Detroit: I Do Mind Dying, A Study in Urban Revolution* (New York: St. Martin's Press, 1975). Paul Buhle's point is made in a letter to the author, January 21, 1991. Nonetheless, an extremely tolerant attitude toward working-class support of the Democratic party can also be found in the 1958 document by James, Grace Lee, and Pierre Chaulieu (Cornelius Castoriadis), *Facing Reality* (Detroit: Bewick Editions, 1974), pp. 147–49.

49. Paul Berman, "Facing Reality," *Urgent Tasks*, Summer 1981, p. 107; Lloyd D'Aguilar, "What Was C. L. R. James' Contribution to Revolutionary Marxism?" *Bulletin in Defense of Marxism*, No. 67, October 1989, p. 30. Some criticisms similar to those raised by D'Aguilar can be found in Baruch Hirson, "Communalism and Socialism in Africa: The Misdirection of C. L. R. James," *Searchlight South Africa*, No. 4, February 1990, pp. 64–73. The position which D'Aguilar attributes to *The Invading Socialist Society* (1947) is not clearly ex-

pressed there—but, on the other hand, see *Facing Reality*, pp. 86–105, 118–23.

50. C. L. R. James, "The Way Out—World Revolution," *Radical America*, Vol. 5, No. 6, November–December 1971, p. 58.
51. Ibid., pp. 59, 58.
52. Johnson et al., *Trotskyism in the United States, 1940–47*, p. 18.
53. James, "The Way Out," p. 60. See Notes 17, 41, 42, and 43 above, for further discussion of these questions.

PART I
Remembering
C. L. R. James

1

C. L. R. James—Thinker, Writer, Revolutionary

CHARLES VAN GELDEREN

C. L. R. James became a legend in his own time. His last home, in London's interracial working-class district of Brixton, became a focus for radicals from all over the world. In his youth in Trinidad, James became known in cricketing circles as a maverick. This term could also be used to describe his impact on Marxism.

Born in Trinidad in 1901, James was first interested in cricket—a sport once considered quintessentially British, but which his native Caribbean has long since made its own. Yet his interests were wide-ranging. He had a passion not only for cricket, but also for Shakespeare, Verdi, and Beethoven, and there was a growing involvement in politics which became central to his life. When an octogenarian with a worldwide reputation, he maintained his interest in these divergent spheres. In the semi-autobiographical *Beyond a Boundary*, he argued that sport (especially cricket), art, and politics are dialectically interrelated.

It was his observations on the cricket field which first awakened him to the injustices of colonial rule in his native Trinidad. Mediocre white players were chosen for the West Indian team simply because they were white. Outstanding players, like Wilton St. Hill, were left out because they were black. In the heated atmosphere of the political debate which followed World War I, James was soon caught up in the mounting criticisms of the colonial regime, and he was particularly drawn to the popular movement led by Andre Cipriani, who was mayor of Port of Spain. One of James's earliest political writings was a biography of Cipriani later republished in a revised version as *The Case for West Indian Self-Government*.

He moved to England in 1932, earning his living as the cricket correspondent for the *Manchester Guardian*. He first settled in Nelson, a Lancashire

41

town with a strong radical tradition. The industrial disputes that were going on at that time were to leave a lasting impression on his mind. The Lancashire workers, as he was to say later, were his educators in the class struggle. Swiftly disillusioned with the moderation of the Labour party, he joined the more militant Independent Labour party (ILP) in 1934, where he came into contact with British followers of Russian revolutionary Leon Trotsky, organized in the Marxist Group. It was in this period that he read Trotsky's *History of the Russian Revolution*, which was to turn him to the study of Marx, Engels, and Lenin. In an interview with Al Richardson and others, published by *Socialist Platform*, James stated quite frankly: "I joined the Trotskyist movement, and I learned Marxism in the Trotskyist movement." He soon became a prominent member of the Marxist Group and its foremost polemicist.

Those of us who were around in those days can still recall his tall, striking figure and his fiery denunciations of capitalism, imperialism, and Stalinism. James's writings became models of Marxist pamphleteering, linking diverse struggles in dialectical unity. He had been a Marxist for only three short years but quickly grasped its essentials. His articles in the ILP journal *New Leader* on Mussolini's invasion of Abyssinia (Ethiopia) still rank among the best and most searing agitational tracts he ever wrote. A similarly formative experience for James was his active role in combating the vicious Stalinist campaign of slander against Trotsky and Trotskyists, which reached its frenzied peak during the Moscow Trials of 1936–1938. James was probably the finest orator our movement has produced, at least in the English-speaking world, and the movement made full use of his talents. In Britain he was the one person feared by the Stalinists as being more than a match for people such as Communist party leaders Harry Pollitt and R. Palme Dutt. Only once did the Communist party pluck up enough courage to engage him in debate. In the Islington Library on Holloway Road he devastated the CP spokesperson Pat Sloan, himself no mean orator.

In 1936 James's novel about West Indian barrack-yard life, *Minty Alley*, was published. The following year saw the appearance of *World Revolution 1917–1936: The Rise and Fall of the Communist International*. This was the first comprehensive study of the rise of the Third International under the leadership of Lenin and Trotsky, and its subsequent fall under Stalin. Some of James's differences with Trotsky were already apparent in this study. Trotsky's comment on the book was that it was good but that its author didn't understand dialectics. This rankled James, and was to lead him into an immense study of Hegelian methodology. The eventual result was his *Notes on Dialectics* (1948), in which he argued that it was Trotsky who misunderstood the dialectic, and that his interpretation of history was flawed. But in the late 1930s, it was James's grasp of Trotsky's theory of permanent revolution which enabled him to write his magnum opus of 1938, *The Black Jacobins*, the history of the struggle led by Toussaint-Louverture in Haiti during the 1790s, the first successful slave revolt since Spartacus. If he had never produced anything else, socialist literature would be richer for this tour de force. In the same year, he also wrote an important world survey, *A History of Negro Revolt*.

James played a major role in the Fourth International, the worldwide revolutionary socialist organization established by those who agreed with Trotsky's basic perspectives. He participated in an important 1936 international conference of Trotskyists and was a delegate to the founding conference of the Fourth International in 1938, and he was elected to the new organization's International Executive Committee. In that year, James left Britain for the United States, where he immediately plunged himself into the work of the Socialist Workers party. He spent some weeks with Trotsky in Mexico, where the Old Bolshevik was exiled, discussing the question of an autonomous black movement. It could be argued that James's most notable contribution in the field of theory was his influence, together with Trotsky himself, in turning the SWP toward a realization of the importance of the black proletariat to the revolutionary process in the United States. James and Raya Dunayevskaya (their party names were J. R. Johnson and F. Forest) were also among the first to see the revolutionary potential of the still-incipient women's movement.

The outbreak of World War II and the crisis that arose within the SWP over its position on the Soviet Union gave James the opportunity to develop his differences with Trotsky. For Trotsky and a majority in the SWP, the gains made by Russia's working-class revolution of 1917 should be defended not only against the Stalinist bureaucracy but also against imperialism. For James, the signing of the Hitler-Stalin Pact in 1939 was the culminating evidence that the Soviet Union was no longer a workers' state that had to be defended. In collaboration with Raya Dunayevskaya, he formed the Johnson-Forest Tendency, which developed theoretical positions that took them further and further away from the traditional positions of Trotsky and the Fourth International. They argued that the Stalinist parties outside the Soviet Union were not the "tools of the Kremlin" but were "an organic product of the mode of capitalism at this stage." The Soviet Union, far from being a deformed workers' state in which the bureaucracy had usurped state power, was seen as being "state capitalist." And while James considered himself a Leninist to the end, he abjured the Leninist concept of the vanguard party. By the early 1950s his break with Trotskyism became absolute.

James also played an active role in support of the growing revolt against colonial rule, especially in Africa. Thanks to his early contact with

Trotskyism, he avoided falling into the Stalinist trap that had initially snared his friend George Padmore. He maintained some contact with the Pan-Africanist movement which Padmore later helped establish. James also played a role in the development of a young radical from Ghana named Kwame Nkrumah, to whom he was introduced by Dunayevskaya. Realizing Nkrumah's leadership abilities, he sent him to George Padmore for political training. He was hopeful that Nkrumah, after leading the victorious struggle for Ghana's independence, would lead the fight for a free and socialist Africa. But Nkrumah's radical nationalism ran up against the stone wall of neo-colonialism. When Nkrumah's regime entered the path of bureaucratic degeneration and personality cult, James did not hesitate to break with him.

Those of us who are part of the Trotskyist movement had serious differences with James, yet he is one of the few people in the late twentieth century who has enriched Marxist theory with original ideas. Some of us continued to value his personal friendship, also feeling that there was a place for him and his radical thoughts in the Fourth International and that we were all the poorer for his departure.

He remained an optimist all of his life. On his eightieth birthday he told a young audience in Chicago: "I will live to see the South African revolution. I don't think I will live to see the American revolution, but when you make your revolution I will find some way of coming here to join you." That revolutionary optimism, that unquenchable belief in the future of humanity, was the characteristic that best sums up C. L. R. James—thinker, writer, revolutionary.

2

C. L. R. James: A Recollection

MARTIN GLABERMAN

One of the great Marxist intellectuals of the twentieth century was buried in Trinidad in June 1989 at the age of eighty-eight. Cyril Lionel Robert James had been living in London after being excluded from the United States for a second time. The remarkable range of his accomplishments has no modern equivalent.

As a young man in Trinidad he wrote short stories and a novel, *Minty Alley*. He also began his dual involvement with politics and with cricket. He wrote a biography of Captain Cipriani, a major figure in Trinidad's development toward independence. An abridged version of that was published in England as *The Case for West Indian Self-Government*. And he played and studied cricket. He went to England in 1932 where he made his living reporting cricket for the *Manchester Guardian* and greatly expanded his political and literary activities. In the 1930s he ghosted a biography of the great West Indian cricketer, Learie Constantine; wrote the classic history of the Haitian revolution, *The Black Jacobins*; published a history of the Comintern, *World Revolution*; and translated Boris Souvarine's biography of Stalin into English.

Politically he moved rapidly leftward and became one of the leaders of British Trotskyism as part of the Marxist Group, active within the Independent Labour party. At the same time, he joined with other West Indians and some Africans to agitate for the independence of Africa and to develop the leadership that later achieved the end of colonialism in most of Africa. This began with the creation of an organization to oppose the Italian invasion of Ethiopia and was expanded with the formation of the International African Service Bureau. James edited its journal, *International African Opinion*.

In 1938 James came to the United States on a lecture tour and became an active participant in the American Trotskyist movement. He had discussions with Trotsky in Mexico and ended up staying in the United States for fifteen years. During that time he created his own tendency within the

45

Trotskyist movement, known, in the peculiar jargon of the times, as the Johnson-Forest Tendency (Johnson was James, Forest was Raya Dunayevskaya), and ultimately broke with Trotskyism to form his own independent democratic revolutionary Marxist tendency.

During those fifteen years he produced a considerable body of Marxist writing—on the theory of state capitalism, on the Negro question (as it was then called), on the nature of the Soviet Union, on organization, on working-class journalism, on the labor movement, and so on. Much of this was written in collaboration with other members of his tendency, especially Dunayevskaya and Grace Lee Boggs. In 1953, after trying to resist deportation by the American government, he left for England voluntarily in order to keep open the option of eventually returning to the United States. During the time that he was imprisoned on Ellis Island he wrote *Mariners, Renegades, and Castaways*, a fascinating study of Herman Melville and the relation of his writing to American civilization. He continued in subsequent years to maintain his ties to his American organization.

In 1958 he went to Trinidad at the request of Eric Williams, the first prime minister of the newly independent nation, to assist in the movement toward independence. When it became clear, however, that Williams was willing to accept subservience to American imperialism as an alternative to British colonialism, James broke with his former friend and student. In 1962 he was involved in a terrible auto accident in Jamaica. He recovered his mental capacities but was never able to restore the physical energy that had always characterized him.

Nevertheless, he contined writing, lecturing, and traveling for many more years. He completed and published *Beyond a Boundary*, which has been described as the greatest book on cricket ever written. It combines autobiography with a study of the relation of cricket to British culture and the struggle for West Indian independence. He wrote a study of the Ghana revolution that showed Nkrumah's inability to move Ghana forward to a genuine democratic society. He wrote and lectured on Shakespeare and on classic and popular culture. And he was an active participant in Pan-African movements and movements for the federation of the West Indies.

He was allowed back into the United States and spent another fifteen years here, teaching at Northwestern University briefly and at Federal City College (now the University of the District of Columbia) in Washington, D.C. In the 1970s he began to receive wider recognition with the publication of much of his writing by Allison and Busby in England. On a trip to London in 1981 to participate in the launching of some of his publications, the American government, once again, refused him a visa to return. He spent his last years in London, associated with the Race Today Collective, in active contact with a new generation of black activists in Britain, the West Indies, and Africa.

This is a very brief and skimpy summary of the life of C. L. R. James. It does not include his massive correspondence. It does not include the tremendous number of associations he had with leading figures of the century—leading figures of the British Left in the 1930s, West Indian poets and novelists, African-American writers of the 1940s and 1950s, African leaders such as Nkrumah, Kenyatta, Nyerere, and so on. In a way it is the very richness of his life that makes an assessment of James more difficult. It is difficult in two ways. In the first place, it is very easy to settle for a subjective judgment: the man was a genius—end of discussion. In the second place, there is the problem of integrating experiences that are intellectually, politically, geographically diverse. Most people, myself included, have not and could not share the range of what James has done. The result is a fragmented James: James as cultural critic, James as Marxist theoretician, James as third world guru, James as expert on sports, etc.

There is another side to the problem. At his funeral in Trinidad I became aware of a reality that violates my usual sectarian instincts. Everyone produces their own James. People have, over the years, taken from him what they found useful and imputed to him what they felt necessary. I listened to the speakers at the funeral, including a minor government functionary, a major novelist, the head of the Oilfield Workers Union, a representative of a cricket team, etc. I talked to, and listened to, others in the days that followed. What had happened to the C. L. R. James that I knew? Well, I lost the patent and have to share him with others. So what follows is one C. L. R. James . . .

I first saw James in 1938 when he spoke to a packed hall in the old Webster Hotel in New York. I was entranced by this tall (six foot, four inch) dark man who kept an audience in his grasp for three hours speaking about the British Empire, striding back and forth across the stage without a podium, without a note. I thought then, and I think now, that he was one of the great orators of the twentieth century. I am saddened by the fact that most of the people who have known him in the last quarter-century will have seen and heard him with his energy and powers diminished by his accident in Jamaica in 1962. It is not simply that he had to sit through lectures rather than stand. It affected his innate graciousness, his willingness to listen to everyone and to respond. He had to husband his strength, which meant that question and discussion periods were limited and, very often, he answered the questions that he felt should have been asked, rather than the ones that were asked.

James visited Trotsky in Mexico and had extended conversations with him. In particular, there emerged James's ideas on the Negro question in the United States. His idea that black struggles had an independent validity that could not and should not be subordinated to the discipline of a revolutionary party was adopted by the Socialist Workers party in name, but not especially in practice. It was a viewpoint that remained identified with James and received considerable justification in the emergence of the civil rights movement of the late 1950s.

A period of crisis began in 1939, for the world and for Marxism. The Stalin-Hitler Pact, the beginning of World War II, and the Moscow Trials of Old Bolsheviks all contributed to the chaos among Marxists throughout the world. The inability of Trotskyism to deal with the crisis only deepened its effect. In the United States it led to a split in the SWP over the question of the defense of the Soviet Union. James went with the newly formed Workers party that was created in 1940. What united the various tendencies in the WP was opposition to defense of the Soviet Union in the war. But within its first year the party had to confront the more fundamental question of the nature of the Soviet Union. In the context of that discussion James, together with Raya Dunayevskaya, formed his own organization and developed his own point of view. He was also convinced by Dunayevskaya to abandon his plan to return to Britain and to stay in the United States.

The new organization was the Johnson-Forest Tendency, a minority grouping in the Workers party and later in the Socialist Workers party. Its existence as a minority until 1953 meant that most of its work would be limited to the internal life of other organizations, published in internal bulletins, discussed in private meetings. The fact that this period was one of the most productive in James's life was essentially unknown until many years later when some of the writings of James and the tendency began to see the light of commercial publication. Johnson-Forest began with a distinct position on the Soviet Union as a state-capitalist society and over the years developed positions on a range of questions which distinguished it from the rest of the Trotskyist movement. But crucial to all of it was a concern with Marxist methodology. The group became notorious for its emphasis on the study of *Capital* and its interest in dialectical materialism as a serious tool rather than the ritual it had become in the Stalinist and Trotskyist movements.

The position on the Soviet Union was ultimately presented as a resolution to the Fourth International and published some years later as *State Capitalism and World Revolution*. Underlying this viewpoint was the rejection of both Russian and American exceptionalism. State capitalism was presented as a new stage of world capitalism, statism, whether in its welfare state or totalitarian state form. It is strange that Paul Buhle, who wrote the introduction to the new edition of that book, did not understand that essential element of the theory. What was attempted was a unified analysis in which both Russian and American state capitalism were presented as fundamentally similar and which viewed Stalinism as a worldwide stage of the labor leadership, even when the form was the CIO in the United States and the Labour party in England. Important to this view was the idea that the fundamental movement of capital in both democratic and totalitarian societies conformed to the laws that Marx had outlined in *Capital*.

This view of state capitalism was then, and remains today, a minority view among Marxists, neo-Marxists, etc. This is not the time or place to try to defend it. What was intriguing at the time that it was first introduced at the 1941 convention of the Workers party was the way the various participants took part in the party discussion. At the time I, together with Raya, was in the Washington, D.C., branch of the Workers party. I was very quickly convinced of the validity of the viewpoint. But I was even more impressed with how the various protagonists fought for their point of view. In the rough and tumble of inner-party debate there were certain unwritten rules—one did not lie, one did not distort quotations, one was fair to one's opponents. We prided ourselves in this distinction from the Stalinist movement. But within those rules there was tremendous pressure for votes. Victory was all, education was very little. The exception to that was C. L. R. James. In his speeches, in his private conversations, in his relations to members who agreed with him or disagreed, the emphasis was always on educating the people he was talking to, on discussion, on methodology, rather than badgering people for votes. I suppose a cynic could say this was easy for him to do since he didn't have a chance of gaining a majority anyway. But the difference existed for too many years to be simply a temporary tactic. Some years later, as organizer of the Detroit branch of the WP (courtesy of my draft board), I witnessed leaders of the organization coming through town during preconvention discussions and debates. I can still remember Max Shachtman, one of the most brilliant debaters the movement ever produced, overwhelming young members and intimidating them with arguments, quotations, etc. When it was clear he could not win their vote, however, he switched to convincing them that they did not know enough to vote at all. The distinction always pointed up to me the essential humanity of C. L. R. James, his concern with people and ideas, rather than votes and power.

Over the years, as a minority in the Trotskyist movement, we developed different positions on more and more questions—on the Negro question in the United States, on the national question in Europe, on the nature of the labor movement, etc. Ultimately, we rejected Trotskyism on the most fundamental question of all—the nature of Marxist organization. James had been approaching that position, the rejection of the vanguard party, for a number of years. In 1948 it was at the center of a document he wrote that was circulated as letters to members of the tendency. Originally known as "The Nevada Document" (that is where James was living temporarily when he wrote it), it was ultimately published as *Notes on Dialectics*. He was attempting to show how, through the use of dialectical methodology, one could trace the historical development of the working class and its organizations. He insisted that the usefulness of the vanguard party was long over, that it had become a counter-revolutionary force. And eight years before the event, he outlined in abstract form what became concretized in the Hungarian revolution of 1956, again in the French revolt of 1968, and again in Poland in 1980.

Most of the formal positions that he developed have become available in published form over the years. But certain questions have remained buried in the essentially private existence of minority currents, or the public existence of tiny groups that have long since disappeared. One of these questions related to the nature of organization. The rejection of the vanguard party was not a rejection of organization as such. Marxists, he believed, had both the right and the duty to organize. But it was necessary to understand the nature of organization. All organizations were made up of three layers—a political or theoretical leadership; a second layer of activist leaders who develop positions of leadership (formal or informal) in the general society, in trade unions, black organizations, peace movements, etc.; and what he called the third layer of rank-and-file members. Democracy within an organization was not simply a matter of free speech and the right to vote. In the ordinary course of events, rank-and-file members would be voting on the views of leaders of the organization. While that was okay as far as it went, it meant that the impulses, needs, and experiences of the rank and file would inevitably be submerged. It was, therefore, a primary function of leadership to draw out from rank-and-file members their feelings, their interests, their attitudes. Only in this way could a Marxist organization truly draw on the resources of rank-and-file workers, blacks, women, youth, etc.

I cannot say that we were very successful in carrying out these ideas. At about the time that James was forced to leave the United States, the tendency left the Trotskyist movement to become independent as Correspondence Publishing Committees. The group had about seventy-five members at the start—and declined steadily (or unsteadily). Dunayevskaya became head of the American group, although James intervened often from abroad. In 1955 she left with almost half the membership to form the organization News and Letters. In 1962 there was another major split led by

James and Grace Lee Boggs and Lyman and Freddy Paine. What was left was less than a handful. In 1970 I proposed the dissolution of the group, then known as Facing Reality, on the grounds that it was too small (twenty-five members nationally, with about half in Detroit) to carry out the minimal functions of a viable organization. James disputed this, but lost, and his connection with an American organization came to an end. I have never been clear on how James related to organization in the years after he left the United States. There was a small discussion circle in his home in London during the 1950s. But he never attempted to form an organization in the United Kingdom that was in any way equivalent to the organization he had formed in the United States. It puzzled me, and still does, that someone who believed so strongly in the importance of organization should make no effort to form one in his country of residence. Years later, after his break with Eric Williams in Trinidad, he indicated that he regretted not having formed a small Marxist group in Trinidad, a group that would not have left him totally dependent on bourgeois nationalists in the struggle for genuine independence of the West Indies.

Another aspect of James relates to revolutionary journalism. He often referred to Trotsky's criticism of the American Trotskyist press as being, although well written, too much centered in a national editorial office. When the break with Trotskyism took place, James attempted to prepare the organization to decentralize its newspaper, *Correspondence*. The Detroit branch was to arrange to write and publish a pamphlet on the working class. The New York branch was to do the same on youth; the Los Angeles branch on women. These publishing activities were to become the basis for these branches taking over the editorship of the relevant sections of the paper. What was tried with *Correspondence* was very definitely new and exciting, but it, too, failed. James tried to revive it with a massive correspondence from London—but what could not be edited adequately from Detroit could not be edited from London. I believe that *Correspondence* was an important experiment, one that can provide lessons even today. It was, so to speak, a fruitful failure. How much of the failure was the result of unfortunate timing is hard to say. *Correspondence* was published during the height of the McCarthy period. We were on the attorney general's subversive list—which made it hard to get subscribers. Unfortunately the whole experience is buried in archives, both the issues of *Correspondence* and the extensive correspondence of James about the paper.

The last fruit of the first American period was his book about Melville, *Mariners, Renegades, and Castaways*. In a way, it did for American civilization through literature what his *Beyond a Boundary* did for West Indian and British civilization through cricket. While they were the peaks that his writing reached on both subjects, they were by no means the end. He continued in articles, lectures, and the like, to expand his views on both subjects.

Leaving the United States in 1953, however, resulted in some fundamental changes. The most important was that he no longer was directly involved with an organization. That was always a two-way involvement. With the considerable assistance that colleagues in an organization could provide, it made him much more productive than he might otherwise have been. This was especially true in the period when he developed his unique vision of a Marxism relevant to the second half of the twentieth century.

It was also important in another way that applied to him as well as to all who came in contact with him. He was fond of encouraging people to develop their ideas, their capacities, their interests to the limit. He would always note that if this led to some people going too far, they could always depend on comrades and collaborators to pull them back. It gave all of us the freedom to raise any questions we pleased, knowing that anything too outrageous would be checked. It applied to him and it applied to us. I believe that both aspects of his relation to an organization were no longer present after he left the United States the first time. And he lost contact with the American working class, which had been so crucial to the development of his ideas in the 1940s and 1950s. Although, when challenged, he continued to insist on the primacy of the working class in the struggle for socialism, he no longer took the initiative to press for it.

This remained true after his return to the United States for another fifteen years. He lectured fairly widely, as widely as his health would permit, and he made and developed considerable contact with black movements in the United States and was the mentor of a substantial group of black intellectuals, some of whom he had first taught at Northwestern University. The body of ideas that he developed from the 1930s on remains as his major legacy. They are joined by the remembrance of a unique, humane personality—a person who always sought to draw people out, to encourage them, to learn from them. As Stuart Hall has noted, James had the capacity to respect and accept people with whom he fundamentally disagreed, people like Paul Robeson, George Padmore, and others.

In 1958 he wrote in *Facing Reality*: "It is true to say that the genuine mass revolution, the twentieth century uprising of the people, has not yet taken place in China, and history has decreed that when it does take place, it will take place against the totalitarian regime." In June 1989, when James was being buried in Trinidad, that revolution had begun. It was a fitting climax to the life of a man who had lived and died as a revolutionary optimist.

3

Nello

JOHN BRACEY

It is a most pleasant task to be able to offer a word or two on the importance of the life and work of C. L. R. James (Nello).

I learned of C. L. R.'s existence when I read *The Black Jacobins* in an undergraduate course on Negro history at Roosevelt University. The book had a tremendous impact on my understanding of the revolutionary process and of revolutionary personalities. It remains after more than fifty years one of the finest works of historical and Marxist scholarship that I have read.

I first met C. L. R. in the fall of 1969, when as one of a number of demands of black student activists at Northwestern University in the wake of a building takeover in the spring of 1968, he was asked to teach West Indian history and politics as one of our new offerings in black studies. He was simply beautiful. He taught a course based on a close reading of *The Black Jacobins* and gave a series of lectures that began with the ancient Greeks—Aristotle's *Politics*, Aeschylus, Sophocles—and ranged far and wide in world history, ending in this century with the social and political writings of Julius Nyerere of Tanzania. The series of lectures published as *Modern Politics* and the essay "Peasants and Workers" (reprinted in his collection *Spheres of Existence*) convey the sweep of C. L. R.'s analysis.

As often as possible C. L. R. would come to dinner with me, my wife, and a few friends on Thursday evenings. He was quite explicit as to when he should be picked up from his apartment, and when he should be returned. We did our best to provide the fare that he suggested, and were even fortunate enough on one occasion to obtain some red snapper, which really made the evening. Those dinner discussions were among the most interesting and intellectually stimulating experiences that I have ever had in or out of academia. What C. L. R. accomplished in his firm but subtle way was to smooth over some of the rougher edges and to loosen up some of the more rigid dogmatism of the views of myself and other young black radicals. C. L. R., now that I think about it, was one of those "soft"

53

Marxists (for lack of a more precise term), very much in the tradition of Raymond Williams, John Berger, and E. P. Thompson in England and, say, William A. Williams in the United States. No base, superstructure, conjunctures, or overdetermination for him. Marxism was a method and a critique: a method to study people and the things that people have done and can do to make their way in the world. The lived experience was the proper focus of attention.

C. L. R. also helped to open up and legitimize our curiosity that ranged far and wide in the general areas of history, politics, philosophy, and culture. He was quite skillful at pointing out the linkages between the experience of blacks and that of the rest of the world. I can recall a discussion where several comrades and I were railing against Europe and its evils. C. L. R. intervened with, "But my dear Bracey, I am a Black European, that is my training and my outlook." C. L. R. said this without apology, and without seeking our acceptance. He was merely (merely?) saying that to reject all things originating in or influenced by Europe would mean rejecting not only people like himself but a significant part of our own cultural and intellectual baggage. The clear implication was that we were much too intelligent to do that. C. L. R., as a good Marxist, upheld the best of what earlier societies produced in terms of literature, art, philosophy, and values.

Two additional incidents stick in my mind concerning C. L. R.'s outlook. First, he cut short a discussion of Marxist humanism by saying that the phrase was redundant. To be a humanist in the twentieth century was to be a Marxist. Finally, shortly after C. L. R. arrived to teach at Northwestern University, we informed him that the library had a copy of his *World Revolution*. At the time a publisher was reprinting it without his knowledge and charging some ridiculously high price. C. L. R. had no copy of this major work of his and expressed a desire to obtain a copy. We offered to "liberate" the copy from the library and give it to him. Our rationale: C. L. R. had created it; it was a product of his labor; and if anyone was entitled to a copy, it was C. L. R. He was horrified at our suggestion. He said that the bourgeoisie could accuse him of working for socialist revolution, but he would never let them accuse him of stealing. C. L. R. James was a gentleman and a scholar in the fullest meaning of those terms.

C. L. R. went on to teach at Federal City College in the District of Columbia and to participate in the Sixth Pan-African Conference. We met frequently over the years. I remember our talks, and our agreements (and disagreements) on the relative merits of various individuals and groups active during the late 1960s. I still teach *The Black Jacobins* in a course on "Revolution in the Third World." I consider myself privileged to have known him as my teacher, colleague, and friend.

4

Marxism in the USA

PAUL BUHLE

The claim that C. L. R. James is a major contributor to revolutionary thought, not only as regards Pan-Africanism but every major aspect of the Marxist legacy, may seem even now exaggerated or mistaken. He has been no demigod of the younger generations, like Herbert Marcuse was for the New Left, and has no European intellectual reputation on the scale of a Sartre; his books do not even sell so briskly as those of his *bête noire* from decades ago, Belgian Trotskyist Ernest Mandel. When I approached a leading American Left book publisher in 1970 with a proposal for a C. L. R. James anthology, the editor politely suggested to me that the author's work could gain attention "on black subjects only." That has been an all-too-characteristic response. Yet I am persuaded that if civilization survives the threat of nuclear annihilation another quarter-century, James will be considered one of the few truly creative Marxists from the 1930s to the 1950s, perhaps alone in his masterful synthesis of world history, philosophy, government, mass life, and popular culture. The retrenchment of revolutionary forces through much of the era, the growth of new conditions which caught party leaders and theoreticians confused and wrong-headed, partly accounts for James's current obscurity. The problem of an emergent alternative beyond Stalinism and Trotskyism, beyond the welfare state and one-party state in every part of the globe, offers the rest of the explanation. The sometimes recondite vocabulary and secluded political context of James's American writings must no longer blind us to the larger significance of what he undertook.

James, first, has been almost entirely outside what Perry Anderson has called "Western Marxism," the drift of Marxist theory from the revolutionary parties to the academies between the 1920s and today. Anderson's *Considerations on Western Marxism* names Lukács, Korsch, Gramsci, Benjamin, Horkheimer, Della Volpe, Lefebvre, Adorno, Sartre, Goldmann, Althusser, and Colleti as those key thinkers who have reshaped the

55

conception of what Marxism is and what it can do. Only Lukács, Gramsci, and Korsch might be remotely considered activists, and they did most of their theoretical work after they had been removed from the center of the fray by prison or exile. Anderson might have included E. P. Thompson or Raymond Williams; he certainly should have included W. E. B. Du Bois. But his schema has a certain logic as the internalization of political defeat, the return to exegetics, to philosophical and aesthetic meditations upon Marxist theory as an end in itself.[1] Missing is an aggressive statement of politics, the working class and its allies *as they move through* these largely disastrous decades, and of their interrelations with the movements of the third world. That was quite beyond most such thinkers, as it has been beyond the functionaries high and low of the socialist, Communist, and anarchist movements in Europe and America who piled formula upon formula without adding greatly to what the generations of Marx and Lenin had set out.

Second, James has been outside the dialogue among the political Left's power brokers for nearly all these years because of his insistence upon two points: the continuing revolutionary potential of the working class and the historic obsolescence of the vanguard party as known in Lenin's time. Had he declined either half of this proposition, he might have garnered interest within a New Left that repudiated class along with party, or in a post–New Left Leninism which returned to the vanguard out of pessimism about the self-organizing capacity of its intended constituency. As far back as the mid-1940s, one of James's sharpest critics complained that he could not comprehend the organizing role of the vanguard and therefore exaggerated "the utter collapse of capitalism" in order to promote "the spontaneous character of the rise of working–class consciousness and the working–class struggle, not merely against capitalism as such, but above all, for such a conscious goal as Socialism."[2] Between James's views and those of neo-vanguardism, or James's views and social democratic reformism, there can be no final reconciliation, any more than the political movements presuming working-class disintegration and obsolescence could have any comfortable agreement with James.

The misapprehension of James's position, the sincere but mistaken reference to it as "syndicalist" or "anarchist" in its treatment of party and state, throws into relief the third and greatest problem. For the essential question of politics as such has been, for James, not merely the form of intervention but the *content* inevitably replete with the heritage of Western thought and world culture, the full range of talents and energies that ordinary people bring to the revolutionary struggle, and the corruption that traditional political institutions (including those of the Left) have suffered. In an age of pessimism, even the statement of a teleology that brings forward the proletariat as the outcome of a vast historical process seems anarchistic—so far has "Western Marxism" fallen. Socialism has been for James concretely, personally, and theoretically what it has been only in general or rhetorical terms for the rest of formal Marxist thought: a question of civilization. This inestimable contribution can be analyzed in a number of ways. Here I will stress the revolutionary problematic most puzzling in the world, for a number of reasons, to Marxist thought: the American scene. The most highly developed of industrial capitalist nations, behemoth of the twentieth century, it has never (and contrary to all orthodox Marxist anticipations) rendered up a European-style mass workers' party, never a third world variety of all-encompassing political organization, and has remained impervious for the most part to the very texture of formal Marxism. Yet it has—in all modesty for any national claims—produced again and again political, social, and cultural movements that surprised revolutionaries and others the world over, supplied heroic personalities, slogans, and songs carried to every section of struggling humanity. Sometimes its labor insurgencies, most recently the Congress of Industrial Organizations (CIO), have shown the way forward. The distance between Marxist political expectation and reality has surely been one of unprecedented proportions. James's contribution has spanned that gap imperfectly, to be sure, but with so much energy and insight that we have yet to measure his work's significance. He accomplished this by comparing European Marxism and West Indian nationalism to the American situation, hardly satisfying those who carried the familiar banners or successfully reaching that massive majority outside the Left political discussion altogether. But the traces are there, and the impact has already been felt in subtle ways.

James could make a unique theoretical contribution because of his own talents and effort, of course, but also because he arrived at a key moment and stood in a special place among those on the American scene. From the late 1930s to the 1950s the political forces of the Left exhausted themselves, lost their following as the immigrant generations aged and no group of workers took their place. From the first years of the CIO to the postwar strikes to the 1950s wildcats, and from the black labor movement and Harlem demonstrations of the 1930s–1940s to the monumental civil rights outbreak of the 1950s, mass movements had gone beyond the leadership that the Left had expected to provide. Meanwhile, and unlike so many other promising intellectuals from the 1930s, James was not to be overwhelmed by Hitler's rampage, Stalin's crimes, and the failure of an immediate revolution after World War II. Historian of colonialism, James had seen greater slaughters, even, than the Holocaust of the Jews, civilizations exterminated and abolished from memory, peoples suffering incalculably from poverty and self-hatred pick themselves up and fight to throw off the oppressor. He stepped out of West Indian and British political life so confident about the colonial revolt and the character of working-class solidarity that he instinctively looked beyond the weakness of the Left to the mobilized forces themselves. Having resisted illusions about the Soviet Union or Stalinism, moreover, he had no hopes in that quarter to lose. He saw the revolutionary process with fresh eyes.

But James's resilience, adaptability, and creative energies are not a matter of race and formal politics only. He remarks in *Beyond a Boundary* that when Trotsky assailed sports as a mere distraction from the class struggle, James knew the thesis to be wrong.[3] Like the American Communists of the 1930s–1940s who, in some of their finest moments, fought for the integration of professional baseball and cheered with Harlem to the profoundly political exhilaration of Joe Louis's ring victories, James recognized the ways in which popular life had in some measure displaced or replaced the literal political intensity of Europe. If he turned to Hegel and the deepest roots of Marxian thought—in tune with Whitman's proclamation of that giant as the "most American philosopher"—James did so because his background and experience drove him to reevaluate the revolutionary process as a whole. Here, where the roads of race and class, popular life, culture, and practice cross, is James's American accomplishment.

I

We can appreciate this better in light of the American Marxism that had existed for some three generations when James came onto the scene. No brief sketch will do justice to a subject that James noted as utterly unique, and the analysis of which he looked upon as a task that should have fallen on shoulders other than his own. A highlighting of some prominent features permits, however, a sense of the crises that James alone addressed directly, in theoretical and practical terms, systematically as his circumstances allowed.

Marxism in the United States had been in the first instance an immigrant sensibility. The reason is not mysterious. The internal strength of collective class self-identification, of tenacity across periods of defeat and isolation, for generations belonged foremost to those who brought with them a heritage of centuries and a set of beliefs and practices that bound up daily habits into a coherent unity. The proletariat stood as a unifying element, but the success of the Left combined small businessmen, professionals, family members, and all conscientious supporters of the ethnic group and its homeland's best interests. Socialists, and later Communists, offered a mediation by which the immigrant could accept the oppressive, discriminatory, chaotic, and frightening American reality as transitory, with international revolution and a common brotherhood of working peoples as the immanent truth of real progress.

The same immigrant radicalisms, singly or together, could not by themselves transform America. Only in some industries did their nationalities hold a commanding position. Outside the industrial Northeast, the Midwest, and pockets of strength elsewhere, they remained alien to the nation. Many did not or could not vote, much less challenge the power of the two-party system. At a still deeper level, they had to compromise the internal dynamics of their movements with the possibilities imposed by the economic system and the waves of labor radicalism, the objective opportunities for alliance with nonproletarian groups (e.g., farmers) and with the contours of the international revolutionary movements. To hold on to their strength and to confront wider America required, more than skill and tenacity, a real sense of what a minority radical movement can do.[4]

The clues were many, but ambiguous. How to balance internationalist aims with desire for influence upon an often racist, xenophobic, exclusively male labor movement? This was not a matter of mere opportunism. Frequently, the very movements that seemed to catch the threads of an impulse beyond that of European labor (like the Knights of Labor, and the Populist, woman's suffrage, and black movements) had the least conscious ideological affinity to Marxism, claimed to organize themselves on nonclass lines, and aimed at something more "American" than socialist. The immigrant communities repeatedly played a decisive role in the struggle for labor advance. But they found their recruits outside their own ranks only in a scattering of intellectuals, political and labor leaders, and short-lived mass constituencies. At times, and in places, this combination nearly dominated American intellectual and cultural life, and promised to help lead the labor movement to a New Jerusalem. Still, something had never connected in the European sense. And Marxism as formal doctrine remained a curious mixture of fumbling exegesis, rote learning, and creative leaps that never quite found a spot to land.[5]

There have been instructive exceptions. W. E. B. Du Bois's *Black Reconstruction*, written only two years before James's *Black Jacobins*, is perhaps one of the classic works of modern revolutionary thought. Perhaps the key methodological truth of the study is that Du Bois brought to Marxism a decisive view of American history, a sense of the U.S. experience in world terms, that the perspectives of Marx and Lenin helped Du Bois to clarify and articulate. Du Bois seems not to have been greatly influenced by other American Marxists. But he stood in a tradition of those who sought to measure the "abstract internationalism" (with a blind eye turned to any distinctions among the proletariat) against the reality of race and ethnic diversity. European Marxist orthodoxy was against a more fluid and adaptive sense of history and practice.[6] In a subtle and complex way, this alternative conception had also been a key to the questions of the state and of culture some time before James came on the scene.

Twenty years earlier, the rise of mass strikes on an unprecedented scale, the aggressive state intervention of Woodrow Wilson's administration, and the prospect of the world revolution coming out of World War I had inspired a real (if diffuse and little-remembered) theoretical breakthrough. Translator of *Anti-Dühring*, theorist of the Industrial Workers of the World (IWW), and perhaps the deepest philosophical thinker of the Socialist movement, Austin Lewis came to concentrate his attentions upon the fierce struggle *within* the working class. The unskilled, foreign-born, and unorganized proletariat had until the strike waves of 1909–1913 and 1915–1919 been under the whip hand of the native-born, skilled American Federation of Labor (AFL) member. Through mass actions, they asserted their own leadership. Now Lewis foresaw the future in the single metaphor of the Mexican-American workers in southern California (for whom he provided legal counsel): lacking any union emblem for a Labor Day parade banner, they had emblazoned the simple slogan "Workers of the World Unite." Likewise, their counterparts among the Eastern European immigrant workers in the new-built factories of heavy industry, brought together by the conditions of production, signified for Lewis the development of a truly modern revolutionary movement. Not the battle against feudal remnants still carried on in Europe; not the backstairs resistance of the fading American petty bourgeoisie against monopolism that had dominated American reform and socialist political mentality; but the machine proletariat in Marx's terms, on its own turf, learning the lessons that only mass production could teach.[7]

Lewis's contemporary William English Walling—a founder of the Niagara movement (forerunner of the National Association for the Advancement of Colored People) and for a time also a propagandist supporter of the IWW—saw the other side of the equation. The state, manipulating the heterogeneity of the work force to draw strength and definition at the moment of ascending monopoly capital, would increasingly tend to pull the petty bourgeoisie, the new white-collar worker, and the surviving labor aristocrat into a formation that unified behind the imperialistic war effort and continued the ruthless exploitation of the basic industrial worker.[8]

Intuitively, and without theoretical elaboration in classic Marxist terms, Lewis, Walling, and a handful of others had guessed at the leap Lenin proposed in *Imperialism*: to explain both the basis for opportunism in the labor movement and the possibilities of a revolutionary outbreak that began from the bottom of the work force and swept away the accumulating state apparatus. Louis Fraina, the first American Communist ideologue and popularizer of the Russian Revolution for an American Left audience, added an element that might be seen best in the United States. Drawn to an examination of mass cultural life even as the Russian events unfolded, Fraina proposed that the dance styles which grew out of black music and provided the immigrant working-class youth measures of freedom in the great metropolitan ballrooms had in themselves an important contribution to make to the revolutionary process. As ordinary working people found the means to express themselves creatively and collectively, across the Old World boundaries, they emancipated themselves for a higher level of consciousness. And—he might have added with his bohemian counterparts in other sections of the Left cultural movement—they came to appreciate at some level that the black contribution would become ever more apparent and essential.[9]

These few writers, looking to their own experience and a partial reevaluation of Marxist basics, had come a long way toward the perception that James broadened into theoretical understanding. Between themselves and him lay twenty years of Left retreat to home base in the immigrant ghettoes, international complications, and a slow but extraordinarily painful learning process in the complexities of American life. The Garvey movement (and the directives of the Comintern) clarified the black experience as central to the United States, past and future, industrial, social, and political. Trade union work showed the levels of contradictions by which downgraded craft workers often led in the unionizing effort, and the industrial union leadership could actually use the inevitable government mechanisms (as the garment workers had already done in World War I) to gain recognition. Meanwhile, the vital, continuing immigrant radicalism demonstrated the tenacious self-identification of militants who remained firm in their basic racial or ethnic differences beyond the factory gates.

The irony of American communism is that these lessons soaked in, became mass initiatives rather than slogans and good intentions, as the Communists entered the New Deal coalition. Anti-fascism, the international popular front, and the atmosphere of progressive democracy enabled sections of the Left to do what the revolutionaries who launched American communism could not have imagined: help develop "Mass Action" (i.e., the sit-down strikes), guide radical popular culture (Woody Guthrie; the public music concerts "From Spirituals to Swing," a black showcase in 1937, and "Socialism in Swing," a Young Communist League spectacle two years later), and ardently support the most downtrodden sectors of labor as mechanisms for advancing Left interests within a state-capitalist regime.[10]

This turnabout, and the steady disintegration of the strategy from 1939, left radicals of all kinds flat-footed. Marxist theory had become among Communists, even more than their rather casual socialist predecessors, a system of political self-justification—strategy, a patchwork with hardly anything in common but general notions of class. The sharp breaks from the Second International parliamentarist expectations before World War I and from the primitive Third International insurrectionism of the early 1920s had been put aside, repudiated, but were never seen as necessary or logical stages in the revolutionary process. In short, nothing had prepared Marxists for the crisis of World War II and after. The development of a dual labor market, the erosion of the first- and second-generation immigrant base of the Left, the advance of cultural questions toward the center of the stage in the postwar working class—these were for the Left a catastrophe hidden only by the more obvious catastrophe of the cold war. Something had come to an end, without the Marxists ever coming to terms with what had been in motion. Enter C. L. R. James.

II

James set foot upon the American scene just as the old ways reached a climactic end to their development. From the "Roosevelt Recession" of 1937 to "Doctor Win the War" and the Truman administration, the ugly side of the welfare state revealed itself step by step: no transition to socialism, but rather a more sophisticated (and potentially more vicious) stage of capitalist hegemony. Although the Communist party reached its numerical peak of 80,000 during wartime, it had become a virtual agent of state capitalism in Russia and America, as its bitter opposition to A. Philip Randolph's planned march on Washington and its avid support of the no-strike pledge and of the Minneapolis Trotskyists' prosecution by the government all attested. Interlocked with the Red Army invasion of postwar Eastern Europe—"revolution from the tank turret" carried out with the imprisonment or murder of opposing radical and democratic forces as if no other form of liberation were now imaginable—the Communist direction showed something more than "betrayal" had taken place. The Party's ethnic and race following, which had in a certain sense compensated for its limited cadre outside the leadership of industrial unions, drifted away. Whatever its future, American radicalism would be something very different from what it had been. James's genius was to perceive this entire political process as a natural and inevitable one (the outgrowth of newer phases of capitalism) and to locate from within the mass of population its dialectical opposite, seeds of a new life within the shell of the old.[11]

The "Negro question," conceived in the broadest terms, can be seen as the illuminating insight that directed James to a fresh perspective. It had been the analysis of the black masses in the West Indies that first gave a political focus to his wide-ranging intellectual interests, helped him not only to write *The Case for West Indian Self-Government* and *The Black Jacobins* but also sharpened his critique of Stalinism in *World Revolution*. The inextricability of the international influence upon any radical prospects; the ability of Lenin to see beyond the party to the potentials of mass stirring and in turn to use the Bolshevik party for the fulfillment of mass democratic prospects; the Communist perception that masses revolt on slogans and for concrete ends rather than from some abstract ideal—all these carried over into James's observations of American blacks. Within a year or so of his American residence, he had outlined a program that confronted not only the Left's handling of the black question per se but also hinted strongly at a very different orientation on a spectrum of strategic matters. Of these, theoretical ramifications would be seen very soon.[12]

James's "Preliminary Notes on the Negro Question" struck at the base of the white Left's previous approach. He insisted that Trotskyists support the "formation of an organization to rally Negroes, which would be reformist at the start, but which would develop at once into militancy." Not an organization with strings pulled by the white Left, as even the best of the Communist "front" organizations turned out to be in moments of political stress, but rather one outside formal socialist ranks, beyond manipulation as a recruiting ground, demanding no specific socialist politics as a condition for membership. In short: an organization with the autonomy that had never been granted ethnic, racial, or other entities within the Left; a fundamental breach of Leninist (or even Second International) concepts of discipline in the name of self-organization. This, and James's opposition to the slogan of black (territorial) self-determination, proved sticking points with Trotsky, who engaged James in a dialogue at Coyoacan in 1939. James wanted revolutionaries to suggest tactics and specific struggles, to aid the formation of a movement, but to remove their hand from the lever and to support the ultimate goals blacks themselves raised up—including self-determination only if they deemed this desirable to emancipation in a multiracial American order. Spontaneity versus organization? In part. But in larger part, American realities against European concepts.[13]

One could draw a straight line from James's observations of Garveyism in his 1938 *History of Negro Revolt* to the culmination of his decade-long wrangling with American Trotskyists in the ground-breaking 1947 conference document "The Revolutionary Answer to the Negro Problem in the United States." James based his high estimation of Garvey's impact not on formal back-to-Africa politics but rather on the sense of pride, the racial and international solidarity against centuries of oppression, that Garvey aroused. What James called the "social service attitude" of the Left could never stoke the "fires that smoulder in the Negro world" showing themselves vividly in social life:

Let us not forget that in the Negro people there sleep and are now awakening passions of a violence exceeding, perhaps, as far as these things can be compared, anything among the tremendous forces that capitalism has created. Anyone who knows them, who knows their history, is able to talk to them intimately, watches them in their churches, reads their press with a discerning eye, must recognize that although their social force may not be able to compare with the social force of a corresponding number of organized workers, the hatred of bourgeois society and the readiness to destroy it when the opportunity should present itself, rests among them to a degree greater than in any other section of the population in the United States.[14]

Through that perception, moreover, James could follow and extend Du Bois in turning the concept of American history around. Blacks had, with their allies the white abolitionists, forced the bourgeoisie toward the Civil War. Only by their emancipation could that struggle have been won, and the South truly reconstructed. Only through their success could a Populist movement have restrained an advancing capitalism. And only by their actual advance could the CIO come into its own. With broadening, deepening relevance to the revolutionary prospect, the independent black movement precipitated the political forces of socialism.

No American radical had gone so far, and none would carry these ideas further until the 1960s. That James's views became gospel for the orthodox Trotskyist movement is a minor (although interesting) concern, with indirect links to white Left recognition of Malcolm X and the early black power slogans. More important, James had set himself against Communist fundamentals in a precise fashion, without renouncing revolutionary intention, Leninist legacy, or direct political involvement.

James's wholly unique perception of the CIO struggle, his analysis of the Communists' support of bureaucratic tendencies within the labor movement, extended the insight into the process of revolutionary transformation and the limitations of the existing Marxist comprehension. With a small group of collaborators within the Trotskyist Workers party, James began to insist that—contrary to the perceptions that cut across other differences among the American Left—the working class was not backward by true Marxist standards. Like the keen observer of early CIO strikes Louis Adamic, who pinpointed in the militant workers the most democratic impulse in the nation, James recognized the instinctual grasping for the universal of socialism—not a change in the form of property but the very negation of the dominant social relations. "More political party than trade union," he was to say later, the CIO embodied the response to the foremost challenge that modern capitalist industry ever set before its exploited.[15]

The system of sweated labor pioneered by Ford evinced a totalitarian economic mentality, scientifically rationalized production with closer inter-capitalist relations, and the intervention of the state as mediator. This marked the culmination of industrial and political development over the centuries and, unchallenged, would signify the subordination of every democratic possibility to the demands of capital. But intertwined with that development, at every step, had been elements of resistance, from the battles of the weavers in the medieval cities to the actions of the ranks in Cromwell's army, to the revolt of the masses in the French Revolution, to the rise of the Paris Commune, and finally to the soviets in Russia. True to Marx, James had seen the proletariat as the embodiment of the revolution-ary prospect. Even his San Domingo slaves of the eighteenth century, "working and living together in gangs of hundreds on the huge sugar factories . . . were closer to a modern proletariat than any group of workers in existence at that time, and [their] rising was, *therefore*, a thoroughly prepared and organized mass movement"[16] (my emphasis). They were not prepared by some external agent, but by the conditions of life and work, with a natural leadership thrown up in self-conscious striving for a better life. The modern class struggle pressed home the ultimate proletarian goals, abolition of hierarchies invested through the division of mental and manual labor. Like Austin Lewis, a generation earlier, observing the mass strikes of unskilled foreign-born workers, James looked at the early, dynamic stages of CIO industrial unionism and declared the shop-floor struggle to be "socialism . . . the only socialism."[17]

And still, the weight of institutions loomed heavier than ever upon the proletarian impulse. As Walling had seen the earliest stages of state capital-ism taking on craft workers as ballast against the unskilled proletariat, James analyzed the next stage as the decisive unfolding of state capitalism. In the United States, the working class had moved forward to institutionalize its power through the unions. But because circumstances had not grown desperate enough or the progressive forces strong enough for revolutionary change, the net result had been the creation of a new intermediary stratum, the labor bureaucracy. That the functionaries were often Communists signaled to James the new level of internal contradictions within the system, generating a political mood that reestablished at the new level the *essential* dichotomy of rulers and ruled.

This symmetry bespoke a weighty analysis, indeed. James had observed in *World Revolution* that Stalin intuitively chose to rely upon the Party bureaucracy or even the bourgeoisie to carry out the interests of the Russian states, as Lenin had chosen the masses in creative moments to override both. As James and his collaborators began to perceive through study of the Russian scene, Stalin was a knave but no fool. He had correctly understood the objective formation of a new power base in the state bureaucracy itself, a perverse extension of Lenin's insights in *Imperialism*. Dramatic change, at least in the West, no longer served a Third International which had, like the Second International before it, been transformed from revolutionary agency to the special interest group of a particular stratum. American Communist union leaders who banked the fires of resistance through crackdowns on wildcats and subtler measures like the dues check-off, who thought in terms of industrial rationalization and international consumer marketing alongside their corporate opposite numbers, constituted the "American bureaucracy carried to its ultimate and logical conclusion"—as state-capitalist functionaries-in-progress. Their willingness to compromise the integrity of the proletarian impulse indicated no necessary corruption or personal gain, but the hankering after a higher logic. They had repudiated private capitalism without believing that the classic proletariat of Karl Marx could in the foreseeable future rule itself.[18]

In later years, James sought to penetrate still further the logic that ruled Communist parties and kept the unquestionably idealistic ranks in a curious stasis between radical and liberal perspectives. "Stalinism is a concrete truth . . . a necessary, an inevitable form of development of the labor movement," he argued by 1948, no distortion of history (in the final sense) but the working out of a logic inherent in the uneven pace of world revolution.[19] The world *was* divided into two camps, the more so after World War II. And yet despite the futility of the Trotskyist polemics against Communist misleadership, despite the rubble of war and the growing fears among non-Communists that revolutionary options had become almost unthinkable, James insisted that a promising stage had been reached.

"The one-party state is the bourgeois attempt to respond to the contemporary necessity for the fusion and transcendence of nation, class, party, state," James argued boldly.[20] The increasing concentration of social and economic power in a few hands, even in the once politically diffuse democracies, pointed in the same direction. When the society as a whole increasingly perceived the forces of production (the working class) to be essentially *social* and not merely economic, the working class stood objectively closer than ever to cutting the Gordian knot. The old categories that had held fast since the beginning of capitalism, the mysterious origin of the commodity in workers' labor power on the one hand and the supposed autonomy of party and state on the other, lost their essential definitions. As Engels had predicted in *Anti-Dühring*, the last major text of the Marxist founding fathers, "concealed within" the very contradictions of this most highly organized capital were "the technical conditions that form the elements of the solution." Working-class elements themselves—and not merely their socialist or Communist political representatives—had become (in Engels's words) "the invading socialist society" at the doorstep of the world order.[21]

Although hardly more than an outline of a world view, this meditation of James's compressed an extraordinary vision of socialism's place in world history into a current political position. As James explained in a 1947 position paper, "Dialectical Materialism and the Fate of Humanity," the philosophical position of Hegel that stood behind Marxism had been no more than a recognition of the human effort to resolve the contradiction between the "abstract universality" (equality, oneness in God's eyes) of the original Christian promise and concrete necessity. Hegel recounted—albeit in idealistic form—the stages of negation through which this struggle had to pass. Marxism gave this understanding, in turn, a material base and a political outlook. Not rationalism, which had served the intermediate classes at every moment of bourgeois revolution, raising up the education, articulateness, and supposed intelligence of the bourgeoisie and petty bourgeoisie against the "backwardness," the "irrationality" of the masses, but the freed expression "by the proletarian millions of their world-historical universality, no longer empirical but completely self-conscious . . . the total mobilization of all forces of society. That and nothing else can rebuild the vast wreck which is the modern world."[22]

So, too, was the prospect altered of what Marxism had meant and would mean to the prospects for socialism. When James's little group published the earliest translations from Marx's *Economic and Philosophical Manuscripts of 1844*, they sought to identify the sense of alienation, below the more obvious poverty and exploitation, that every modern working person suffers. "Be his wages high or low," as Marx wrote, that alienation remained fundamentally intolerable. Lenin had, in his finest moments, recognized the limitation in any change of property form as such. Trotskyism, the closest thing to a revolutionary succession, carried over the party form without that awareness and unwittingly returned to what Marx had blasted as the "vulgar communism" of mistaking transcendence of private property for real socialist social relations. Now the Marxist group, if not to fall upon the same pointless contest to become the "real" vanguard, had to take up the deeper purpose of demonstrating to the masses of people the power of their own creativity, "the socialism that exists in the population, the resentment, the desire to overturn and get rid of the tremendous burdens by which capitalism is crushing the people."[23] Or there would be no Marxism, no socialist or communist movement, worthy of consideration at all. From the young Marx laboring under Hegelian influence to the final socialist impulse, the circle would be closed by Marxists who had come to grips with the world around them. The revolutionary movement would become explicitly what it had been implicitly, the amalgam of every progressive impulse in the history of the species, the vindication of humanity not for any external end (not even "progress") but for its own sake.

Did James delude himself or disguise for political reasons the extent to which this constituted a break from all that historic Marxism (since, at least, the young Marx) had been? In one specific sense, yes. "Trotsky declared that the proletariat does not grow under world capitalism and declines in culture. This is absolutely false," James wrote in 1950.[24] One may find hints in this or that Marxist literary commentary about the existence of a "cultural question." Never, by the orthodox Marxists of the First, Second, Third, or Fourth Internationals, not even during the drive for a "proletarian culture" in the Soviet Union and abroad from the late 1920s to the mid-1930s, was the proposition of culture *in itself* put forward as the basis for the revolutionary transition. Yet, understood in the broadest sense, it was the glue for James's philosophical, economic, and political perspectives, his observation of workers' lives as a whole, their articulated and ill-expressed subjectivity being the disproof of their supposed "backwardness." When he argued in his own last major theoretical document before his deportation that Captain Ahab of *Moby Dick* was the consummate bureaucrat ("abstract intellect, abstract science, abstract technology, alive, but blank, serving no human purpose") while the crew constituted the indestructible working class embracing risk, nature, and spontaneity, James believed the task of the true revolutionary was to understand that cultural dichotomy above all and to choose Life over the promise of Power. Marxism at its best had implied this difference all along; but almost never had the cultural logic become the ground for a real communism.[25]

In another, quite intimately related sense, James had stated the basic propositions of an American socialism that had never been the text of the formal Marxist parties. For James had cracked the nut of radicalism's relation with the racial, ethnic, social, and cultural forces that had never fit into the smaller Marxism but nonetheless directed the potential of the revolutionary movement. The force of blacks upon American political life seems in retrospect an almost obvious insight, but the implications that they arrived in politics under their own steam and brought socialism to center stage stood outside all conventional wisdom. The struggle within the class struggle that this interpretation implied defied the best of the Communists' "Black and White, Unite and Fight" perspective. And it was the logical outcome of the conflict between American- and foreign-born, skilled and unskilled, which, as Austin Lewis had shrewdly perceived, reflected the final vestiges of a small-property tradition (translated into skill as a form of property) that reached back centuries against the totality of modern manufacture. The resolution to this conflict stood ultimately beyond the adjustments that state-regulated capital could make to the condition of the wage earner.

There was much to American radicalism that James did not and could not see from the secluded corner of the Trotskyist movement, isolated from other great elements of American reform. The significance of the ethnic strains, which had provided the immigrant with the taste of the socialist future in the warmth of family and class ties, James glimpsed from afar. Not until the mid-1940s did he begin to write about that force that stood coequal with blacks in the abolitionist movement, that bolstered ethnic radicalisms and contributed in large part the moral sensibility, the grass-roots impetus to native socialism: the women's movement. That the struggle (as James put it) against "an authority which inculcated the authoritarian character of the society as a whole" within the family circle might have an importance hardly less than that of the struggle for emancipated labor—this was a leap too far in one direction, too precise in totality for James's central conceptions.[26] Here as in other areas like the profound effect of religious moralisms, or the unfolding of a radical aesthetic, one must say that the great questions of American socialism received only an abstract answer at James's hands.

But he achieved no small thing. The path he illuminated broadens out to a wide road that passes through valley and dale of theory and practice, the high mountain passes of profoundest human hope, and the dark cities of toil and trouble. James made his contribution to American radicalism, as a variant of the European experience. But, foremost, from the onset of his career, James placed international responsibilities upon the agenda, showing them to be inevitable as the connections between capitalism and the labor market worldwide. If he returned Marxist theory from the darkness of exegetical lumber rooms, it is because he saw the working out of the deepest global schema in the lives of ordinary people across the globe.

III

Many of the same themes reached a wide reading public, first in a pessimistic, then a more hopeful, and then again more pessimistic vein. The rife alienation that James and his collaborators perceived in American life, if one can believe Albert Camus, grew out of the detective novel into the entire existentialist philosophy. Ralph Ellison's *Invisible Man*, building upon themes that James's friend Richard Wright had developed earlier, pointed up what James had written about Communists in Harlem—but without proposing any solutions. Slowly, over generations, the Hegelianism of the young Marx played a role in the revival of another Left, as did the vision of corporate liberalism (a general approximation of state capitalism and rationalist totality). By the late 1960s, the connection between culture and radicalism had become an all-pervasive topic of discussion, and not only within the Left; culture was now recognized as a powerful agent, if by no means coherently perceived. And in the time that has followed, the congruence of social history and radical commitment has been made abundantly evident, indeed become the Marxist scholarly commitment of hundreds who emerged with university training from the 1960s: a vision of ordinary people in the United States and everywhere, searching urgently for the means to remake the quality of their existence. The New Left, the women's movement, and above all the black movement seemed at points to be expressing in political logic the insightful kernel James had opened up in his venture beyond orthodox Leninism. And the turn toward the working class by the New Left during the early 1970s carried along his imperative, to relocate the blue-collar source of a future soviet.[27]

James's specific contribution and the totality of his view, with the partial exception of that emphasis on black initiative and self-activity, seemed to have been lost on the cutting-room floor. Part of the rationale surely resides in the groupuscule character of James's earlier efforts, their publication and language so restricted by the Trotskyist context that twenty years hence the confused Fourth Internationalists whom James singled out for critique took the aspect of ghosts from some vanished political dynasty. And his books were, aside from *The Black Jacobins*, for all practical purposes physically unobtainable.

There is also a deeper reason that goes back to the conflicts of the 1940s. When James redressed Trotsky's estimation of proletarian physical diminution and spiritual decline under later capitalism, he militantly defended the "thesis of Marx that in the very crisis of capitalism the proletariat is . . . prepared socially for its tasks, by the very mechanisms of capitalist production itself."[28] A few years after World War II, nearly every avowed radical movement, whatever its formal ideology, shared Trotsky's pessimism. Stalinism and social democracy in particular had gone over to the belief that armies, bombs, political maneuver, and foreign policy, rather than the working class, would rule the fate of the world. In James's own Workers party, the thesis of "retrogressionism," as one key writer put it, placed "a question mark over the ability of the proletariat to reassemble a revolutionary leadership to take power before it is overtaken and destroyed by the disintegrative tendency of capitalist civilization of which threatening atomic war is the most potent force."[29] Against this defeatism every instinct of James rebelled. But his voice cried into the wind.

By and large—with the exception of some rather brief political periods and some groups—the fundamental pessimism as regards the working class has never lifted. Indeed, one can say that it has permeated the best as well as the worst of political writing on the Left, from the philosophy of Herbert Marcuse to the social economics of Michael Harrington to the cultural ruminations of Ishmael Reed. When today a noticeably undoctrinaire socialist writer looks to the possible futures of "a semi-corporatist liberalism," "a technocratic, authoritarian neo-conservatism," or (in the best case) a "radical-democratic liberalism with populist elements," he cites as his future-looking guide the same Daniel Bell whom James leveled against in 1949 for substituting technical for human solutions, and for excluding the socialist possibility altogether.[30] Even at the mundane level of tactics, many of James's complaints—the Marxist response to a widespread backwardness and assertions that it was not backward but needed the leadership of a (still unformed) vanguard—have not been essentially outdated in forty years.

The obscurity of James's contributions, beyond the problems of verbiage and context, can be summarized in the proposition that Marxists have not yet reconciled themselves with the subjectivity of the revolutionary subject. Whether this be the *locus classicus* proletariat is not even the essential matter. James often glimpsed moments when the peasantry, entering into a transition to the modern order, can take the leadership of the whole social matrix. And he stressed that in the outbreaks of the future in the industrialized nations, students, women and other self-defined groups will represent themselves in the councils of transformation. Meanwhile, among the Marxist political groups, not even the most "spontaneist" have become seriously interested in popular life as a whole, beyond the factory gates, save to deplore consumerism, to place "real" (i.e., economic) class struggle against such delusions, to cite a left-wing (generally socialist realist) artist here and there who has supposedly captured the palpitating dynamics of contemporary conflict. Only among the smallest minority have the (once) widely accepted notions of black proletarian combativity been linked with a concept of that as lever for the rest of the working class and broader society, means for insight about the cultural particularities and possibilities across the demographic map. James, be it recalled, never elicited guilt from white workers; he made it clear that for them (and the rest of the nation) to accept black equality in the fullest sense meant an acceptance of dramatic change in the whole social order. Meanwhile, as the world revolutionary process continued to accelerate, things remained in a stasis for more than two generations. Socialists were committed to one version or another of the state, with its perpetuation of mental versus manual labor, while Communists waited for the working class to join some sort of Communist party en masse. Bypassed or in the future, James's contributions have never seemed quite timely.

James's perspective defies empirical proof, in the sense that nothing but barbarism or socialism can finally demonstrate such political conclusions.

During World War II, James presciently referred to "socialism or barbarism," alive at the same moment, battling toward a finish that has only been postponed all these decades. But there is something more that James wrote from a deep sense of history and that the Left, and the intelligentsia as a whole, have been unable or unwilling to absorb:

> We do not idealize the workers. . . . But the very bourgeois society which has produced its most gifted body of thinkers and artists has also given birth to a proletariat which instinctively demanded the application to itself of every value which the philosophers and the various classes they represented had demanded throughout the ages. . . . Spinoza and Kant would stand aghast at what the average worker takes for granted today. But he does not demand them as an individual or in the primitive manner the early Christians did. . . . These are the values of modern civilization. They are embodied in the very web and texture of the lives of the masses of the people. Never were such precious values so resolutely held as necessary to complete living by so substantial and so powerful a section of society. Socialism means simply the complete extension and fulfillment of these values in the life of the individual.[31]

This is even more than the prophets had foreseen, since the continuation of class society nourished a variety of liberational forces that might have been anticipated on the morrow of the Revolution. Yet it is also the ancient dream of Utopia realized.

To James, who early saw the human truth behind the civilized falsehoods about his West Indian people's capacities, this promise has never been a matter of dogma or blind faith. "We live our daily lives in the upper reaches and derivative superstructures of Marxism," he wrote in 1943. "We are not academicians and must perforce spend most of our time there. But the foundations and lower floors are huge unexplored buildings which we enter if at all in solitude and leave in silence. They have been shrines too long. We need to throw them open, to ourselves and to the public."[32] Perhaps no Marxist had dug deeper into the subsoil of the socialist heritage, from its distant origins to the philosophic foundation stones to the fructifying columns and arches which have been considered the holiest of holy additions. From the colonial background of the West Indies to metropolitan London, from Harlem to Detroit to Africa, James felt his confidence in the basic capacities and desires of plain people to be justified. "The unending murders, the destruction of peoples, the bestial passions, the sadism, the cruelties and the lusts, all the manifestations of barbarism . . . are unparalleled in history. But this barbarism exists only because nothing else can suppress the readiness for sacrifice, the democratic instincts and creative power of the great masses of people," as James wrote.[33] The task of revolutionaries, to build upon those perceptions, those desires, has been often and sadly disappointed. But nothing short of nuclear holocaust encompassing the whole planet can obliterate the revolutionary option.

Notes

1. Perry Anderson, *Considerations on Western Marxism* (London: New Left Books, 1976).
2. Albert Gates, "Politics in the Stratosphere," *New International*, Vol. 9, November 1943, p. 311.
3. C. L. R. James, *Beyond a Boundary* (London: Stanley Paul, 1963), p. 151.
4. See my *Marxism in the United States*, 2nd ed. (London: Verso, 1991) for an exploration of this topic, especially chapters 1 and 4.
5. This subject is approached many times, from many angles, in Mari Jo Buhle, Paul Buhle, and Dan Georgakas, eds., *Encyclopedia of the American Left* (New York: Garland, 1990). See also *Marxism in the United States*, chapters 2, 3, and 6.
6. See Paul Richards, "W. E. B. Du Bois and American Social History: Evolution of a Marxist," *Radical America*, Vol. 5, November 1970.
7. Lewis's writings are scattered through the *New Review*, *International Socialist Review*, and other publications. His most incisive single text is *The Militant Proletariat* (Chicago: Charles H. Kerr, 1911).
8. Walling's major works were *Socialism as It Is* (New York: The Macmillan Company, 1913), *The Larger Aspects of Socialism* (New York: The Macmillan Company, 1913), and *Progressivism—and After* (New York: The Macmillan Company, 1914).
9. See my forthcoming biography of Louis Fraina/Lewis Corey (Atlantic Highlands, NJ: Humanities Press).
10. See the *Encyclopedia of the American Left* entries, for instance, on "Woody Guthrie," "Hollywood Left," "Popular Culture," and "Sitdown Strikes."
11. George Lipsitz's incisive volume, *"A Rainbow at Midnight": Class and Culture in Cold War America* (New York: Praeger, 1981) and a special issue of *Radical America*, Vol. 9, July–August 1975. This view of the 1940s CP is argued best in this special issue of *Radical America* on the 1940s, and most especially in Stan Weir's reminiscence, "American Labor on the Defensive: A 1940s Odyssey."
12. I treat this subject, as those in the rest of the essay, at greater length in my *C. L. R. James: The Artist as Revolutionary* (London: Verso, 1988). James gave some important clues to the origins of his historical analysis in *Letters on Organization* (Detroit: Facing Reality, n.d.), p. 12.
13. The discussion has been reprinted in *Leon Trotsky on Black Nationalism and Self-Determination* (New York: Pathfinder Press, 1970) and in *At the Rendezvous of Victory* (London: Allison & Busby, 1984).
14. James's resolution is now most accessible in *The Future in the Present* (London: Allison & Busby, 1977), quotation from pp. 126–27.
15. Louis Adamic, *My America* (New York: Harper, 1938). James's observation was stated many times in different ways, but perhaps is clearest in *State Capitalism and World Revolution* (Chicago: Charles H. Kerr, 1986), chapter 5.
16. C. L. R. James, *The History of the Pan-African Revolt* (Washington: Drum and Spear Press, 1969), p. 188.
17. See my efforts to wrestle with the context of this conclusion in *C. L. R. James: The Artist as Revolutionary*, chapter 3.

18. See Scott McLemee's essay in this volume, and my own introduction to the latest edition of *State Capitalism and World Revolution* (Chicago: Charles H. Kerr, 1986). Like a number of other documents from the time, this work was in fact a collaboration with Grace Lee (now Grace Boggs) and Raya Dunayevskaya. See also C. L. R. James, *The Invading Socialist Society* (Detroit: Bewick Editions, 1972), co-authored with Lee and Dunayevskaya.
19. *Notes on Dialectics* (London: Allison & Busby, 1980), p. 30.
20. Ibid., p. 178.
21. *The Invading Socialist Society*, p. 62. See also Fredrich Engels, *Anti-Dühring* (Moscow: Progress Publishers, 1969), pp. 328, 331.
22. Reprinted from the Johnson-Forest Bulletin in *Spheres of Existence* (London: Allison & Busby, 1980). I published a shortened pamphlet edition of this essay as *Dialectic of History* (Cambridge, MA: Radical America, 1972).
23. Best articulated in C. L. R. James, *Perspectives and Proposals* (Detroit: Facing Reality, 1966), p. 39.
24. *State Capitalism and World Revolution*, p. 31.
25. C. L. R. James, *Mariners, Renegades, and Castaways* (London: Allison & Busby, 1985), p. 22.
26. Reprinted in Selma James, "The American Family: Decay and Re-Birth," *Radical America*, Vol. 4, February 1970, p. 3.
27. This viewpoint was expressed in *Radical America*, more than in any publication in the United States during the late 1960s and early 1970s. I try to recapitulate it in *Marxism in the United States*, chapter 7.
28. *State Capitalism and World Revolution*, pp. 40–41.
29. Ernest Erber, "The Class Nature of the Polish State," *New International*, Vol. 11, August 1947, p. 100.
30. David Plotke, "The United States in Transition: Toward a New Order?" *Socialist Review*, No. 54, November–December 1980. This essay, as it turns out, was the opening shot of a large-scale political retrenchment of social democracy (including a former section of the New Left) into a neo-liberal quest for social control and national competitiveness. The U.S. victory in the cold war consolidated the development, but its origins can be clearly traced to the liberal/conservative banishment of "utopianism" (i.e., radical democratization) in favor of a corporate capitalist future, during the later 1940s.
31. C. L. R. James, "Laski, St. Paul and Stalin," reprinted in *The Future in the Present* (London: Allison & Busby, 1977), p. 100.
32. C. L. R. James, "Production for the Sake of Production—A Reply to Carter," *Workers Party Bulletin*, No. 2, April 1943, Raya Dunayevskaya Papers.
33. *The Invading Socialist Society*, p. 14.

PART II
Writings for the
Trotskyist Press
(1939–1949)

5

Revolution and the Negro

The Negro's revolutionary history is rich, inspiring, and unknown. Negroes revolted against the slave raiders in Africa; they revolted against the slave traders on the Atlantic passage. They revolted on the plantations.

The docile Negro is a myth. Slaves on slave ships jumped overboard, went on vast hunger strikes, attacked the crews. There are records of slaves overcoming the crew and taking the ship into harbor, a feat of tremendous revolutionary daring. In British Guyana during the eighteenth century the Negro slaves revolted, seized the Dutch colony, and held it for years. They withdrew to the interior, forced the whites to sign a treaty of peace, and have remained free to this day. Every West Indian colony, particularly Jamaica and San Domingo and Cuba, the largest islands, had its settlements of maroons, bold Negroes who had fled into the wilds and organized themselves to defend their freedom. In Jamaica the British government, after vainly trying to suppress them, accepted their existence by treaties of peace, scrupulously observed by both sides over many years, and then broken by British treachery. In America the Negroes made nearly 150 distinct revolts against slavery. The only place where Negroes did not revolt is in the pages of capitalist historians. All this revolutionary history can come as a surprise only to those who, whatever International they belong to, whether Second, Third, or Fourth, have not yet ejected from their systems the pertinacious lies of Anglo-Saxon capitalism. It is not strange that the Negroes revolted. It would have been strange if they had not.

But the Fourth International, whose business is revolution, has not to prove that Negroes were or are as revolutionary as any group of oppressed people. That has its place in agitation. What we as Marxists have to see is the tremendous role played by Negroes in the transformation of Western civilization from feudalism to capitalism. It is only from this vantage-ground that we shall be able to appreciate (and prepare for) the still greater role they must of necessity play in the transition from capitalism to socialism.

What are the decisive dates in the modern history of Great Britain, France, and America? 1789, the beginning of the French Revolution; 1832, the passing of the Reform Bill in Britain; and 1865, the crushing of the slave-power in America by the Northern states. Each of these dates marks a definitive stage in the transition from feudal to capitalist society. The exploitation of millions of Negroes had been a basic factor in the economic development of each of these three nations. It was reasonable, therefore, to expect the Negro question to play no less an important role in the resolution of the problems that faced each society. No one in the prerevolutionary days, however, even faintly foresaw the magnitude of the contributions the Negroes were to make. Today Marxists have far less excuse for falling into the same mistake.

THE NEGRO AND THE FRENCH REVOLUTION

The French Revolution was a bourgeois revolution, and the basis of bourgeois wealth was the slave trade and the slave plantations in the colonies. Let there be no mistake about this. "Sad irony of human history," says Jaurès, "the fortunes created at Bordeaux, at Nantes by the slave trade, gave to the bourgeoisie that pride which needed liberty and contributed to human emancipation." And Gaston-Martin, the historian of the slave trade, sums it up thus: though the bourgeoisie traded in other things than slaves, upon the success or failure of the traffic everything else depended. Therefore when the bourgeoisie proclaimed the Rights of Man in general, with necessary reservations, one of these was that these rights should extend to the French colonies. In 1789 the French colonial trade was 11 million pounds, two-thirds of the overseas trade of France. British colonial trade at that time was only 5 million pounds. What price French abolition? There was an abolitionist society to which Brissot, Robespierre, Mirabeau, Lafayette, Condorcet, and many such famous men belonged even before 1789. But liberals are liberal. Face to face with the revolution, they were ready to compromise. They would leave the half-million slaves in their slavery, but at least the mulattoes, men of property (including slaves) and education, should be given equal rights with the white colonials. The white colonial magnates refused concessions and they were people to be reckoned with, aristocrats by birth or marriage, bourgeois by their trade connections with the maritime bourgeoisie. They opposed all change in the colonies that would diminish their social and political domination. The maritime bourgeoisie, concerned about their millions of investments, supported the colonials, and against 11 million pounds of trade per year the radical politicians were helpless. It was the revolution that kicked them from behind and forced them forward.

First of all the revolution in France. The Girondins, right wing of the Jacobin club, overthrew the pro-royalist Feuillants and came to power in March 1792.

And secondly the revolution in the colonies. The mulattoes in San Domingo revolted in 1790, followed a few months later by the slave revolt in August 1791. On April 4, 1792, the Girondins granted political and social rights to the mulattoes. The big bourgeoisie agreed, for the colonial aristocrats, after vainly trying to win mulatto support for independence, decided to hand the colony over to Britain rather than tolerate interference with their system. All these slave owners, French nobility and French bourgeoisie, colonial aristocrats and mulattoes, were agreed that the slave revolt should be suppressed and the slaves remain in their slavery.

The slaves, however, refused to listen to threats, and no promises were made to them. Led from beginning to end by men who had themselves been slaves and were unable to read or write, they fought one of the greatest revolutionary battles in history. Before the revolution they had seemed subhuman. Many a slave had to be whipped before he could be got to move from where he sat. The revolution transformed them into heroes.

The island of San Domingo was divided into two colonies, one French, the other Spanish. The colonial government of the Spanish Bourbons supported the slaves in their revolt against the French republic, and many rebel bands took service with the Spaniards. The French colonials invited Pitt to take over the colony, and when war was declared between France and England in 1793, the English invaded the island.

The English expedition, welcomed by all the white colonials, captured town after town in the south and west of French San Domingo. The Spaniards, operating with the famous Toussaint-Louverture, an ex-slave, invaded the colony from the east. British and Spaniards were gobbling up as much as they could before the time for sharing came. "In these matters," wrote the British minister, Dundas, to the governor of Jamaica, "the more we have, the better our pretensions." On June 4, Port-au-Prince, the capital of San Domingo, fell. Meanwhile another British expedition had captured Martinique, Guadeloupe, and the other French islands. Barring a miracle, the colonial trade of France, the richest in the world, was in the hands of her enemies and would be used against the revolution. But here the French masses took a hand.

August 10, 1792, was the beginning of the revolution triumphant in France. The Paris masses and their supporters all over France, in 1789 indifferent to the colonial question, were now striking in revolutionary frenzy at every abuse of the old regime and none of the former tyrants were so hated as the "aristocrats of the skin." Revolutionary generosity, resentment at the betrayal of the colonies to the enemies of the revolution, impotence in the face of the British navy—these swept the Convention off its feet. On February 2, 1794, without a debate, it decreed the abolition of Negro slavery and at last gave its sanction to the black revolt.

The news trickled through somehow to the French West Indies. Victor Hugues, a mulatto, one of the great personalities produced by the revolution, managed to break through the British blockade and carried the official notice of the manumission of the mulattoes and blacks of the West Indian islands. Then occurred the miracle. The blacks and mulattoes dressed themselves in the revolutionary colors and, singing revolutionary songs, they turned on the British and Spaniards, their allies of yesterday. With little more from revolutionary France than its moral support, they drove the British and Spaniards from their conquests and carried the war into enemy territory. The British, after five years of trying to reconquer the French colonies, were finally driven out in 1798.

Few know the magnitude and the importance of that defeat sustained at the hands of Victor Hugues in the smaller islands and of Toussaint-Louverture and Rigaud in San Domingo. Fortescue, the Tory historian of the British army, estimates the total loss to Britain at 100,000 men. Yet in the whole of the Peninsular War Wellington lost from all causes—killed in battle, sickness, desertions—only 40,000 men. British blood and British treasure were poured out in profusion in the West Indian campaign. This was the reason for Britain's weakness in Europe during the critical years 1793–1798. Let Fortescue himself speak: "The secret of England's impotence for the first six years of the war may be said to lie in the two fatal words of San Domingo." British historians blame chiefly the fever, as if San Domingo was the only place in the world that European imperialism had met fever.

Whatever the neglect or distortions of later historians, the French revolutionaries themselves knew what the Negro question meant to the revolution. The Constituent, the Legislature, and the Convention were repeatedly thrown into disorder by the colonial debates. This had grave repercussions in the internal struggle as well as in the revolutionary defense of the Republic. Says Jaurès, "Undoubtedly but for the compromises of Barnave and all his party on the colonial question, the general attitude of the Assembly after the flight to Varennes would have been different." Excluding the masses of Paris, no portion of the French Empire played, in proportion to its size, so grandiose a role in the French Revolution as the half-million blacks and mulattoes in the remote West Indian islands.

THE BLACK REVOLUTION AND WORLD HISTORY

The black revolution in San Domingo choked at its source one of the most powerful economic streams of the eighteenth century. With the defeat of the British, the black proletarians defeated the mulatto Third Estate in a bloody civil war. Immediately after, Bonaparte, representative of the most reactionary elements of the new French bourgeoisie, attempted to restore slavery in San Domingo. The blacks defeated an expedition of some 50,000 men, and with the assistance of the mulattoes, carried the revolution to its logical conclusion. They changed the name of San Domingo to Haiti and declared the island independent. This black revolution had a profound effect on the struggle for the cessation of the slave trade.

We can trace this close connection best by following the development of abolition in the British Empire. The first great blow at the Tory domination of Britain (and at feudalism in France for that matter) was struck by the Declaration of Independence in 1776. When Jefferson wrote that all men are created equal, he was drawing up the death-warrant of feudal society, wherein men were by law divided into unequal classes. Crispus Attucks, the Negro, was the first man killed by the British in the war that followed. It was no isolated or chance phenomenon. The Negroes thought in this war for freedom, they could win their own. It has been estimated that of the 30,000 men in Washington's army 4,000 were Negroes. The American bourgeoisie did not want them. They forced themselves in. But San Domingo Negroes fought in the war also.

The French monarchy came to the assistance of the American Revolution. And Negroes from the French colonies pushed themselves into the French expeditionary force. Of the 1,900 French troops who recaptured Savannah, 900 were volunteers from the French colony of San Domingo. Ten years later some of these men—Rigaud, André, Lambert, Beauvais, and others (some say Christophe also)—with their political and military experience, would be foremost among the leaders in the San Domingo revolution. Long before Karl Marx wrote "Workers of the world, unite," the revolution was international.

The loss of the slave-holding American colonies took much cotton out of the ears of the British bourgeoisie. Adam Smith and Arthur Young, heralds of the Industrial Revolution and wage-slavery, were already preaching against the waste of chattel-slavery. Deaf up to 1783, the British bourgeoisie now heard, and looked again at the West Indies. Their own colonies were bankrupt. They were losing the slave trade to French and British rivals. And half the French slaves that they brought were going to San Domingo, the India of the eighteenth century. Why should they continue to do this? In three years, the first abolitionist society was formed and Pitt began to clamor for the abolition of slavery—"for the sake of humanity, no doubt," says Gaston-Martin, "but also, be it well understood, to ruin French commerce." With the war of 1793, Pitt, cherishing a prospect of winning San Domingo, piped down on abolition. But the black revolution killed the aspirations of both France and Britain.

The Treaty of Vienna in 1814 gave to France the right to recapture San Domingo; the Haitians swore that they would rather destroy the island. With the abandonment of the hopes for regaining San Domingo, the British abolished the slave trade in 1807. America followed in 1808.

If the East Indian interest in Britain was one of the great financial arsenals of the new bourgeoisie (whence the diatribes of Burke, Whig spokesman, against Hastings and Clive), the West Indian interest, though never so powerful as in France, was a cornerstone of the feudal oligarchy. The loss of America was the beginning of their decline. But for the black revolution, San Domingo would have strengthened them enormously. The reformist British bourgeoisie belabored them, the weakest link in the oligarchical chain. A great slave revolt in Jamaica in 1831 helped to convince those who had doubts. In Britain "Better emancipation from above than below" anticipated the Tsar by thirty years. One of the first acts of the victorious reformers was to abolish slavery in the British colonies. But for the black revolution in San Domingo, abolition and emancipation might have been postponed another thirty years.

Abolition did not come to France until the revolution of 1848. The production of beet sugar, introduced by Bonaparte, grew by leaps and bounds, and placed the cane sugar interests, based on slavery in Martinique and Guadeloupe, increasingly on the defensive. One of the first acts of the revolutionary government of 1848 was to abolish slavery. But as in 1794, the decree was merely the registration of an accomplished fact. So menacing was the attitude of slaves that in more than one colony the local government, in order to head off the servile revolution, proclaimed abolition without waiting for authorization from France.

THE NEGRO AND THE CIVIL WAR

1848, the year following the economic crisis of 1847, was the beginning of a new cycle of revolutions all over the Western world. The European revolutions and Chartism in England were defeated. In America the irrepressible conflict between capitalism in the North and the slave system in the South was headed off for the last time by the Compromise of 1850. The political developments following the economic crisis of 1857 made further compromise impossible.

It was a decade of revolutionary struggle the world over in the colonial and semi-colonial countries. 1857 was the year of the first war of Indian independence, commonly miscalled the Indian Mutiny. In 1858 began the civil war in Mexico, which ended with the victory of Juárez three years later. It was the period of the Taiping revolution in China, the first great attempt to break the power of the Manchu dynasty. North and South in America moved to their predestined clash unwillingly, but the revolutionary Negroes helped to precipitate the issue. For two decades before the Civil War began, they were leaving the South in thousands. The revolutionary organization known as the Underground Railway, with daring, efficiency, and dispatch, drained away the slave owners' human property. Fugitive slaves were the issue of the day. The Fugitive Slave Law of 1850 was a last desperate attempt by the federal government to stop this illegal abolition. Ten Northern states replied with personal liberty laws which nullified the heavy penalties of the 1850 law. Most famous perhaps of all the whites and Negroes who ran the Underground Railway is Harriet Tubman, a Negro who had herself escaped from slavery. She made nineteen journeys into the South and helped her brothers and their wives and three hundred other slaves to escape. She made her depredations in enemy territory with a price of $40,000 on her head. Josiah Henson, the original of Uncle Tom, helped nearly two hundred slaves to escape. Nothing so galled the slave owners as this twenty-year drain on their already bankrupt system.

It is unnecessary to detail here the causes of this, the greatest civil war in history. Every Negro schoolboy knows that the last thing Lincoln had in mind was the emancipation of the Negroes. What is important is that, for reasons both internal and external, Lincoln had to draw them into the revolutionary struggle. He said that without emancipation the North might not have won, and was in all probability right. Thousands of Negroes were fighting on the Southern side, hoping to win their freedom that way. The abolition decree broke down the social cohesion of the South. It was not only what the North gained but, as Lincoln pointed out, what the South lost. On the Northern side 220,000 Negroes fought with such bravery that it was impossible to do with white troops what could be done with them. They fought not only with revolutionary bravery but with coolness and exemplary discipline. The best of them were filled with revolutionary pride. They were fighting for equality. One company stacked arms before the tent of its commanding officer as a protest against discrimination.

Lincoln was also driven to abolition by the pressure of the British working class. Palmerston wanted to intervene on the side of the South but was opposed in the cabinet by Gladstone. Led by Marx, the British working class so vigorously opposed the war, that it was impossible to hold a pro-war meeting anywhere in England. The British Tories derided the claim that the war was for the abolition of slavery; hadn't Lincoln said so many times? The British workers, however, insisted on seeing the war as a war for abolition, and Lincoln, for whom British nonintervention was a life-and-death matter, decreed abolition with a suddenness which shows his fundamental unwillingness to take such a revolutionary step.

Abolition was declared in 1863. Two years before, the movement of the Russian peasants, so joyfully hailed by Marx, frightened the Tsar into the semi-emancipation of the serfs. The North won its victory in 1865. Two years later the British workers won the Second Reform Bill, which gave the franchise to the workers in the towns. The revolutionary cycle was concluded with the defeat of the Paris Commune in 1871. A victory there and the history of Reconstruction would have been far different.

THE NEGRO AND WORLD REVOLUTION

Between 1871 and 1905 the proletarian revolution was dormant. In Africa the Negroes fought vainly to maintain their independence against the imperialist invasions. But the Russian Revolution of 1905 was the forerunner of a new era that began with the October Revolution in 1917. While half a million Negroes fought with the French Revolution in 1789, today the socialist revolution in Europe has as its potential allies over 120 million Negroes in Africa. Where Lincoln had to seek an alliance with an isolated slave population, today millions of Negroes in America have penetrated deep into industry, have fought side by side with white workers on picket lines, have helped to barricade factories for sit-down strikes, have played their part in the struggles and clashes of trade unions and political parties. It is only through the spectacles of historical perspective that we can fully appreciate the enormous revolutionary potential of the Negro masses today.

Half a million slaves, hearing the words Liberty, Equality, and Fraternity shouted by millions of Frenchmen thousands of miles away, awoke from their apathy. They occupied the attention of Britain for six years and, once again to quote Fortescue, "practically destroyed the British army." What of the Negroes in Africa today? This is a bare outline of the record.

French West Africa: 1926–1929, 10,000 men fled into the forest swamps to escape French slavery.

French Equatorial Africa: 1924, uprising. 1924–1925, uprising, 10,000 Negroes killed. 1928, June to November, rising in Upper Sagha and Lai. 1929, a rising lasting four months; the Africans organized an army of 10,000.

British West Africa: 1929, a revolt of women in Nigeria, 30,000 in number; 83 killed, 87 wounded. 1937, general strike of the Gold Coast farmers, joined by the dockers and truck drivers.

Belgian Congo: 1929, revolt in Ruanda Urundi; thousands killed. 1930–1931, revolt of the Bapendi, 800 massacred in one place, Kwango.

South Africa: 1929, strikes and riots in Durban; the Negro quarter was entirely surrounded by troops and bombarded by planes.

Since 1935 there have been general strikes, with shooting of Negroes, in Rhodesia, in Madagascar, in Zanzibar. In the West Indies there have been general strikes and mass action such as those islands have not seen since the emancipation from slavery a hundred years ago. Scores have been killed and wounded.

The above is only a random selection. The Negroes in Africa are caged and beat against the bars continually. It is the European proletariat that holds the key. Let the workers of Britain, France, and Germany say, "Arise, ye children of starvation" as loudly as the French revolutionaries said Liberty, Equality, and Fraternity, and what force on earth can hold these Negroes back? All who know anything about Africa know this.

Mr. Norman Leys, a government medical officer in Kenya for twenty years, a member of the British Labour party, and about as revolutionary as the late Ramsay MacDonald, wrote a study of Kenya in 1924. Seven years later he wrote it again. This time he entitled his work *A Last Chance in Kenya*. The alternative, he said, is revolution.

In *Caliban in Africa*, Leonard Barnes, another milk and water socialist, writes as follows: "So he [the South African white] and the native he holds captive go spinning down the stream fatally, madly spinning together along the rapids above the great cataract, both yoked to one omnipotent hour." That is the revolution, wrapped in silver paper.

The revolution haunts this conservative Englishman. He writes again of the Bantu, "They crouch in their corner, nursing a sullen anger and desperately groping for a plan. They will not be many years making up their minds. Time and fate, even more prevailing than the portcullis of the Afrikaner, are driving them on from the rear. Something must give; it will not be fate or time. Some comprehensive social and economic reconstruction must take place. But how? By reason or by violence?"

He poses as alternatives what are in reality one. The change will take place, by violence and by reason combined.

"WE HAVE A FALSE IDEA OF THE NEGRO"

Let us return again to the San Domingo revolution with its paltry half a million slaves. Writing in 1789, the very year of the revolution, a colonist said of them that they were "unjust, cruel, barbarous, half-human, treacherous, deceitful, thieves, drunkards, proud, lazy, unclean, shameless, jealous to fury and cowards."

Three years later Roume, the French Commissioner, noted that even though fighting with the royalist Spaniards, the black revolutionaries, organizing themselves into armed sections and popular bodies, rigidly observed all the forms of republican organization. They adopted slogans and rallying cries. They appointed chiefs of sections and divisions who, by means of these slogans, could call them out and send them back home again from one end of the province to the other. They threw up from out of their depths a soldier and statesman of the first rank, Toussaint-Louverture, and secondary leaders fully able to hold their own with the French in war, diplomacy, and administration. In ten years they organized an army that fought Bonaparte's army on level terms. "But what men these Blacks are! How they fight and how they die!" wrote a French officer looking back at the last campaign after forty years. From his dying bed, Leclerc, Bonaparte's brother-in-law and commander-in-chief of the French expedition, wrote home. "We have . . . a false idea of the Negro." And again, "We have in Europe a false idea of the country in which we fight and the men whom we fight against." We need to know and reflect on these things today.

Menaced during its whole existence by imperialism, European and American, the Haitians have never been able to overcome the bitter heritage of their past. Yet that revolution of a half-million not only helped to protect the French Revolution but initiated great revolutions in its own right. When the Latin American revolutionaries saw that half a million slaves could fight and win, they recognized the reality of their own desire for independence. Bolívar, broken and ill, went to Haiti. The Haitians nursed him back to health, gave him money and arms with which he sailed to the mainland. He was defeated, went back to Haiti, was once more welcomed and assisted. And it was from Haiti that he sailed to start the final campaign, which ended in the independence of the five states.

Today 150 million Negroes, knit into world economy infinitely more tightly than their ancestors of a hundred years ago, will far surpass the work of that San Domingo half-million in the work of social transformation. The continuous risings in Africa; the refusal of the Ethiopian warriors to submit to Mussolini; the American Negroes who volunteered to fight in Spain in the Abraham Lincoln Brigade, as Rigaud and Beauvais had volunteered to fight in America, tempering their swords against the enemy abroad for use against the enemy at home—these lightnings announce the thunder. The racial prejudice that now stands in the way will bow before the tremendous impact of the proletarian revolution.

In Flint during the sit-down strike of two years ago seven hundred Southern whites, soaked from infancy in racial prejudice, found themselves besieged in the General Motors building with one Negro among them. When the time came for the first meal, the Negro, knowing who and what his companions were, held himself in the background. Immediately it was proposed that there should be no racial discrimination among the strikers. Seven hundred hands went up together. In the face of the class enemy the men recognized that race prejudice was a subordinate thing which could not be allowed to disrupt their struggle. The Negro was invited to take his seat first, and after the victory was won, in the triumphant march out of the factory, he was given the first place. That is the prognosis of the future. In Africa, in America, in the West Indies, on a national and international scale, the millions of Negroes will raise their heads, rise up from their knees, and write some of the most massive and brilliant chapters in the history of international socialism.

DECEMBER 1939

6

Native Son and Revolution: A Review of *Native Son* by Richard Wright

Black Bigger Thomas, native son, stifled by and inwardly rebellious against white America's treatment of him, by accident murders a white girl. For him this murder is the beginning of a new life. In striking such a blow against his hated enemies, in the struggle to outwit them and evade capture, his stunted personality finds scope to expand. Before he is sentenced to death, the sincere efforts of two white Communists to save him teach him that all whites are not his enemies, that he is not alone, that there is a solidarity of all the oppressed.

Such, finely audacious and magnificently simple, is the theme, sprung from such a wealth of emotional vitality and presented with such power of literary realization that it forces discussion and unwilling reconsideration of the world's number one minority problem, the Negro question in America. The book therefore is not only a literary but also a political event. Here we are concerned with a revolutionary interpretation of Bigger Thomas, an aspect, not unnaturally, neglected or misunderstood by all reviewers, "Marxist" or otherwise. The career of Bigger Thomas is a symbol and prototype of the Negro masses in the proletarian revolution.

Bigger hates white people with a consuming hatred. So do the great masses of Negroes. Quite often the hate is hidden, sometimes it is buried deep out of sight, sometimes it is twisted into its opposite, a passionate religiosity. But it is there, and speakers, particularly Negro speakers, can always elicit it from any Negro gathering. It represents ten generations' experience of injustice, of humiliation, of suppressed resentment and bitterness. But if Negroes hate whites, they also fear them, their knowledge, their power, their ruthlessness—also the accumulated experience of the generations.

88

THE SLEEPING VOLCANO

This hate will be one of the most powerful forces in the Negro revolution. In the South whites know quite well what fires smoulder behind the deference and the humility. "If you let a nigger forget himself, you will have to kill him" is one of their commonest expressions. As long as society in the South maintains its integrity, the Negroes will continue to be docile. But if the solid South does not remain solid, if that society ever goes to pieces, then, wherever the Negroes outnumber the whites, we shall see some of the bloodiest massacres that this continent has ever known. Whoever doubts this should study the slave revolts of Spartacus, and the black revolt in San Domingo: the end of the San Domingo revolt was the complete annihilation of the white population.

America differs from San Domingo in one important respect: the Negroes are a minority and in a proletarian revolution the white proletariat of the North will be dominant. Its aim will be to tear the poor whites of the South from the leadership of the Southern landlords and capitalists, by precept and example to make them aware of their solidarity with the Negroes. The strength and organization of the Northern proletarians, and the extent of the social disintegration in the South driving blacks and poor whites closer together, will shape the course of the struggle.

In a profound sense Bigger Thomas is a "typical" Negro. His hatred of whites, his sense of his wrongs and forcibly limited life, his passionate desire to strike at his enemies, all this is racial. He is different from other Negroes only in the fact that his nature is such that he cannot contain himself.

Bigger, having killed by accident, now has to save himself. He must match his wits against this whole powerful white world, which has hitherto held him chained, and in this conflict he finds himself. The murder of Mary is an accident, rooted though it is in the social order. But his acceptance of full responsibility for it is a revolutionary act. To scheme, to plan, to fight—this is to be free. In this bold stroke, the central theme of his book, Wright has distilled the very essence of what is in the Negro's future. The great masses of Negroes carry in their hearts the heavy heritage of slavery, and their present degradation. Such has been their past, it is their present, and, as far as they can see, it is their future. It is the revolution which will lift these millions from their knees. Nobody can do it for them. Men, personalities, will be freed from the centuries of chains and shame, as Bigger's personality was freed, by violent action against their tyrants. It is on the evening after the battle, with smoking rifle and bloody bayonet, that the Negro will be able to look all white men in the face, will be able to respect himself and be respected. Wright notes that Bigger had no confidence in other Negroes; they were too afraid and conscious of fear to trust one another. That confidence in himself which Bigger earned by the unwitting murder of Mary, millions of Negroes will gain only by the revolution. There is no other way for them.

BIGGER'S FIGHT

The finest passages in the book describe Bigger's fight against capture, and it is curious how blind all have been to the overwhelming significance of this. What hero in what literature ever fought his fight with such courage and such determination? As he reads in the paper that the crime has been pinned on him, "his right hand twitched. He wanted a gun in that hand. He got his gun from his pocket and held it. He read again." Thenceforward he fights. The murder of Bessie, his girl friend, is subordinate to his great purpose, to fight against these tyrants and torturers. He couldn't leave Bessie behind and he couldn't take her. Therefore he had to destroy her. In the abstract it is a revolting crime. But whoever has entered into the spirit of the new Bigger must see it as he saw it. Eight thousand white men with guns and gas were looking for him. Without bravado, without self-pity, he fought.

A small black object fell near his head on the snow, hissing, shooting forth a white vapor, like a blowing plume, which was carried away from him by the wind. Tear gas! With a movement of his head he knocked it off the tank. Another came and he knocked it off. Two more came and he shoved them off. The wind blew strong, from the lake. It carried the gas away from his eyes and nose. He heard a man yell.

"Stop it! The wind's blowing this way! He's throwing 'em back!"

The bedlam in the street rose higher; more men climbed through the trapdoors on the roof. He wanted to shoot, but remembered that he had three bullets left. He would shoot when they were closer and he would save one bullet for himself. They would not take him alive.

"Come on down, boy!"

He did not move; he lay with gun in hand, waiting. Then, directly under his eyes, four white fingers caught hold of the icy edge of the water tank. He gritted his teeth and struck the white fingers with the butt of his gun. They vanished and he heard a thud as a body landed on the snow-covered roof. He lay waiting for more attempts to climb up, but none came.

"It's no use fighting, boy! You're caught! Come on down!"

He knew that they were afraid, and yet he knew that it would soon be over, one way or another; they would either capture or kill him. He was surprised that he was not afraid. Under it all some part of his mind was beginning to stand aside; he was going behind his curtain, his wall, looking out with sullen stares of contempt. He was outside of himself now, looking on; he lay under a winter sky lit with tall gleams of whirling light, hearing thirsty screams and hungry shouts. He clutched his gun, defiant, unafraid.

More than the mere desire to live was at stake. It was the bursting pride of a spirit long cramped and oppressed that found itself free at last. All students of revolutionary history know it: the legions of Spartacus, Cromwell's Ironsides, the Paris enragés, the Russian workers defending Petrograd against Yudenich, the Spanish workers defending Madrid, the march of the Chinese Communists across China in 1936. That was the spirit of defiance and determination in which Bigger fought.

In prison, fighting for a clear realization of what has happened to him, Bigger attains the highest stage of his development: he learns that the two white Communists are his friends. They prove it in action. Here again Bigger's experience typifies another important revolutionary truth. Masses learn by experience, not by propaganda, and the Negro masses in particular will have to be shown solidarity in action and not logic. There will be many Negroes in the revolutionary party, but the vast majority will in all probability learn the lesson of class solidarity as Bigger learned it.

WRIGHT AS A REVOLUTIONARY NOVELIST

Did Wright consciously epitomize Negro revolutionary struggle in the career of Bigger Thomas? The question is irrelevant. The artist, by methods compounded of conscious logic and his own intuition, observes society and experiences life. He comes to his conclusions and embodies them in character, scene, and dramatic situation. According to the depth of his penetration and the sweep of his net, his capacity to integrate and reproduce, he writes his novel, paints his picture, or composes his symphony. Psychologist, historian, politician, or revolutionary, drawing on his own experience, sees symbols, parallelism, depth and perspective unsuspected by the creator. The artist can see the truth and nothing but the truth, but no one can expect him to see the whole truth.

In our age literature, especially literature of this kind, cannot be divorced from politics. Wright is a Stalinist. In this novel a scrupulous artistic integrity enables him to draw white Communists, if not with the same success as Negroes, yet without bias or subservience to the Stalinist conception of the party and the party "line." But he treads a dangerous road. Stalinism has destroyed the literary and artistic life of Russia, it has ruined Malraux, one of the most gifted of contemporary writers. In that evil garden nothing creative flourishes. The artist in uniform soon ceases to be an artist. The Stalinists are past masters in the art of suborning, corrupting. It will be a pity if they succeed in perverting and blighting this splendid talent.

MAY 1940

7

Trotsky's Place in History

The bourgeoisie, perforce lacking historical method and suborning all aspects of life to the maintenance of power, has not only confused the proletariat but has confused itself in the estimation of what constitutes greatness in contemporary men. Woodrow Wilson, Poincaré, Stanley Baldwin, and similar mediocrities have all been crowned with the laurel, not excluding Nicholas Murray Butler, on the score presumably that he dined often with the others. So often and so conspicuously have the bourgeois theorists blundered that in the face of a skeptical world they confess bankruptcy: always to their biographies and obituary notices they add a saving clause, that posterity alone can tell.

No such tendentiousness, hesitancy, hit-or-miss judgment have discredited the estimates of those who use the method of historical materialism. Marx and Engels judged their contemporaries, Darwin, Proudhon, Abraham Lincoln, Napoleon III, Balzac and Dickens, Palmerston, Gladstone, Thiers, Bismarck, Shaw, with incisiveness and precision, and their judgments have stood the test of time. The most famous of all their pronouncements on persons, Engels's judgment on Marx, "mankind is shorter by a head, and the greatest head of our time at that," would have seemed presumptuous to many, the usual exaggeration of a friend, a collaborator, and a Communist fanatic. Today that judgment might be questioned by some but with caution and respect. Marx's name rings incessantly in the ears of all, capitalists and workers alike. His book *Capital* is high on the sales list of popular classics. Stanley Baldwin, the English prime minister, on his retirement, indicated what he considered the main characteristics of his period: "In the year that I was born two events occurred which were the beginning of the two forces competing in the world today; the one was Disraeli's Reform Bill with its doctrine of expanding freedom and the other the publication of *Capital*, with its doctrine of economic determinism." Thus Marx had at last arrived, being recognized as a world force by a Conservative prime minister only fifty years after his death.

Trotsky is easier to recognize immediately. All men, Marxist or otherwise, will agree that between 1917 and 1923 he played a great role in the history of our times. Before that his life had made no exceptional impression on the general consciousness. During his last decade he was an exile, apparently powerless. During those same ten years, Stalin, his rival, assumed power such as no man in Europe since Napoleon has wielded. Hitler has shaken the world and bids fair to bestride it like a colossus while he lasts. Roosevelt is the most powerful president who has ever ruled America, and America today is the most powerful nation in the world. Yet the Marxist judgment of Trotsky is as confident as Engels's judgment of Marx. Before his period of power, during it, and after his fall, Trotsky stood second only to Lenin among contemporary men, and after Lenin died in 1924, was the greatest head of our times. That judgment we leave to history.

THE THEORY OF THE PERMANENT REVOLUTION

Trotsky's first claim to the attention of mankind is his theory of the permanent revolution, and if he had fallen dead after correcting the last proof over thirty years ago, his place in political thought was safe. Marx and Engels for fifty years had made their profound and brilliant predictions of the future disintegration of capitalist society. Engels in 1887 had predicted the 1914 war, the revolution in Russia first, the revolutions in Europe and crowns rolling with no one to pick them up, the formation of the Third International. In 1889 Plekhanov declared that the coming revolution in Russia would be a revolution of the working class and could be no other. But in 1905 Trotsky, then twenty-six years old, in an essay of a few thousand words, unfolded the course which history was to follow.

Let us consider the mental climate of that period. Previous to that time, 1905, Europe and America had seen no revolutions of any importance since the Civil War of 1861 and the Commune of 1871. The Civil War was not then recognized for what it was, and what Charles Beard has since called it, the Second American Revolution. The Commune, except to the Marxists (and the French bourgeoisie), had seemed an unpleasant episode growing out of the war. In 1905 the specter of communism was not haunting Europe, and the bourgeois writers and statesmen of those days, Viscount Bryce, the expert on democracy, Maximillian Herden, Lloyd George, Theodore Roosevelt, Woodrow Wilson, Benedetto Croce, Anatole France, Miliukov, the *Manchester Guardian*, the *New York Times*, the *London Times*, the *Corriere del Sierra*, all the finest bourgeois thinkers, and the distinguished organs of bourgeois thought, what a monumental pile of rubbish and nonsense they, reactionaries and progressives, were producing in this very 1905 about the world and its future. They and their successors are a little more sensible today, though to do them justice they lie more. From those bourgeois who took notice of it, the theory met with derision. Miliukov, the Russian savant, gave it a name and thus "Trotskyism" was born.

Despite all the evidence piled up under his eyes, the bourgeois of today cannot accept the theory; far less the bourgeois of 1905. Capitalism, said this theory, was approaching its end and society was ripe for the socialist revolution. This view Trotsky held in common apparently, but only apparently, with all Marxists. But, and here he broke sharply with all of them, Lenin included, Russia, the most backward of the great European states, would be the scene of the first socialist revolution. Where all the great European Marxists looked upon the coming Russian revolution as one which would give Russia a bourgeois republic, Trotsky stated that this was impossible. A revolution in Russia, to be successful, would have to be a socialist revolution. True, Russia, a backward country with a hundred million peasants, was not ready for socialism. Left to itself the Russian Revolution would certainly collapse. But the Russian Revolution would unloose proletarian revolutions in Europe which would come to the assistance of the Russian. It would initiate the era of permanent social revolution until the establishment of worldwide socialism. Either this, or the collapse of capitalist civilization into barbarism.

In analytical power and imaginative audacity the theory is one of the most astounding productions of the modern mind. The bourgeoisie makes a great to-do about de Tocqueville, who foresaw that America would one day free itself from England; Goethe, who recognized the significance of Valmy; and Seward, who foretold "the irrepressible conflict." How pitiable these are beside the work of Trotsky, who foretold the future of a world. Except in the work of Marx, Engels, and Lenin there is no comparable piece of political prophecy anywhere. After Marx's discoveries political thinkers were limited to the use of his method. It has never been better used. As for the bourgeoisie, its writings of 1905 remind us of the day when all the young men were for Racine, so remote are they from the terrible modern reality.

THE VERDICT OF THE YEARS

What is more important for us than the limitations of the bourgeoisie is the limitations of the Marxists. They wrote and taught the socialist revolution but we know today that in reality Kautsky, for instance, did not believe in any such thing. Trotsky himself relates the deadly politeness of the Austro-Marxists when, an exile in Vienna, he ventured to suggest to them the coming collapse of the world they knew. Such was 1905. In the genuinely revolutionary wing of socialism the theory met with fierce opposition. Lenin never ceased to deride it. As late as November 1915 he was slashing at Trotsky "who repeats his original 1905 thesis without stopping to think why life during a whole decade has passed by this beautiful theory . . . amusing example . . . incorrect . . . To what limits Trotsky's confusion goes . . ." Lenin believed that the revolution in Russia would be a democratic revolution, though he as confidently as Trotsky expected that it would unloose the socialist revolution in Europe, without which, he stated over and over again, the Russian democratic revolution would collapse. Trotsky refused to concede an inch. To the Mensheviks who preached that the Russian bourgeoisie would lead the revolution he said that the counter-revolutionary character of their ideas would show itself before the revolution. To the Bolsheviks who taught that the proletariat would destroy tsarism but install the bourgeoisie in power he said that the counter-revolutionary character of their theory would appear after the revolution. The years have justified him. The Russian Revolution followed his road. After it came the postwar revolutions in Germany, Austria, and Hungary, in Turkey and Italy, in Egypt and India, in China, in Spain. The Russian and other proletarian and nationalist revolutions have shaken the structure of capitalism. Two-by-four political thinkers attribute it all to "the war." As if the war fell from the sky and was not itself a product of capitalist disintegration; as if Lenin, long before 1914, had not watched the growing industrialization of India and China and predicted the coming proletarian struggles in those countries. But for these upheavals the socialist revolution in Russia would have been annihilated. True, the socialist cause has suffered a succession of defeats. But the struggle is not over. In every chancellory in the world, Stalin's included, the specter of communism, grown to Arabian Nights proportions, sits at every conference. Read the bourgeois press carefully. Always between the lines and sometimes in them snarls the fear that the coming years will see the consummation of the audacious theory put forward by the young Marxist thirty-five years ago.

TROTSKY'S CREATIVE POWER

The theory of the permanent revolution was no isolated spurt of inspiration. In abstract creative imagination and range of thought Trotsky excelled Lenin. Today we accept the idea of the single economic plan as an indispensable part of the socialist reorganization of society. Trotsky first put it forward in his little history of the Russian Revolution written during spare moments at Brest-Litovsk. Lenin at first opposed it as he opposed the theory of the permanent revolution. But that most realistic of men, though often wrong, was never wrong for long in the face of reality, and soon he recognized the value of the single economic plan as opportunely as he had accepted the permanent revolution in April 1917.

Besides the theory with which his name will always be associated, the outstanding example of Trotsky's analytic and creative power was *The New Course*, the outgrowth and flowering of the single-plan proposal. It is characteristic of him that, immersed in his work, he never saw the dangerous growth of the bureaucracy until Lenin, with an agonized urgency, pointed it out to him and asked for help. Lenin's immediate preoccupation was to take the political and practical steps necessary to break up Stalin and his clique. Here Trotsky failed completely—we shall deal with that later—but in the course of a few months he outlined a course of action which is one of the most profound and masterly plans of reconstruction ever laid before the rulers of a state in crisis.

A succession of good harvests was dangerously increasing the weight of the peasantry and capitalism. Unless checked this would lead inevitably to the overwhelming of the proletariat and the soviet power. The last great turn Lenin had given to the party had been toward the appeasement of the peasantry. But the retreat had gone far enough. It was necessary to embark on a bold plan of industrialization. Collectivization, in proportion to the strength of the industrialization, should be the aim. Inseparably intertwined with the industrial was the political reorganization. He analyzed the dangers of bureaucracy, its causes and consequences, the relation of the youth to the older party comrades, the role of the masses in maintaining the revolutionary morale and integrity of the party. He called for a systematic education of the peasantry in the aims of the soviet power. He set the whole against the background of the struggle for world socialism under the leadership of the Communist International. It is one of the classic documents of socialist literature. Socialism in a single country is impossible, but Victor Serge, who knew Russia well, has drawn attention to what would have been the result of such a program not only in Russia but among the peasant millions of Central Europe. With Lenin's authority and the political skill which Trotsky so sadly lacked, such a plan would have altered the whole history of Russia and the world. Trotsky fought for it for five years, and it received its final and most perfect expression in the *Platform* of the Left Opposition. It was only in 1929 that Stalin, having brought Soviet Russia to the brink of disaster, adopted some parts of it and carried them out with the brutality and exaggerations of the Third Period. Today the Russian Five-Year Plans, the New Deal (Roosevelt's New Course), the Goering Four-Year Plan, Petain's Three-Year Plan, all are the misshapen offspring, conscious and unconscious, of the ideas contained in *The New Course*. But in the multifarious writings which expound these experiments, nowhere appears a hint of the comprehensive grasp of society as a whole, the political penetration, the breadth, and the humanity that are contained within the pages of that slender volume which is concerned more with the political approach than the actual economic plan. *What Is to Be Done?*, *The State and Revolution*, and *Imperialism* are Lenin's greatest books, all analytical, all, profound as they are, compact of determination for immediate action. Trotsky's *Results and Prospects*, in which is contained the theory of the permanent revolution, and his *New Course*, though written in the heat of action, broaden out, the first on an international and the second on a national scale, into the perspectives of the future. Here he was excelled by only two men in history, Marx and Engels, and by them only because they covered so much ground that they limited the range of all successors.

LENIN'S SUCCESSOR

With the death of Lenin, the prime responsibility for Marxist analysis of contemporary events devolved upon Trotsky. He tells us himself that he had learnt from Lenin and the evidence is clear in his work. To his faculty for synthesis, of seeing history from a height, he had by now added a closer coordination between the general line of development and the immediate practical conclusions to be drawn at the different stages, though he never attained Lenin's superb mastery in this field. How deeply he had absorbed the lessons of the Russian Revolution and Lenin's method is visible in his analysis of the Chinese Revolution, not so much in his *Problems of the Chinese Revolution* as in the essays in *The Third International after Lenin*. There is, as always, the same wide sweep and comprehensive generalization, but there is also a precision, a definiteness, and a certainty in the handling of the specific problems which are absent from the pre-October works. The chief weakness in the presentation of the theory of the permanent revolution, the slurring over of the bourgeois-democratic stage, is brilliantly corrected.

We do not propose to give here any connected or complete account of Trotsky's work. Trotsky wrote on all the great issues of the day, turned them inside out, so that students of his writings have cinematic X-rays into the physiology and anatomy of twentieth-century society. But some example of his mature method must be given in any evaluation of his place in history. The first that springs to mind is that of the Soviet bureaucracy. Despite the differences which developed between Trotsky and the Workers party in the very last year of his life, despite unceasing criticism of his methods and his conclusions from all quarters, the fact remains that over the years, there is simply no analysis of the Soviet Union worth bothering about except his own.

It is a lesson in Marxism to read not only Trotsky, but also "educated opinion" on the Soviet Union from 1917 to the present day. The howls of coming disaster at the NEP; the struggle of the Left Opposition (when Trotsky was exiled to Turkey the *London Times* said that Stalin had sent him there to organize a revolt in the Near East); the colossal sneers at the *Platform* and Trotsky's plans for industrialization, to be followed by bulging eyes and hyperbole at Stalin's fabricated statistics; Sidney and Beatrice Webb on Russia in 1923 and then in 1933; Louis Fischer and Vincent Sheean; the thousands of "trained observers" who went to Moscow and saw for themselves through Stalin's spectacles; Barbusse and Romain Rolland; the bourgeois intellectuals on the Moscow Trials, those clumsy, brazen, incredibly impudent falsifications which were exceeded in stupidity only by the comments of the intelligentsia—as one looks back in Trotsky's writings on the one hand and the rows of dustbins on the other, one realizes what it is to be a Marxist in these days.

But there are Marxists and Marxists. In the revolutionary Marxist movement his writings on Russia stand alone, for we are still without (perhaps shall be forever without) the works of Rakovsky, Sosnovsky, and others persecuted by Stalin. Outside of Russia there is nothing. Many people opposed what Trotsky wrote. They had a brief importance only through opposition to him. This one opposes Trotsky in 1934 on this point, another opposes him in 1936 on that. But a connected body of comprehensive thought in opposition? It does not exist. This, the strongest part of his theoretical work, is, however, so closely intertwined with the struggle for the Fourth International, that it can be treated adequately only in a special article or rather series of articles. It is more convenient and more opportune to illustrate Trotsky's role after his expulsion from Russia by his analysis of the rise and victory of German fascism. To read those half-dozen slender volumes today is to wonder how a voice so strong and so clear should have cried in the wilderness.

The First Four Congresses on Fascism

He did not start from scratch. The first four congresses of the Communist International, in which he took so preponderant a part, laid the foundation for all future analysis of the economics and politics of our age. The *Platform of the Communist International* (1919) in its second paragraph repeated the then familiar thesis of Lenin. "Monopoly supplants free competition. The isolated capitalist is transformed into a member of a capitalist association. Organization replaces wild anarchy." From the First Congress there is an insistent reiteration of the tendency to complete statification of all aspects of society by the imperialist state. The *Manifesto* of the Congress laid down the line. "If the absolute subjection of political power to finance capital has led humanity to the imperialist butchery, this butchery has given finance capital the chance not only to militarize the state completely, but to militarize itself in such a manner that it can continue to fulfill its economic functions only by fire and blood." The military state, what Lenin called "the vast state-capitalist military trust and syndicate," was the ultimate to which capitalism was moving. These states would inevitably seek "wholesale military decisions of a violent nature." It was from there that Lenin and Trotsky began, while all the democrats carolled about parliamentary democracy and the League of Nations. Of German parliamentary democracy, specifically, the Second Congress (1920) said that "it is merely a gap between two dictatorships." It would be no parliamentary dictatorship. The Second Congress, using its eyes, pointed out that besides the capitalist state, "other counter-revolutionary organizations of a private character, formed under its aegis and placed at its disposal, work to put a violent end to strikes, to commit provocations, to bear false witness, to destroy revolutionary organizations, to do away with communist institutions, to massacre, and to set afire and take measure to defend private property and democracy." The personnel of these bandits consisted of "the sons of the big proprietors, big bourgeois, petty bourgeois who do not know what to do with themselves, and, in general, declassed elements . . . the twenty thousand officers of the Hohenzollern army." These counter-revolutionaries would be destroyed only by "the smashing hammer of the dictatorship of the proletariat." This was in 1920. In that year the great masses were following the Communist party. But by 1921 the revolutionary wave had subsided and at the Third Congress came the theses on the united front. In 1922 Italian fascism took power and at the Fourth Congress, in 1923, a section in the resolution on tactics analyzed the danger of fascism. "Legal methods of constraint no longer are sufficient for the bourgeoisie . . . the fascists are not only fighting organizations, mainly counter-revolutionary and armed to the teeth, but they try by means of social demagogy to create for themselves a base among the masses in the peasantry, in the petty bourgeoisie, and even in certain parts of the proletariat, utilizing adroitly for their own counter-revolutionary ends the disillusionment provoked by so-called democracy."

It can't happen here and can only happen there? Lenin and Trotsky knew that, barring the socialist revolution, it is going to happen everywhere. The Fourth Congress stated that there was a danger of fascism among other countries besides Italy. It could happen in Germany; and "under one form or another Fascism is no longer impossible in countries like France and England." Such was the leadership that the great Bolsheviks gave to the international proletariat. Today one has to listen to solemn and presumptuous idiots who will tell you that Marxism has failed or is lacking in understanding of the modern world. We may pass them by. Lenin stopped work in March 1923. One year afterward, Stalin, having seized the power, informed the world that social democracy and fascism were twins. One can appreciate therefore the motives of those who, using the name of Marx, complacently ask, "What difference would it have made to Russia if Trotsky had won in the struggle with Stalin?" We shall soon see what difference it would have made to the German proletariat. Behind the sham determination of their determinism, these enemies of Bolshevism conceal a genuine determination to defend bourgeois society.

THE MENACE OF HITLER

Such was the basic analysis. Therefore when in the September 1930 elections in Germany, Hitler's vote jumped from 800,000 in 1928 to 6 million, Trotsky, an exile in Turkey, was immediately on the alert. He knew at once what millions are now learning in blood and suffering and death. We do not propose to spend time here on the Stalinist crimes and responsibilities of that period. What we want to recall is that the Marxist method in the hands of a great master applied to a social crisis which has since grown so that it dominates the world.

Writing after the September elections, Trotsky indicated the menace which Hitler represented, and called upon the Communists to stop their attacks on social democracy as the twin of fascism and to struggle for the united front. But in the course of the following months Stalin held the Communist party of Germany to its course and in August 1931 forced it, against its own wishes, to form an alliance with the Fascists against the Social Democrats. Social democracy, in its turn, preached an abiding faith in one god, democracy, with Bruening as its prophet. Later they would exchange Bruening for Hindenburg. More than any other living being Trotsky saw the whole frightful catastrophe which loomed, and in November 1931 he finished his first great document on fascism, *Germany, The Key to the International Situation*. He calls it "hastily sketched reflections." There was no false modesty here. He merely wrote down what seemed to him the crying obviousness of the situation.

He begins with the Spanish revolution which was then eight months old. How the pseudo-Marxists and the liberal democrats beat the air when Hitler and Mussolini intervened in Spain! Trotsky *begins* his essay on Germany with Spain where he sees the struggle as likely to be of a more or less protracted character. England also shows the possibility of years of partial ebbs and flows. France occupies a secondary role in world economics, with immense privileges and pretensions in world politics. This contradiction will heap dangers upon dangers and upset the internal stability of France. In

America the economic crisis has laid bare frightful social contradictions. At the first sign of a rise in the economic depression, the trade union movement will acutely feel the necessity of tearing itself loose from the claws of the despicable AF of L bureaucracy. (Here is the CIO predicted.) American capitalism itself will enter an epoch of monstrous imperialism, uninterrupted growth of armaments, of interventions in the affairs of the entire world, of military conflicts and convulsions. Japan's adventure in China can lead to revolution in Japan, for the Chinese, despite their weakness, will always improvise new armies. This is the background on which stands out in bold relief the situation in Germany. On the solution of the German crisis hangs the fate not only of Germany but of Europe and the entire world. Socialist constriction in the USSR, the revolution in Spain, the fate of France and Britain, China and India, the development of the working-class movement in America, all this rests "directly and immediately" on who will be victorious in Germany: fascism or communism. The Communist party, said Trotsky, must announce the danger, must unite the working class by a struggle for the united front with the social democratic leaders. It must let the international proletariat and the Red Army know in advance, "Fascism can come into power only after a merciless, annihilatory civil war to the bitter end."

The German Communist party had at one period over 300,000 members. It was more than enough. But instead of seeking the united front, Stalin's minions declared every minute of the day that the social democracy, not Hitler, was the main enemy. They were counseling a retreat. Let Hitler come to power. After will be our turn. They got that from Stalin who did not want to be bothered with any German revolution. It was in response to this that Trotsky uttered a warning which is the most poignant in all the historic literature of our times, and day by day rolls louder in our ears:

> The coming into power of the German "National Socialists" would mean above all the extermination of the flower of the German proletariat, the disruption of its organizations, the extirpation of its belief in itself and its future. Considering the far greater maturity and acuteness of the social contradictions in Germany, the hellish work of Italian Fascism would probably appear as a pale and almost humane experiment in comparison with the work of the German National Socialists.
>
> Retreat, you say, you who were yesterday the prophets of the "Third Period"? Leaders and institutions can retreat. Individual persons can hide. But the working class will have no place to retreat to in the face of Fascism, and no place where to hide. If one were really to assume the monstrous and improbable to happen: that the Party will actually evade the struggle and thus deliver the proletariat to the mercy of its mortal enemy; this would signify only one thing: the gruesome battles would unfold not *before* the seizure of power by the Fascists but *after* it, that is,

under conditions ten times more favorable for Fascism than those of today. The struggle of the proletariat, taken unawares, disoriented, disappointed and betrayed by its own leadership, against the Fascist regime, would be transformed into a series of frightful, bloody, and futile convulsions. Ten proletarian insurrections, ten defeats, one on top of the other, could not debilitate and enfeeble the German working class as much as a retreat before Fascism would weaken it at the given moment, when the decision is still impending as to the question of who is to become master in the German household.

HOW TO STOP FASCISM

The Fascists consisted of the petty bourgeoisie, and the new middle class, artisans, shopkeepers, the technical personnel, the intelligentsia, the impoverished peasantry. One thousand Fascist votes equaled one thousand Communist votes on the scale of election statistics. But on the scales of revolutionary struggle, a thousand workers in one big factory represent a force a thousand times greater than a thousand petty officials, clerks, their wives, and their mothers-in-law. "The great bulk of the Fascists consist of human rubbish."

Away from the center of things, dependent upon newspapers days old, and unable to feel the pulse of the masses, as he complained, Trotsky followed events as best he could and in the next twelve months produced a succession of articles which were like a series of powerful searchlights in the prevailing darkness. Never for one moment did Trotsky falter on the supposed division between different sections of the bourgeoisie and the possibility of Bruening crushing Hitler or controlling him. He based himself on the crisis of German capitalism which demanded that the bourgeoisie get rid of the workers' organizations, to demolish all the defensive bulwarks of the proletariat, and to uproot whatever has been achieved during the three-quarters of a century by the social democracy and the trade unions. German capitalism had reached that stage. Since 1918 he and Lenin had been awaiting it and only the proletarian revolution could stop it. (Look and learn if you can, while there is still time, Messrs. Democrats of 1940, look and learn.) Trotsky wasted no breath in shouting imprecations on Fascist brutality and sadism, or making psychoanalytic researches into Hitler's ambition. He knew what the German capitalist economy needed in order to survive. It would be overthrown by a socialist revolution or it would smash everything before it. In Germany and outside Germany, before Hitler and after his rise to power, the fools and the wise men, some very exalted statesmen indeed, besides the usual riff-raff of bourgeois intellectuals, speculated on the control that would be exercised over Hitler, on the pressure from the left, the balance of the center, the restraint of the right.

Trotsky kicked this out of the way almost without looking at it. "What relationship would develop in the early days between Hitler, Schleicher, and the Center leaders, is more important for them than it is for the German people. Politically, all the conceivable combinations with Hitler signify the dissolution of the bureaucracy, courts, police, and army into Fascism."

It would take too long to detail how, article by article, he foresaw move after move, and prescribed the course of action necessary to unite the Stalinist and the social democratic workers in common struggle against the Fascist bands. Together these workers had 40 percent of the votes. In actual struggle they were overwhelmingly the strongest section of the country. They controlled transport, production, and distribution. The transport workers could paralyze the small Reichswehr. Millions of workers were trained for war by their experiences in 1914–1918.

HITLER AND THE OUTSIDE WORLD

On the international scale he was as usual at his best. A special conference of the Communist International to place the crisis before the revolutionary workers everywhere; a joint plan for coordination of Soviet and German industry to be worked out by German and Soviet engineers with the participation of the German working-class movement; a declaration by Stalin that in view of the repeated expressions of hostility to the USSR by Hitler, the Soviet government would consider Hitler's accession to power as a threat to its future existence and would mobilize the Red Army on the borders of Poland. Trotsky had done the same thing under similar circumstances in 1923. In 1932, the economic crisis had every country by the throat, none more so than the "new society" of Italian fascism. A fierce bitterness against the imperialistic governments burned in the hearts of millions of workers in every country. The revolution crackled in Spain, ready to blaze; a tremendous revolutionary ferment was shaking India. Never at any time was there less fear of capitalist intervention in a revolutionary Germany. Of the success of a Communist Germany the bourgeoisie had no doubt. Doubt it left to the intellectuals. Lloyd George said, after Hitler's coming to power, that it was just as well, for these Germans know how to manage their communism.

Trotsky made some mistakes, e.g., in *Germany, The Key to the International Situation*, he thought that, in the first period of its rule if victorious, German fascism would be the tool of France. But this—and nearly all his other mistakes—flowed from a constant incapacity to acknowledge, perhaps even to himself, the full depravity of Stalinism. He did not think it possible that the Stalinists in Germany would capitulate so completely as they did. Who else thought so? About the social democratic bureaucrats he had no illusions. He knew and said in advance that their upper layer preferred the victory of fascism to the socialist revolution. When Wels, Liepart, and company offered their services to Hitler it was no surprise to Trotsky. Knowing the future that awaited Europe, he had to sit and watch the catastrophe unroll itself before him.

He wrote rarely on bourgeois foreign policy. Every line in *What Next?* and *The Only Road*—the two brochures in which were collected the articles which followed *Germany, The Key to the International Situation*—is addressed, like ninety-nine percent of his writings, to the workers. They could stop fascism; nobody else could.

But some months after Hitler came to power he completed his analysis in a pamphlet, *What Hitler Wants*. Hitler had astonished the world by a most pacific speech, which, following on a bellicose piece of rhodomontade by Von Papen, fell like a soothing lotion on Europe's troubled ears. Trotsky, with mathematical precision, itemized Hitler's foreign policy. The inevitability of the new conflict between Germany and France; his immediate aim: to restore the military power of Germany; the use of Italy, "but with the Italian crutch alone German imperialism will not rise to its feet"; the splitting of England from France by the coming German departure from the League of Nations; England to be bribed by Hitler taking upon itself "the protection of European civilization, of the Christian religion, of the British colonies, and other moral and material values, against Bolshevik barbarism . . . Hitler is convinced that on the scales of Great Britain the danger of German Fascism to Western Europe weighs less than the danger of the Bolshevik Soviets in the East. This evaluation constitutes the most important key to the whole foreign policy of Hitler." Hitler would strive to unite the vanquished nations, only the more pitilessly to crush them after; and rearmament being accomplished, should the East be difficult, the explosion might take place along a different direction. "For if it is still possible to discuss to what degree offensive means are distinguished from defensive means, it is already beyond dispute that the military means suitable for the East are equally suitable for the West."

The essay ended with another warning: Europe needs a new organization. But woe betide it if this work falls into the hands of fascism. The historians of the twenty-first century would then have to write that the war of 1914, called the "war for democracy," soon led to the triumph of fascism which became the instrument of the destruction of Europe's economic and cultural organizations. He hoped that the old continent had enough vital strength to open for itself a different historical road. This is the man who three years afterwards was accused by Stalin and Browder of being in alliance with Hitler. And the intellectuals read and shook their heads and said, "It is possible." He made only one serious error. He laughed to scorn the idea of an alliance between Hitler and Stalin and that is a question that demands detailed treatment. Enough for the moment that Trotsky was writing in the summer of 1933. He knew then that Stalin had openly asked for the alliance in March. And Hitler had refused. The Soviet Union of 1933 was not the Soviet Union of 1939.

Idiots and bourgeois scoundrels always emphasize Trotsky's personal brilliance whereby they seek to disparage Trotsky's method. The two are inseparable. His natural gifts were trained and developed by Marxism and he could probe these depths of understanding and ascend to these peaks of foresight because he based himself on the Marxian theory of the class struggle and the revolutionary and predominant role of the proletariat in the crisis of bourgeois society. The choice is still yours, Messrs. Democrats, the choice between fascism and socialism. And if you say that instead you choose democracy, then the lesson of the rise of German fascism is still lost upon you, though you know every detail of German history since 1933 and can point to all the absurdities of *Mein Kampf.*

THE ORGANIZER

It is difficult, it is impossible to write about the career and achievements of this extraordinary man without the constant use of superlatives, and yet they are rigidly and soberly applicable. Marx and Engels were the guiding spirits of the First International but their work was largely literary—the exposition of ideas. In that field Lenin and Trotsky continued and developed on foundations which had been well and truly laid. But history prevented Marx and Engels from being men of action on the grand scale. Trotsky, his theoretical writings apart, belongs to that small company of human beings who have been instruments in assisting new worlds to be born. We have no need to detail here the leadership of the Russian Revolution which earned him the title of the Man of October, or his organization of the Red Army. What we have to do in order to get an approximate evaluation of his historical significance is to compare his role with that of other great political figures at similar historical crises.

The Russian Revolution is the greatest revolution in history; and among the political events which have been decisive in altering the course of human society, come what may, it takes high place. As we look back over the history of Western civilization, we can see the high spots, the German Reformation, the Thirty Years' War which ruined Germany and laid the basis of modern Europe, the English revolution, the first American Revolution, the French Revolution, Bolívar's liberation of Latin America, the American Civil War. There are others, and there is scope for argument, but it is incontestable that each of these marks the beginning of a new epoch in human relations. The dynastic wars of the eighteenth century, even such a war as the Franco-Prussian, shrink into insignificance as time marches on. It did not extensively matter to the world who conquered India, the British or the French, but it was a matter of life and death to Western civilization whether the North conquered the South or vice versa in the American Civil War; it is not spleen that makes Hitler foam at the mouth when he speaks of the Northern victory. The success of the Russian Revolution ushered in a period of crisis for Western civilization such as never existed before since the third century of the Roman Empire. And this time not only Western civilization but the fate of the world is at stake. Among the men who played the decisive parts at these historic climaxes Trotsky easily takes his place as one of the foremost.

He is not in the very first rank. Cromwell and Lenin stand towering above all others. Lenin organized the Bolshevik party, was the strategist of October, and again and again saved the Revolution. Cromwell was indispensable, statesman and soldier as well. But Marat was a journalist and agitator of genius and that was all he did; Robespierre was a politician; Danton was a politician but his chief contribution was his tactical leadership of the revolution. Washington was a soldier and much of the politics of the American Revolution was in other and more capable hands. Lincoln had the enormous advantage of always being in control of the state power. He had neither to overthrow nor to rebuild. Trotsky on the other hand was second in command of those who planned the greatest overthrow of the existing order recorded in history. During the crucial months the tactical decisions on which depended success or failure were entirely in his hands. War and revolution are the two greatest social crises. At this great business of leading a revolution he showed himself a great master, all the more because, twelve years before, he had correctly disentangled the main motive forces and direction of the revolution: he masters tactics best who most profoundly masters strategy. And as if that were not enough he proceeded almost overnight to show himself one of the greatest war ministers in history. Any historical study or analysis of war and armies must of necessity give a high, in some respects a unique, place to Carnot, the "organizer of victory." But Carnot was no politician. He was a trained army officer. Trotsky, previous to the revolution, having done his share of the work done by Rousseau, Voltaire, and Mably, then turned to the revolution to do the work of Danton, immediately dropping that to do the work of Carnot, all this on a scale infinitely surpassing the limitations of eighteenth-century France, at the helm of a revolution which directly changed the lives of over 150 million people and administered a shock to society the echoes of which are still reverberating in its remotest corners. Prickly and poisonous as are such analogies to handle, yet they are indispensable in arriving at any conclusion as to the historical stature of any great actor on the human stage. But by these or any other standards one conclusion emerges. Trotsky was one of the most powerful agents of social dynamics who has lived in this or any other time.*

THE MAN OF IDEAS

Here is a list of achievements which can challenge comparison with that of most men in history, even without our taking into account the *History of the Russian Revolution.* There is no need to dilate on his intellectual and physical endowments, his iron self-discipline, his devotion. And yet this superbly gifted theoretician, executive, and leader of men on the grand scale, who achieved so much in the realm of politics, was a very defective politician. We do not refer to the fact that he had built no organization of importance before 1905. There was no room for a second Bolshevik party in Russia. Lenin might be wrong on the imminence of the socialist revolution in Russia. But his party was the proletarian party and Trotsky, who repudiated the Menshevik doctrine and the Bolshevik practice, was of necessity left in a no-man's-land of small dimensions: two Bolshevik parties in any country at the same time is impossible. Nor do we refer to the weakness of the Fourth International to which he devoted his last years. It is possible to differ with Trotsky on some of the organizational conflicts of the Fourth International during the last period, and yet it is easy to recognize for what they are, those who place the responsibility for the smallness of our forces on him and his "methods" and his weakness. They are for the most part disgruntled backsliders or people looking for excuses to get out of the movement. But recognition of his genius does not preclude the obvious fact that 1905 found him outside of an organization; 1917 found him again without an effective organization in which to function; in 1923, at the greatest crisis of his career, though he was, after Lenin, the most famous and popular leader of Russia in the party, among the proletariat, and among the peasantry, Trotsky found himself pushed out of power as if he were a fourth-rate bureaucrat. It was Trotsky's reputation with the great masses of the people that Stalin and his friends of the moment feared and systematically destroyed. Actual power Trotsky had none. Second-raters like Zinoviev and Kamanev were rooted, the one in the Leningrad soviet, the other in the

---

*There is a characteristic and diverting passage in *My Life* (p. 358) on Trotsky's estimate of his work as War Commissar. He says that if anyone could be compared with Carnot it is his assistant, Skylansky. Trotsky knew that the natural comparison was not Skylansky but himself, and knowing Carnot's role in the French Revolution was important but confined, carefully disentangled himself by giving the role to Skylansky. He need not have worried. But he was always careful of the verdict of history.

Moscow soviet. Stalin had to do a deal of digging to get them out. Trotsky was rooted nowhere, not even in the army he had built from the ground up. No sooner was Lenin ill than Trotsky's power in the party was seen for what it was—a glittering shell. Such failures were not due to superficial characteristics. If they were, a man of his devotion and his will would have conquered them. They were organic and his work is not fully comprehensible without seeing them as an essential part of the man he was and the things he did. The weakness was not all on the debit side.

Let us look at his style, for words were his greatest weapons as a man of action. He expressed himself always amply, completely, and with care, writing and rewriting and rewriting. Man of action though he was, the whole of him is contained in his books.

> The false way in which the chairman of a soviet district committee approaches the kulak is only a small link in the chain whose largest links are constituted by the attitude of the Red trade unions towards the General Council [of the British Trade Union Congress], or of the Central Committee of the CPSU towards Chiang Kai-Shek and Purcell.

How magnificent it is. Range and precision, but above all range. These and similar superb generalizations are scattered all over his works. He could bring the whole world situation to bear upon the single point he was discussing. Here is a longer example:

> Caesarism, or its bourgeois form, Bonapartism, enters the scene in those moments of history when the sharp struggle of two camps raises the state power, so to speak, above the nation, and guarantees it, in appearance, a complete independence of classes—in reality, only the freedom necessary for a defense of the privileged. The Stalin regime, rising above a politically atomized society, resting upon a police and officers corps, and allowing of no control whatever, is obviously a variation of Bonapartism—a Bonapartism of a new type not before seen in history.
> Caesarism arose upon the basis of a slave society shaken by inward strife. Bonapartism is one of the political weapons of the capitalist regime in its critical period. Stalinism is a variety of the same system, but upon the basis of a workers' state torn by the antagonism between an organized and armed Soviet aristocracy and the unarmed toiling masses.
> As history testifies, Bonapartism gets along admirably with a universal, and even a secret, ballot. The democratic ritual of Bonapartism is the *plebescite*. From time to time, the question is presented to the citizens: *for* or *against* the leader? And the voter feels the barrel of the revolver between his shoulders. Since the time of Napoleon III, who now seems a provincial dilettante, this technique has received an extraordinary development. The new Soviet constitution which establishes *Bonapartism on a plebescite basis* is the veritable crown of the system.

In the last analysis, Soviet Bonapartism owes its birth to the belatedness of the world revolution. But in the capitalist countries the same cause gave rise to Fascism. We thus arrive at the conclusion, unexpected at first glance, but in reality inevitable, that the crushing of Soviet democracy by an all-powerful bureaucracy and the extermination of bourgeois democracy by Fascism were produced by one and the same cause: the dilatoriness of the world proletariat in solving the problems set for it by history. Stalinism and Fascism, in spite of a deep difference in social foundation, are symmetrical phenomena. In many of their features they show a deadly similarity. A victorious revolutionary movement in Europe would immediately shake not only Fascism, but Soviet Bonapartism. In turning its back to the international revolution, the Stalinist bureaucracy was, from its own point of view, right. It was merely obeying the voice of self-preservation. (*The Revolution Betrayed*)

One writer alone of modern times had the same range—Spengler.* A horizon separated him from Trotsky in precision. We who know his work may perhaps be a little dulled by familiarity. That page, however, is the summary of two thousand years of history ending in judgment of the two major phenomena in modern society, which are as startling as a picture suddenly flashed on a screen and as incontrovertible as a proof in geometry. Trotsky, man of action, was therefore, above all, an intellectual, a man of theory. Thus he was a man for whom ideas had far more reality than people. Vulgar minds like Louis Fischer say that he had his head in the clouds. There is just a germ of truth in it. But he was never dreaming or admiring himself. He was always conscious of the panorama of history, not as an antiquarian but in its bearing on the problem in hand. He said so. He deplored his weak memory for faces but admitted to his memory for ideas. That sentence in his autobiography tells us as much. He has made still more revealing confessions. He says openly that for him power was an inescapable burden. "In prison with a book or a pen in my hand, I experienced the same sense of deep satisfaction that I did at the mass-meetings of the revolution." Such a spirit is absolutely foreign to the genuine *homo politicus.* He even goes so far as to say that he found prison a perfect place for writing: "It was so quiet there, so eventless, so perfect for intellectual work." It was the one place were he was certain not to be arrested. It is a joke, but a joke perfectly in harmony with his general approach to life. In the midst of one of the most difficult periods of the revolution he had on his desk some of the latest books on science and chafed that he could find no time to read them.

---

*And Spengler had it not only in the history of society but in music, art, and literature. It is to be hoped that the fog of mysticism does not obscure for Marxists the colossal learning, capacity for synthesis, and insight of Spengler's book.

(Joseph Stalin, we may be sure, was not worried at his ignorance of Einstein's theory.) After the October Revolution, when Lenin asked him what position he wanted, he had never thought of it because he had always wanted to be a writer. That was his trend of mind. In a different age he would not have been a politician at all.

Compare Lenin who never finished *The State and Revolution* because, as he gaily writes in the introduction, it was far more enjoyable to be going through a revolution than to be writing about it. Lenin, it is known, loved conventions, conflicts over resolutions, the wear and tear and hurly-burly of political strife. Trotsky, it is clear, hated them. He would have preferred to be elsewhere, at his desk. His political work was a duty. He saw the moving forces of history and played his part. Conscious that it was a great part, he was glad to be able to give so much in a struggle where gifted men are so few. He would throw his cloak about his shoulders in superb style as when, at a difficult moment in the *History*, he remarks: it seems easier at times to have captured Petrograd in 1917 than to write the history of the event. (How his small bright blue eyes would have gleamed just before he said it.) But in this consciousness of himself there was not the slightest meanness or conceit. His writings against Stalin are evidence. There is rage and indignation at the degradation of the Russian Revolution, but there is not one line, not a comma, of personal bitterness. The confinement irked him but he was as happy at his desk in Coyoacan as he was in the Kremlin. It was true, too true, too true. He loved learning, knowledge, theory for their own sake, whereas Lenin, more learned and more profound than Trotsky, loved them for the sake of the revolution. He could not resist a theoretical disquisition. "What constitutes the essence of a dual power? We must pause upon this question, for an illumination of it has never appeared in historical literature." There follows a rather lengthy digression in the *History* and, feeling guilty, he is at pains to assure the reader at the end to have patience, it will be worth it. "It may seem as though this theoretical inquiry has led us away from the events of 1917. In reality, it leads us right into the heart of them. . . . Only from a theoretical height is it possible to observe it fully and correctly understand it." At the tensest moments of revolution and war he was always looking at events from a theoretical height. Stalin, his rival, never ascended to any theoretical height. He was always crawling down below. And to be successful, politicians must learn to grub.

THE MAN OF FEELING

That is one key to Trotsky's character and his work. Another was his attitude to the masses. He had a passionate faith in them and no great work for socialism, theoretical or practical, can be done without it. On one occasion he spoke of them with an unsurpassable dignity and restraint. "Mr. Attorney," he told Finerty during the sessions of the Dewey Commission,

France and Great Britain are not my allies. They can be the allies of the Soviet state. My allies are the workers of all countries, and the only allies I recognize are the workers of all the other countries. My politics are established not for the purpose of diplomatic conventions, but for the development of the international revolutionary movement of the working class. I cannot put hopes in the allies of the Soviet Union, in France and England. They can betray one another. They can separate from one another. But I am sure that the workers who understand very well the situation — they will be free and they will win one hundred workers, and the hundred workers a thousand soldiers. They will be victorious at the end of the war. It seems to me very simple, but I believe it is a good idea.

But though he had no illusions about them his general attitude was one of explosive indignation at their oppression and sufferings.

Workers to the shops! Such is the iron-clad egotism of the educated classes, liberals and socialists alike. These people believed that millions of workers and soldiers lifted to the heights of insurrection by the unconquerable pressure of discontent and hope, would after their victory tamely submit to the old conditions of life.

More than once the *History* refers to the freedom from drudgery of the domestic servants. Of many passionate outbursts in the *History* one of the most remarkable is the description of the horny hands and hoarse voices of the Paris workers intruding themselves on the political stage where the silken gentlemen are settling the fate of the nation. His chapters on the revolution in the autobiography are instilled with a hot sympathy for the masses. It is often a characteristic of the gifted intellectual, and particularly of men who are somewhat aloof from their fellows. It is the chief ingredient in the complex of psychological traits which make the great mass orator. You can feel it in every page of Burke and Demosthenes. But neither of these were great politicians in the small sense of that word. Most young men have it. Trotsky never lost it. The possessor of it can usually lead men to accomplish the impossible, but a certain tendency to rashness goes with it. With all his self-discipline Trotsky's feelings could outrun his discretion. To demonstrate the contrast, read Lenin's writings. There is the same passion but it is controlled. Rage at Mensheviks and petty-bourgeois radicals? Yes. But outbursts of moral indignation, of outraged sympathy, are singularly few. But if he was never the orator that Trotsky was, he was never the man to be swept off his feet. He lost his head only once, and that in a personal question.

And finally, quite in keeping with Trotsky's passion for ideas, his generous indignation at injustice, was his sense of personal rectitude, his idealistic
approach to life. All who knew him intimately even when he was one of the
rulers of Russia speak of it. Max Eastman and also Boris Souvarine, who,
though a fierce opponent of Trotsky's politics, has said of him that there
was nothing "mesquin" in his character, not a trace of rascality. It is a
noticeable characteristic of many great writers and philosophers, but a fatal
weakness in a politician. You can see it in all his writings. Was any other
politician of similar eminence capable of saying the following at a public
investigation?

> I can say that never in my life did I take the interest—take the contrary of
> the truth. If you will, in plain words, a lie. I believe, in our society, which
> is very contradictory, that the conventional rules of conduct in family,
> society, or corporation—everybody is obliged from time to time not to
> say the truth. I committed it sometimes. I believe the question can be
> decided only by comparison of the lies I was obliged to give, and the
> truth. I believe that in the balance my truths are more heavy than the lies.
> It seems to me so in the more important questions, the decisive questions,
> in the questions upon which depend the actions of many people, of
> friends, of their fate—it seems to me that I never committed such crimes.

Trotsky had been through much, but the fundamental honesty of his
character, his inner sensitiveness, as he quite unconsciously expresses them
here, are very moving, but very revealing also. He was a materialist but
none of the great idealist philosophers ever surpassed the conclusion of his
address to the Dewey Commission.

> Esteemed Commissioners! The experience of my life, in which there has
> been no lack either of successes or of failures, has not only not destroyed
> my faith in the clear, bright future of mankind, but, on the contrary, has
> given it indestructible temper. This faith in reason, in truth, in human
> solidarity, at the age of eighteen I took with me into the workers' quarters
> of the provincial town of Nikolaiev—this faith I have preserved fully and
> completely. It has become more mature, but not less ardent. In the very
> fact of your Commission's formation . . . in this fact I see a new and
> truly magnificent reinforcement of the revolutionary optimism which
> constitutes the fundamental element of my life.

Caesar, Cromwell, Napoleon, Lenin, men of deeds, his place is among
them. But he was not one of them really. By nature and inclination he
would have preferred the company of Plato, Aristotle, Spinoza, and
Goethe. History was not unkind to him personally. He got his chance
before he died and took it with both hands. Men make history and to
understand history we must understand men.

LENIN AND TROTSKY

With an understanding of Trotsky as that type of person we can now better understand his successes and his failures. After the 1905 revolution, he met Lenin in Finland. They discussed politics and found themselves in general agreement against the Mensheviks on the political issues of the day. Lenin, always suiting the action to the word, taunted Trotsky with refusing to join the Bolsheviks. Trotsky preferred to wander around for twelve years between Bolsheviks and Mensheviks. He remained untaught by his experience of 1905 when the Mensheviks and Bolsheviks divided between them the leadership of the proletariat. Especially after 1905 a man intent on political power, on political influence, which is the first business of any politician, would have joined one or the other of these parties. Trotsky could not. And his reasons were essentially the reasons of a man repelled by Lenin's toughness and what seemed to him the unscrupulousness of the Bolsheviks. How bitterly he complains!

During the past three to four years of intense party frictions, the life of very many committees has consisted of a series of *coups d'état* in the spirit of our court revolutions of the eighteenth century. Somewhere way up on top somebody is incarcerating, replacing, choking, somebody else, somebody proclaims himself something—and as a result, the top of the committee house is adorned by a flag with the inscription, "Orthodoxy, centralism, political struggle."

He accused the central apparatus itself of starting a new discussion every month:

. . . the apparatus supplies the topic for it, feeds it by false materials, draws its summary, dispenses justice, postpones a congress for a year, and is now preparing a congress from among its own apparatus workers previously appointed, who are to authorize the people on top to continue this work in the future as well.

Thus 1917 found him in an insignificant organization. But for the Bolshevik party, created by Lenin, he would have been helpless, and his grasp of the situation and his gifts would have run to waste. Trotsky has stated emphatically that without Lenin there would have been no October Revolution. He was fully capable of leading a revolution alone, but all the evidence points to the fact that without Lenin he would not have been able to handle the Bolshevik party. Trotsky never minimized the personal weakness which kept him out of the Bolshevik party till 1917. Lenin mitigated its consequences while he lived. When he died Trotsky paid heavily.

Trotsky rendered inestimable services to Russia but twice his enthusiasm, his love of the idea, nearly wrecked the Russian Revolution. Despite the somewhat ingenuous explanation of Brest-Livotsk in *My Life*, the fact remains that he made a terrible error in 1918. That Russia would be saved by the international revolution Lenin knew as well as he. Lenin knew as well as he also that the October Revolution had to hold itself free of any stain of imperialist dealing. But Lenin said, "Peace now, for we cannot fight." Trotsky persisted in chasing a mirage of his own imagination and his obstinacy cost Russia dearly. Had he voted with Lenin earlier the peace would have been signed weeks before. He tries in places to balance Lenin's mistakes in urging the attack on Poland in 1920 with his own in 1918. The comparison is quite false. Soviet Russia could afford a gamble in 1920. The whole point of 1918 was that the country was on the edge and could not take the slightest chance. In 1920 during the dispute on the trade union question, oblivious to the reality, he let his imagination run away with him again. He did not want to militarize labor as the Stalinist liars report, but he wanted to fuse the trade unions with the state administration. His basic argument was that Russia was a workers' state and therefore the trade unions, as the workers' organizations, could administer the state. Lenin's reply was devastating. "Comrade Trotsky says that Russia is a workers' state. Excuse me, that is an abstraction." Had Trotsky had his way he would have placed the Soviet state in mortal peril.

Lenin saved Russia from the political consequences of such a blunder. He could not save the party from the organizational consequences. Trotsky had taken up the cause with his usual enthusiasm, single-mindedness, and the emotional drive which had swept everything before it in 1905, in 1917, and in the formation of the Red Army. For a moment Lenin was in a minority. But Trotsky had to be stopped, and Lenin fell back on Zinoviev, Stalin, and others who had long been waiting their chance to discredit Trotsky. The falseness of Trotsky's position, the recklessness with which he advocated it, and Lenin's political generalship soon put an end to Trotsky's adventure. But Lenin, though recognizing Trotsky's invaluable qualities, sought to guard against any more of these volcanic eruptions. There was a reorganization of party functionaries. Krestinsky, Proebrazensky, and others of Trotsky's supporters, were "distributed." Less than two years afterwards, Lenin fell ill and at the crisis which followed his incapacitation, Trotsky, never concerned with his strength in the party organization, found himself isolated. The whole episode is one of the most instructive in the history of the Bolshevik party, and in the political biography of Trotsky. He brought it on himself not only in the political error—during the debates Lenin carefully pointed out they, all of them, had made theoretical errors—but in the way he behaved.

TROTSKY WITHOUT LENIN

Finally, in the crisis of 1923, Trotsky conducted himself like a philosopher who had spent his life in a study and had suddenly been asked to take charge of a policy at a party conference. We do not wish here to raise the question of whether this policy by Trotsky or that could have succeeded or had better results than the one he followed. He himself, and, for the immediate political aim, very rightly, always insisted on the economic and social factors at work, minimizing the personal factors. But his political naiveté and the idealism of his character are almost incredible but for his own unsuspecting documentation. Trotsky tells us how, over forty, with his head packed with history and a lifetime of political struggle behind him, he hesitated to make a bid for power because he did not want people to think he was too anxious to step into Lenin's shoes. The rest of his strategy is no less amazing. In the hands of Kamanev and Stalin he was a child. Exaggeration? Then characterize these two incidents. Lenin sent him a private letter dealing with an urgent political question in which Stalin and his clique of the moment were intensely interested. Trotsky immediately proposed to show the letter to Kamanev and would have done so but that Lenin stopped him, pointing out that Kamanev would show the letter to Stalin who would inevitably deceive them. All who knew Stalin knew him for what he was. Trotsky knew that Stalin had attempted to poison Lenin's mind against him. He knew all the intrigues that were going on even before Lenin had the final stroke. Yet read his autobiography. He himself reports not one single action of his own to counter Stalin's intrigues. Instead he sent the following message to Stalin by Kamanev. "I am against removing Stalin. . . . But there must be an immediate and radical change. Let (Stalin) not overreach himself. There should be no more intrigues, but honest co-operation." Never was the leopard more sincerely asked to change his spots.

This is not being wise after the event. Lenin saw to the ultimate end what Stalin stood for. His last writings show it without possibility of argument and it is only within recent years that we have been able to understand their full urgency. Trotsky, warned and warned and warned again, wandered about like a child in a forest of wild beasts. An embittered American anti-Trotskyite, George Marlen, gives meaning to his life by ceaseless attacks on Trotsky as having entered into a pact with Stalin to deceive the Russian people. Undoubtedly owing to the political situation Trotsky, rightly or wrongly, submitted to the suppression of Lenin's testament, and assisted Stalin to get out of the hole he was in on the national question. But such compromises, though there can be arguments and differences of opinion about them, are inevitable in the most principled party in the world, and no political party was ever more concerned with principle than the Bolshevik party in its heroic days. What this critic fails to see is that whatever policy Trotsky was following, whatever tactical compromises he found it necessary to make, he himself, being the man he was, was bound to fail. That he was able to use his magnificent gifts in the way he did was due to the fact that Lenin had created the Bolshevik party. Who does not understand that does not understand the letter B in Bolshevism.

The last of his blunders which may be conveniently dealt with here was his political position on the Russian invasion of Poland and, particularly, of Finland. As in 1920, pursuing an idea to the end, he repeated his formula: Russia is a workers' state and must be defended. Unfortunately for his followers he did not stop there. He condemned the invasion and perhaps for the only time in his long career found himself in an insoluble intellectual contradiction. For if Finland was an outpost of imperialism and Stalin was justified in crushing it then Trotsky's condemnation of the invasion was a mere gesture to the widespread disapproval and dismay of the workers. But sharp as were the differences between the present Workers party which was expelled from the Socialist Workers party, a split was not necessary on this question alone. Trotsky knew that, but despite his unwillingness he was cunningly maneuvered into a position in which his authority and energy were unscrupulously used to an aim he did not have in mind. When he recognized what was happening, it was too late. To the end he remained what he was, a man incapable of leaving his main work and concentrating his powerful intellect on the tricks and dodges which are inseparable from politics. Unscrupulous men not fit to clean his pen could gain his confidence and get the better of him. Not the least significant was the tragic circumstances of his death. He had been warned against his murderer but this GPU agent earned his favor by an exaggerated devotion to Trotsky's political position. For six months he discussed politics with the greatest living master of politics and Trotsky never detected a false note, apparently set no trap for him. We can be certain that whoever else might have been deceived by an imposter, Mr. Joseph Stalin would not have been.

In the end the idea expressed was more important and interesting to Trotsky than the person expressing it. It was his strength, the cause of some of his greatest triumphs, but it was his weakness, the cause of some of his greatest failures. We must have him as he was. If you agree with this interpretation of his political character, then you will agree that the power of will and self-discipline with which he devoted himself to a type of work for which he so often expressed a personal distaste is, like so much about him, probably unsurpassed by any other figure of similar stature.

"FROM A THEORETICAL HEIGHT"

What we are trying to do here is to make an historical evaluation of Trotsky and his work. Nowhere is it so necessary and fruitful as in a consideration of the *History*. The bourgeoisie, particularly, in this age, lives from hand to mouth. Philosophy it has none. Mussolini's writings on fascism enjoy a merited obscurity. *Mein Kampf* is no more than the political card-sharping of Machiavelli, adapted to the age of mass production, finance capital, and imperialism. No bourgeois critic can properly evaluate Trotsky's book. For any kind of historical evaluation you need an end—for example, socialism; a material force—the revolutionary proletariat and the colonial peoples; a political method—Bolshevism. This is ours, it is from there that we begin; others may have their own and are welcome to it. But having nothing the bourgeoisie is at a loss not only with politics but with writing of all kinds. Today the Fascists are making history and the Stalinists with them. Why have they not had anything very important or interesting to say? Molotov's "Fascism is a question of taste" is at least original. Even that cannot be said of Stalin's also solitary contribution to recent literature: the brilliant phrase that Russia would not pull anybody's chestnuts out of the fire.

Against this and similar curiosities set the body of Trotsky's writings. On the one hand brutality, hypocrisy, lies and cunning, clumsily and coarsely expressed; on the other strength, honesty, high aspiration and a sparkling intelligence, dynamic power, all portrayed through the medium of a style whose miracles we know even in translation.* The bourgeois critic will explain it in terms of personal ability. A patent and far-reaching error. The style is the man, and men like Hitler and Trotsky speak for a social order. An age, a class, a political system expresses itself through its great books. The Declaration of Independence and Lincoln's Gettysburg Address are two of the greatest pieces of writing in any language. Beside them Winston Churchill's rhetoric is shoddy. Yet Churchill is a greater master of language than either Jefferson or Lincoln and wants to win his war as much as they wanted to win theirs. His weakness lies in his historical circumstances. They had enormous historical confidence. Churchill has none. He is doubtful of the past, fearful of the future.

It is historically that we must approach Trotsky's *History of the Russian Revolution*. We do not only take it as our own and judge it by its own standards. We compare it to other literary and political writings of this and other ages. We make a genuinely historical comparison. We shall find that

---

*This does not mean that this writer, for instance, is in complete agreement with everything Trotsky wrote. There are not negligible sections to which he is absolutely opposed. These will be taken up in good time. But the disagreements are family disagreements.

in the same way as Marx and Engels stand above all who have concerned themselves with the analysis of society, as Lenin and Trotsky rank with the greatest of those who have helped to alter the lives of large masses of human beings, so Trotsky's *History* is far more than a brilliant history of a great event. It is the greatest history book ever written and one of the most stupendous and significant pieces of literature ever produced in any language.

We do not intend merely to assert. We shall demonstrate. But we must not be so shortsighted about these things. These tremendous achievements were the achievements of men, but these men could do the things they did because they represented something—a method, a system of ideas; they could do them because they were the advance guard of something infinitely greater than their individual selves—a new society. At a time when our forces are small we need to maintain the Marxist tradition ready for the day. The best way to maintain it is to understand it, and one sure way to understand is through the *History*.

But your pseudo-Marxists will certainly ask: What use is it that Trotsky wrote so well and Hitler and Stalin write so badly? What does it prove? It proves a hundred times over the historic significance of the ideas which Trotsky stood for. Great books do not drop from the sky. Messrs. pessimists are soused to the marrow in the vinegar of bourgeois empiricism and trained from childhood to worship the established fact. That is why to the greatest problem of the present day, the future of Marxism, they come armed with the scientific weapon of primitive man: the philosophy of simple addition. The Marxists have six hundred members here, eighty here, and twenty there. And on the other side look at Hitler's thousands of airplanes and millions of men. Obviously, oh, how obviously the Fourth International is doomed to failure. Trotsky, looking at Marxism since 1840 and all that it had done, faced the future with confidence and looked upon the ready reckoners as a man looks upon little boys playing at marbles. They do no harm until they try to introduce their infantile accounts into the records and perspectives of mature men. We cannot judge history by its own probable effect upon our own tender hides. Any hillbilly in the wilds of Arkansas can do that. We must have historical perspective, look a long way back and a certain distance forward. It will not then be difficult to see what the *History of the Russian Revolution* represents. It is the climax of two thousand years of European writing and study of history. It is these and similar things that were in Trotsky's mind when with his last words he said that he was confident of the victory of the Fourth International.

WESTERN CIVILIZATION AND HISTORY

First a brief review of the historical hierarchy. Herodotus was the first. And he set himself to tell the history of the war between the Greeks and Persians before the material was forgotten. He was not an Athenian citizen. He was a very impressionable intellectual, widely read and widely traveled, who was caught by the romance of history. He wrote down what he gathered and from that day he has been the model and inspiration, whether they know it or not, of countless historians, inside Europe, inside Asia, and inside everywhere else. But we lose sight of what is essential in him if we allow his love of the picturesque to obscure the purpose—the victory of Greece over Persia. It was the defense of civilization against barbarism, the greatest peril that the Greeks had ever faced. He had a great theme, one which every civilized man on the Mediterranean coast could understand and feel.

Thirty years after, Thucydides, in his very first paragraph, repudiated Herodotus. With singular acerbity for so urbane a man, Thucydides says that before the Peloponnesian War nothing of importance had ever happened. It was as if a modern American historian watching the world situation had called upon the American people to stop reading about Columbus and to study his history of the 1914 war. Man of affairs, politician, soldier, this sober Athenian was sick of all this old tale-telling in the face of the threat to Athens. He wrote a book which to this day is not excelled for gravity, lucidity, proportion, and knowledge of politics. He wrote with one aim—the glorification of Athenian democracy. "Our country is governed in the interests of the many instead of the few. That is why it is called a democracy." How those words have echoed down the years, drowning the sighs and groans of Athenian slaves!

The great Romans, Livy and Tacitus, wrote within a few years of each other. They hated the autocracy and depravity of the Empire, and Livy, in particular, glorified the constitution of the Roman republic and the stern virtues of ancient Rome. He gives one of his best speeches to Cato denouncing a law which allowed freedom of attire to Roman women. As Rome went to pieces without any future, men clung to the past which Livy had idealized by forty years of labor. Rome fell but Latin literature remained and when the Renaissance brought back the study of the classics, all the growing forces of liberalism in Europe nourished themselves on the vivid artistry and republican sentiments of Thucydides, Livy, and Plutarch and cursed tyranny in the language of Tacitus. By the end of the nineteenth century Livy had been translated some five hundred times. The Elizabethan age was famous for its translations. Amyot translated Plutarch and North translated Amyot, giving Shakespeare rich material for plays. To all these people Livy and Plutarch were far more important than Holinshed and Froissart. The heroes of the French Revolution conceived themselves as heroic Romans of the republican days. So did Babeuf. The finer shades of European history are a closed book without an understanding of what the classics meant to all the educated classes. For generations they learned nothing else at school. The climax came with Gibbon, who gathered together all the learning and classical consciousness of centuries in his justly celebrated book. But a hundred years ago Guizot knew that for the scientific history of Rome you had to look elsewhere than in the *Decline and Fall*. Gibbon's history was the historical peak of the age of enlightenment. He was a member of that cosmopolitan society of Voltaire, Frederick the Great, Catherine, and the French aristocracy which flourished before the French Revolution. Even the Bourbon monarchy enjoyed this culture and Gibbon's devastating attack on Christianity was characteristic of educated society in his day, not excluding French bishops. Aristocrat though he was, he represented progress. Voltaire was a prolific historian of the same school.

Two generations after Gibbon, Michelet wrote of the French Revolution with an erratic passion that made him a French classic. Macaulay made his political reputation in the struggle for the Reform Bill of 1832 and his history so dominated bourgeois English thought for a century that it is only since October 1917 that the Whig tradition has ceased to reign over all English academic writing. Yet he was so biased that his great history is fittingly called a Whig pamphlet in four octavo volumes. Green was less crude, but of the same school. His *Short History of the English People* first made history popular among all classes. All the English prejudices of the last sixty years, their belief in English history as one long struggle for liberty culminating in the British constitution, their conception of themselves as a Germanic people born to freedom, the Magna Carta legend, the Cromwell protestant legend, all come straight from Green. These histories are some of them good, some of them bad. Green, the most popular, is very bad. But that is not their importance. What they do is to hold not a mirror but a banner up to society. They give society or more often a class an image of itself, not as it was but as it thought it was, or as it would have liked to be. In them is written the history of an age, but not in the sense that they thought they were writing. Gibbon portrays eighteenth-century Europe as well as the Roman Empire.

These writers were great artists, powerful personalities, preaching a cause, and "they wrote so well because they saw so little."* But all of them represented some powerful progressive idea, and the great classics first, and

---

*See the introduction to *The Black Jacobins* by C. L. R. James. [Editors' note: The article was signed by James with his pseudonym, J. R. Johnson. This is one case of his reference to a text published under his proper name.]

these and their satellites after, dominated the thought of the bourgeoisie for over four hundred years. Even Gibbon, aristocrat though he was, was an *English* aristocrat and praised the Roman constitution in which he thought he saw the model of the British. Then suddenly, with Michelet and Macaulay the line comes to a dead stop and is taken up again only with Trotsky. Why? A few dates will help us.

Michelet's book appeared in 1847–1850 and the fiery *History of the French Revolution* was directly inspired by the 1848 revolution, the events leading up to it, and his own belief in communism. Macaulay's first volume of the *History of England* appeared in 1848. But 1848 was the year when the *socialist* revolution first appeared. It was the year of *The Communist Manifesto*. The specter began to haunt Europe. Sharp eyes were watching, and the call for liberty vanished from bourgeois historical writing on the grand scale. Mommsen's *History of the Roman Republic* appeared in 1854, six years after 1848. Not at all accidentally, he was a German. He loved parliamentary democracy but he hated the proletariat, especially after 1848. There was only one refuge for him, Bonapartism, and the climax of his learned work on Rome is his description of Caesar as "the entire, the perfect man." Bismarck and Napoleon III did their best to emulate if not the perfection at least the entirety of Caesar. Carlyle before 1848 had been so sympathetic to the workers as to win favorable notice from Marx and Engels, but 1848 drove him into the reaction and henceforth he was the advocate of the hero, essentially Mommsen's entire and perfect man. The domination of the world market enabled Britain to be a little more liberal and Green published in 1874. But six years after Green came Seeley's *The Expansion of the British Empire*, whose idiotic thesis that the British founded their empire in a fit of absence of mind did not prevent his book from being one of the most widely read of the day. Mahan's *Influence of Sea Power in History*, though not widely popular, was scarcely less influential. Mommsen, Carlyle, Bismarck, Nietzsche, Seeley, Mahan, all that they had to say of political importance was gathered into one tremendous volume—Spengler's *Decline of the West* which was completed in 1917. During the very hours that Spengler was writing finis to bourgeois civilization, Lenin was completing *The State and Revolution* and *Imperialism* in preparation for the Russian Revolution. In the face of the grandiose movement of social revolution, the slow accumulations, the dramatic confrontations, statements of position, retreats and advances, battles across a world for the future of society, in the face of all this how mean and piddling are the smug calculations of our sneering accountants, blind to the historical process as a whole and unable to rise above their own insufficiency!

It is, as Trotsky would say, from this theoretical height that we can see what the *History* has restored to historical writings. To Gibbon, to

Macaulay, to Trotsky, liberty meant different things. Trotsky's conception is the widest. That is not the point at issue now. What matters is that the proletariat at least calls for liberty. The bourgeoisie cannot find one great writer to do so. Marx's claim that the future of society rests with the proletariat is demonstrated as clearly in historical writing as in economic analysis. This guarantees nothing. To show where the future of any liberty that we may look forward to lies, is no guarantee of its success. But this reactionary and cowardly sentiment, masquerading as realism, draws strength as reaction always does, from ignorance. There is something very concrete to the great historians, propagandists though they were. Not a single broad political step forward in modern European history has ever been taken in the name of tyranny. The exalted sentiment of the popular historians always related to economic expansion and political progress. Even Christianity, the ideological successor to the Roman Empire, spoke in the name of the liberty of the individual, his right to the disposition of his own soul, opposed to the Roman state and slavery. The Reformation saw itself as a revolt against papal tyranny. The absolute monarchy was the first political resource of the bourgeoisie against the feudal lords. Its misconceptions of Thucydides, Livy, Plutarch, and Tacitus seemed like heaven on earth to the bourgeoisie. No taxation without representation; life, liberty, and the pursuit of happiness; liberty, equality, and fraternity; government of the people, by the people, and for the people—these contained falsities, conscious and unconscious, but they broke monstrous and avowed tyrannies. Workers of the World Unite aims at doing the same. But for the first time for over five centuries, a political system with a great fanfare of newness and solution to crisis, makes a political virtue out of tyranny, inequality; class, racial and national prejudice; and decries everything that European civilization has striven for, in theory at least, since the Renaissance. During Europe's worst periods of reaction, the period of the Counter-Reformation and the Holy Alliance, the most reactionary writers could find something plausible to say in defense of their cause. German imperialism plunders in order to live. Fascism is the decline of the West and its protagonists know it in their souls. Their writings on all subjects except the seizure of power are nothing else but lies and nonsense, cold-blooded deliberate falsification. Not a flower blossoms on their arid heaths. There is no soil in which anything can grow. They are just a thin cover for exhausted bourgeois society. They can have nothing to say. Mommsen and Carlyle said all when the bourgeoisie still could guarantee some illusions. If Trotsky's *History* does not guarantee the inevitability of socialism, *Mein Kampf* guarantees the fraud of fascism as a solution to the ills of capitalist society.

NOT ONLY ART BUT SCIENCE

We have carefully avoided hitherto dealing with the scientific aspect of Trotsky's *History*. It is familiar to all Marxists, and gives the final endorsement to its value as propaganda on the grand scale. For whereas the other historians in the pursuit of their aim shaped their material as an artist shapes his figures, Trotsky claimed and irrefutably demonstrated that his history was scientific in that it flowed from the objective facts. He challenged anyone to question his documentation and the challenge has never been taken up. In method and presentation the book is as scientific as *The Origin of Species*. It may be challenged as Darwin was challenged, but on concrete not on abstract grounds. No herald of liberty and progress ever stood more firmly with both feet on the earth. And yet in pure style, this materialist, as rigid with fact as Scaligar, is exceeded in no sphere by any one of his ancestors, not by Thucydides in proportion and lucidity, nor by Tacitus in invective, nor by Gibbon in dignity, nor Michelet in passion, nor by Macaulay, that great bourgeois, in efficiency. There is a profound lesson here not only in history but in aesthetics.

And finally, the book is not only a propagandist tract, the expression of an attitude to society, and a scientific thesis. It is, besides, what none of the others is. It is a summons to action. It is not only a banner and a blueprint. It is a roll of drums. Through it breathes not only the spirit of "this is what we aimed at, this is the way it was done," but also, "this is the way to do it." Every aspect of the struggle is scientifically analyzed and expounded, and the reader is not so much rhetorically exhorted to join up, but as he sees the difficulties and feels the unbounded confidence and unshakable will which attacks and overcomes them, the knowledge and the power, he becomes part of this wonderful adventure. Resentment at oppression smoulders in hundreds of millions of people all over the world. What they lack is confidence in their own powers. How can we fight and win? The answer is in the *History*. And by and large, the advance guard of this generation have been ready for that answer. In translations, it has sold thousands upon thousands of copies. On the shelves of many rank-and-file Social Democrats it occupies an honored place, and it has penetrated into the homes of numerous Stalinists, the only book by Trotsky since his exile to do so, despite their copious denunciation of all his writings. This is not one of its least triumphs.

Had the Third International been a revolutionary organization, this book, with its knowledge, its confidence, and its will, would have inspired, directly and indirectly, millions of political leaders all over the world. History has deemed otherwise, but it is another proof of what we know in so many other fields, that it is Stalinism above all which confuses the working class and keeps away from it that knowledge and understanding without which it cannot conquer. The new class is willing to listen. An excrescence stands in the way. Powerful though it is, it is still an excrescence. To see the *History* in perspective is to realize that it is Stalinism which is the accident and that the proletariat and its spokesman are a sequence in the movement of European life and thought as we have known them for five centuries.

HOW A CLASSIC IS BORN

Now a book could be a propaganda tract on the grand scale, an attempt at a scientific treatise, and a summons to action; could be written by a highly gifted participant in a great event; and yet be merely one of many other books. The memoirs of all who took part in the last war are there to show that these are not sufficient to write a great book. That the *History* is what it is, is due certainly to Trotsky's power as a writer. There is no substitute for a great artist. But that for us is the least consideration.

With *The Communist Manifesto* began something entirely new in historical method. Specifically to show how the new method should be used, Marx deliberately wrote *The Eighteenth Brumaire*, but afterward he and Engels wrote specifically on history only as the occasion presented itself, and always to the point and no more. Bernstein and Kautsky wrote historical works which were illuminating but academic. The Marxist method enables you to write a scientific history. But it is not a talisman. Kautsky and Bernstein were bureaucrats, the one a concealed and the other an avowed reactionary. And Marxist method or no Marxist method, only passionate conviction can write a great book. Neither Lenin nor Rosa Luxemburg wrote history. Men of action must cease being men of action to write history, which demands a certain tranquility. But during all these years, there was accumulated in books, articles, and correspondence, a vast amount of thinking on history; isolated sketches, scholarly works, deductions and observations about classes, states, insurrections, mass movements, which formed the Marxist corpus. It was not collected anywhere but the students of Marxism knew it. It was in the background of Lenin's mind always. He studied the proceedings of Cromwell's Long Parliament and the proceedings of the Paris Commune during the French Revolution, and thus tested and amplified the principles laid down by Marx. Trotsky followed this example, only whereas Lenin seemed by nature inclined to economic and statistical studies, Trotsky's natural instincts as we have seen drove him to history and writing. Trotsky also had met and talked with all the great European Marxists of his time. In 1905 came the theory of the permanent revolution, and from that time on, not to mention the earlier years, how the

Russian Revolution would develop was the main preoccupation of the Social Democrats in Russia and of European Marxists as a whole. But whereas everyone, according to his gifts and opportunities, contributed and analyzed, no one, not even Lenin, analyzed more deeply than Trotsky. He had his theory to test and to defend and he was above all a man of theory. Thus the structure and movement of the Russian Revolution was the very structure of his mental make-up, the axis around which he lived intellectually and emotionally. Came 1917 and for seven intense months, first outside and then inside Russia, he saw and helped and guided. Thus it is safe to say that no previous writer was ever so much completely master of a great subject as Trotsky was of the Russian Revolution. Politically mankind came of age with the Russian Revolution. Caesar, Cromwell, Marat, Robespierre, and other famous men had worked largely by instinct. For the first time in history, a man had foreseen the main lines of a great historical event, and had himself been instrumental in carrying it through to a successful conclusion. Lenin had to revise his conceptions. Not Trotsky. Any writer, any artist would know the extraordinary power and confidence, the certainty of direction, that would be Trotsky's when he sat down to write. Such was the background. The interplay of class as a whole and individual artist are fused here as nowhere else that we know in writing. But that is only half the book.

A revolution is the greatest event in the life of all those who experience it. It alters the food that you eat, the way you eat it, the clothes that you wear, even the way of a man with a maid. And never were so many people jerked so far and with such violence as were the people of Russia by the October Revolution. Thus from 1917 onward an unending stream of reminiscence, memoirs, documents, conferences, conversations, contributed unceasingly to the consciousness of the leaders of a historical event who from the beginning were as conscious of their historic selves as no other leaders in history. Politicians, diplomats, aristocrats, and merchants wrote, the official historians collected, but worker-Bolsheviks, ordinary workers, ordinary peasants, ordinary soldiers, all poured their contributions in. How often Trotsky must have talked about the Revolution to ordinary folks! How glad they were to talk to the man of October! Too much material can swamp. But to Trotsky, who since 1905 had the main lines of the map clear, it defined, clarified, enriched, illustrated. Had he remained a ruler of Russia, the book would never have been written. But driven into exile he settled down to it. (He was at his desk at last, with a pen in his hand.)

Into the book went all the historical knowledge and understanding which Marx and Engels had started to accumulate, and which the Marxists had continued, step by step, as the proletariat and peasantry of the whole world moved slowly forward. All that Marx and Engels and Lenin had written and thought about great revolutions in the past and Trotsky's own discoveries,

Lenin's studies of 1905 and the period in between 1905 and 1917, all the erudition, conflicts, thoughts of the Russian social democracy, the writings and analyses that followed 1917, of Lenin, of Bukharin, of Rakovsky, and scores of other gifted men, and of all the millions of the Russian people, all this Trotsky gathered together. The artist in him, suppressed for forty years by the needs of the revolution, now opened out, and with the same personal force, discipline, and will which always distinguished him, he hammered this mountainous mass of facts and ideas around the theme of the class struggle into one of the most powerful, compact and beautiful pieces of literature that exists in any language, prose or poetry. Milton says that a great book is the precious life-blood of a master spirit. True. But in the *History* is the precious life blood of many master spirits; and also of the Russian people, of the French proletariat, in 1848 and 1870, of Ironsides and Jacobins and *sansculottes*, of the abortive German revolution of 1918, and the Chinese and other nationalist revolutions. All, all are there. All had contributed their sufferings, their hopes, the wisdom that was drawn from their experiences. A hundred years of socialist thought and proletarian struggles have gone into the making of that book, the first of its kind. No one will ever be able to write like it again for generations. Historians will write, their wine will be new, but their bottles will be old. It is the first classic of socialist society and it will never be superseded. For there may come a time when *Capital* will be of historic interest only, when *What Is to Be Done?* will be pondered over by students who will seek in vain to recapture the remote circumstances which produced Bolshevism of the imperialist age. But the *History* will remain the bridge between the long line which leads from the Old Testament and Homer, Greek tragedy, Dante and Cervantes, to the books which will be written when, in Marx's famous phrase, the history of humanity begins.

THE VOICE OF THE REVOLUTION

With the conclusion of the *History*, it might have seemed that Trotsky had done enough for one man. And yet, infatuated exaggeration though it may sound, his last phase is the most unprecedented of his wonderful career. He was the most powerful and celebrated exile in history. Napoleon at St. Helena was out of it. Bismarck walked down the gangway and was rowed into oblivion. Napoleon III finished like the last discord of a modern jazz composition. Kaiser Wilhelm added a beard to his moustache. These men ruled tremendous empires for many years and then sank from public affairs like stones. As for the social democratic rubbish, the Kerenskys, the Chernovs, the Bauers, Caballeros, Negrins, and Prietos, what a miserable down-at-heel assortment of discards, old curs with scarcely spirit enough to yelp at the moon—for nobody wants to hear them. All of them, kings and bureaucrats, could find a place to stay. Great organizations, sometimes great states, backed them. Yet all added together they amount to nothing. Trotsky could not rest anywhere. No country wanted him until Mexico added luster to its history by giving him a home.

He was pursued by all the resources of the Soviet state. Despite the devoted solicitude of his supporters he was often in financial straits, for though their devotion was unlimited, their numbers were few. Yet from all these difficulties he emerged as a veritable tribune of the international working class, speaking for the proletarian revolution and for socialism as no private individual ever spoke for any public cause. First was the gigantic conflict with Stalin and the Soviet bureaucracy. Never did any state spend so much time, energy, and resources to blacken the reputation and silence the ideas of a single individual. His supporters were systematically murdered. Unprecedented trials were arranged for the purpose of getting rid of internal enemies and utterly discrediting him. Huge political parties all over the world carried out the orders and repeated the slanders of Moscow. Almost single-handed, Trotsky, aided only by a small and devoted band of followers (they did a great historic work) fought Stalinism to a finish and inflicted upon it a resounding defeat. Today the whole world knows that Stalin lied, that Trotsky was no enemy of the Soviet Union, that he stood for the revolution as it was originally conceived, and though they hate him for his unswerving devotion to revolution, yet his sincerity and his loyalty to the cause of socialism are not questioned.

He fought for that, not on account of his personal reputation—he was always confident of the judgment of history—but because he knew that in attempting to discredit him, the Stalinists, inside and outside Russia, sought to discredit the ideas for which he stood—the ideas of revolutionary socialism. Periodically the front pages of every newspaper in the world were covered with the records of this great conflict, and Stalin, the ruler of 170 millions, and Trotsky, *primus inter pares* of a few scattered thousands, met as equals on the arena of world public opinion. It will be said that historical events helped him to win his final victory. What infinite wisdom! As if Trotsky did not know that history was moving in a certain direction, as if all his efforts were not directed toward hastening and clarifying the process.

The Stalinists claimed that he gained all this publicity because he was an enemy of the Soviet Union and the bourgeoisie used him. It is a pitiable self-deception. At the time of the Moscow Trials, the *Manchester Guardian* was advocating an alliance between Great Britain and the Soviet Union. Yet it threw open its pages to him, for in the confusion all felt that only one man could help to elucidate the mystery and that man was Trotsky himself. That was the secret of his power. He could clarify the world bourgeoisie, in the confusion in which it finds itself. It learned something from him. He was prepared to speak whenever asked, because he knew the limitations of bourgeois wisdom; through their organs he spoke to the workers about every important event, not only on revolutions on which he was an authority, but on every development in the steady progress to war. Journalists came from all over the world to interview him, certain that people would read eagerly what he said. His books were literary events, simultaneously reviewed everywhere and pondered over.

To attribute it all to his personal brilliance, the vigor and incisiveness of his expression, is an absurdity we have already dealt with earlier. Trotsky represented something—represented it adequately, magnificently, with a power that was all his own, but yet he was only a representative. He represented the proletariat in the period of the decay of capitalism. The proletariat is a mighty force in the modern world. If the radical intellectuals do not know it, the bourgeoisie does. The bourgeoisie listened to Trotsky because whether it recognized this or not he represented the point of view of the world revolution. The bourgeoisie does not accept Marxism. It cannot. But it was obvious to many bourgeois thinkers that on any knotty tangle of international politics he always had something of value to say. Why had Hitler come so easily to power in Germany? What was the significance of Hitler? Why, why the Hitler-Stalin Pact? How would the war end? He told them what he thought. They listened to his predictions because these turned out so often to be true. But if they were hazy as to the source of his ideas, they had no illusions as to what use he intended to make of them, and they carefully excluded him from their shores. When he died, in their news columns and obituary notices they recognized the greatness of the figure that had so dominated a social epoch; in their editorials they vented their spleen against the implacable enemy of their society.

For those who can understand history there is a tremendous significance in this last period of Trotsky's life. Like some bold reconnoiterer he forced his way into the enemy's camp, and using every trick, wile, and dodge at his command, and giving away practically nothing, he carried on the battle, cleared paths, exposed dangers, charted a course, knowing that though the great armies had fallen behind and were stumbling, they were coming, slowly but inexorably they were coming. And that almost alone he could do so much was a testimony not only to his personal qualities but to the great forces which he represented. How little some of his friends knew it, and how well his enemies! Stalin, aware of the state of his regime and in what a tottering world he lived, did not count Trotsky's meager following and then sit back in comfort. He knew that as long as Trotsky lived and could write and speak, the Soviet bureaucracy was in mortal danger. In a conversation just before war broke out, Hitler and the French ambassador discussed the perils of plunging Europe into conflict and agreed that the winner of the second great war might be Trotsky. Winston Churchill hated him with a personal malevolence which seemed to overstep the bounds of reason. Those men knew his stature, the power of what he stood for, and were never lulled by the smallness of his forces. If some of our radical intelligentsia will not learn from Marxism, perhaps they will ponder on the view of Trotsky held by Stalin, Hitler, and Churchill.

THE FOURTH INTERNATIONAL

And yet his work as a spokesman of the revolution was not his main occupation in this period. Not at all. For him that was secondary. What interested him most was getting his ideas directly to the masses through revolutionary organizations. This work is a chapter in itself. It is almost unknown to the general public. All of it is included in the words "the struggle for the Fourth International." We of the Fourth International know what was the quality and quantity of that work; the enormous labor, the knowledge and wisdom, the enthusiasm that he put into it. Always he saw history from a great height. Yet a dispute between ten struggling young comrades, five thousand miles away from him, whom he had never seen or heard of until they wrote to him, would occupy his devoted attention for hours and hours at a time. People accuse Trotsky of impatience and domineering. They do not know what they are talking about. He had his opinions and fought for them. In ideological struggles he was a relentless foe. With him theories were not interesting ideas to be played with, as is the detestable habit of the bourgeois intellectuals. They were weapons in the class struggle. But to know and to appreciate his powers and his past, the enormous force of this many-sided and yet perfectly integrated personality, and to see him listening patiently to some inexperienced comrade putting forward his inexperienced ideas, to read letters in which he took up some apparently minor point and elaborated it meeting all possible objections one by one, was to have a great lesson in the difference between the superficial arrogance which often characterizes essentially sensitive men, and the ocean of strength, patience, and resiliency which can come from complete devotion to a cause.

That is the secret of his life and achievement—we cannot state it too often—the fact that he was not only gifted above his fellows but that he early abandoned a bankrupt society and embraced a cause which used all that he had and placed no limits on his development. Bourgeois society limits and cramps and distorts. Winston Churchill is a man who in energy and diversity of natural gifts, courage, and spirit, executive ability, and artistic instinct could not have been anything if at all inferior to Trotsky.

Yet look at the result. His whole great British Empire has throttled instead of developing him. It has debarred him from understanding history; he has no historical method. He was at the head of the British navy in the last war and knew everything from the inside, yet his *World Crisis* is commonplace, and full of windy rhetoric. His recent speeches are far above anything bourgeois democracy has produced in this crisis. He describes with clarity and style. Yet, at the conclusion of one of his best efforts, all he can tell the British people is so to bear themselves that if they lived a thousand years, men shall say this war was their finest hour. It is not a chance phrase. Men in such times as these do not use chance phrases. Perspective he has and can have none, unless, like Hitler, he turns himself definitely and consciously round and tramples upon everything that humanity has aimed at, however unsuccessfully, in thousands of years of painful effort. All the gifts in the world would not have saved Trotsky from a similar fate had he limited himself to bourgeois society. Being determines consciousness. In the struggle for socialism he strides through the world, a titan among men, excelling in every field he touched. An exile half his life, persecuted as no man has been persecuted, he lived the fullest life of any human being hitherto. The field of being which he chose developed his consciousness to a pitch reached by few men. That consciousness he did his best to pass on to us. It is ours to guard, from each according to our abilities. Let us see to it that we do our share. He himself now belongs to history and this is an historical evaluation. But his death is recent enough and each of us is personally indebted to him for too much to exclude a personal note. Motley closed his noble history of the Dutch Republic by saying of William the Silent that for thirty years he was the guiding star of a whole great nation, and when he died the little children cried in the streets. Whatever the fate of our movement, whatever its successes or failures, whatever our personal lives may hold, to us who knew him and worked with him, now that he is dead, the world will never be the same again.

SEPTEMBER 1940

8

Imperialism in Africa

The great war for democracy (or, from Hitler's point of view, the great war for fascism) is being fought out in Africa as fiercely as anywhere else. It is not only a question of strategy. The competing imperialisms want Africa, first and foremost, for the sake of Africa, a fact which the democratic propagandists disregard with the Olympian sublimity of complete ignorance or complete hypocrisy. Hitler at any rate says plainly that he wants his living space. But let that pass. What we want to do here is to state a few facts about Africa and its role in imperialist economy, and its future in a socialist world. So tightly knit is the world market which capitalism has created that we shall find ourselves dealing with the fundamental problems of modern society and the solution of the permanent crisis not only in Africa but on a world scale.

Up to 1914 the British bourgeoisie had not the faintest idea of the revolutionary violence which capitalism was nursing in its bosom, particularly in the colonies. An obscure Russian revolutionary exile named Lenin wrote confidently about the inevitable emergence of the proletariat in India and China as the leaders of the coming nationalist revolutions. But which British politician or world publicist worried himself about that? It is most valuable to reread what these wise men of thirty years ago used to say about the world and what we used to say. But first the Russian Revolution and then the wave of nationalist revolutions which swept through the British and French empires after the war gave the British bourgeoisie a fright which goes far to explain their insatiable desire for appeasement. All the cunning, all the lies, the violence, the sanctimonious cruelty, which have so distinguished the British ruling class through the centuries, proved powerless to stifle the great Indian revolution, and though Churchill says little in public about India, he thinks about it only less than he thinks about Germany.

INDIA AND AFRICA

The Indian revolution took British imperialism by surprise, but, as the full disintegration of capitalist society and its colonial consequences began to

131

force itself upon the British bourgeoisie, a very distinctively enunciated current of thought took shape: We have been taken by surprise in India; if we do not act in Africa, we shall be taken by surprise there also. The climax was the formation of an African research society under the auspices of the Royal Institute of International Affairs, the disguise the British government assumes when it wants to investigate economic and political questions without official responsibility. A powerful commission was appointed, consisting of the ablest men who could be found in England for the task. An economic adviser to the Bank of England, an Oxford professor of colonial history, the editor of *Nature*, Julian Huxley, Arthur Salter, Lord Lugard (after Cecil Rhodes the greatest of African proconsuls) and some others, all under the chairmanship of that well-known liberal, admirer of fascism, and defender of the British and American way of life. We refer to the late Lord Lothian. The committee decided to make a complete survey of colonial Africa [*African Survey*] and appointed Lord Hailey, the governor of the united provinces in India, to carry it out. Special researches were commissioned preparatory to the actual work in Africa, the most important being a study of capitalist investment in Africa [*Capital Investment in South Africa*] by professor Frankel of Johannesburg. The survey (1,837 pages) and Frankel's volume (487 pages) were published in 1938 by the Royal Institute. They constitute an indictment of capitalist civilization impossible to find outside the pages of Marxist writers.

Frankel writes with the freedom of one without official responsibility. Hailey has the caution of an old civil servant, with the understatement of the Englishman and the evangelical mode of expression which is part of the British imperialist burden. Both, however, come to identical conclusions. Imperialism in Africa is bankrupt. There is only one way to save the situation, and that is to raise the standard of living, culture, and productivity of the native Africans. The full significance of this economic conclusion can only be understood against the *political* background of Africa, for it is the first law of existence and self-preservation of every European in Africa, that the existence of European civilization in Africa (and by European civilization these people mean, of course, European imperialism) depends upon one fact, the maintenance of the African in the position of inferiority, segregation, and backwardness in which he is at present. In this bourgeois thought, by the process of separating what is dialectically inseparable, has reached the conclusion that, to save itself it must destroy itself.

What Is Africa?

Lord Hailey's survey comprises all of Africa south of the Sahara and was not confined to the British colonies, for the British wanted to find out officially all that there was to be found out about Africa. The African population of this territory is estimated at 100 million. Of this, the European population is about 2.25 million. Of these, over 2 million are in the Union of South Africa alone. For the rest, you can find figures like these: French West Africa, population in round figures, 14 million, white population 19,000; Belgian Congo, population 10 million, white population 18,000. In Kenya, which is supposed to have areas particularly suited to white colonization, African population 3 million, white population 18,000. In Nigeria, African population 19 million, white population 5,000. North of the Zanibes the white population is barely 100,000. The area of the territories is about 8.26 million square miles, three times the size of the United States of America. Colonial Africa is for the most part one vast concentration camp, with a few thousand white slave drivers. In India there is an Indian industrial and landowning class, in China the same. In Africa there are just slaves and overseers. The British government three years ago awoke (theoretically) to the fact that this cannot go on, for it does not pay.

THE RAILWAY FIASCO

The mercantilist system had exploited Africa as a field of commerce: first, slaves, and secondly, *pacotille*, the beads, colored cotton, and other rubbish for which Negro slaves were exchanged. With the decline of the mercantile system, after the American war of independence, Africa receded out of the picture of European imperialism until the period for capital export. By 1935, the total capital investments from abroad amounted to $6,111 million. Of this amount, 77 percent is *in British territories* and *British investors have supplied 75 percent of this total*. In trade it is the same. In 1935 the total trade of British territories formed 85 percent of the total trade of Africa. In 1907 it was 84 percent and for years it has never fallen below 80 percent.

Britain dominates the whole of native Africa, the French, Belgian, and Portuguese colonies being merely satellites of this swollen imperialist monster. Of the total of over 6 billion dollars invested from abroad in Africa, nearly one-half consists of loans and grants to governments, while a little less than a quarter of the whole, $1,335 million, to be exact, has been invested in railways, which hang like a weight of chains on European capitalists and black labor in Africa. Africa did not need them. Railways must serve flourishing industrial areas, or densely populated agricultural regions, or they must open up new land (as in the United States) along which a thriving population develops and provides the railways with traffic. Except in the mining regions of South Africa, all these conditions are absent. Yet railways were needed, for the benefit of European investors and heavy industry, for some vague purpose known as the "opening up" of the continent, and for the all-important strategic purposes. The result is that in nearly every colony today railways have been developed by the governments and, up to today, only governments can afford to operate them. Most of them have been overbuilt. As a result of this expenditure the railways have been burdened with large interest obligations which cause excessively heavy rates on imported or local traffic.

CAPITAL AND SLAVERY

In the attempt to improvise the production for export which is necessary to meet these heavy interest charges, various types of uneconomic production have been embarked upon. Uneconomic in themselves, chiefly of the one-crop type, and subjected to the fluctuations of the world market, some of these have now become burdens upon the territories concerned. As a result, Frankel comes to the following remarkable conclusion: "Governments have been brought up time and time again against the fundamental difficulty that capital investment in itself cannot lead to economic development, but requires a concomitant expansion of other factors of production. Capital alone cannot solve the economic problem." In other words, capital cannot expect to flourish if the African native remains a slave. In colony after colony the complaints are the same. In 1934 the general manager of the Nigeria Government Railways reported:

> The trade of the colony is not yet developed to anything like the transport capacity of its railway route mileage. No private railway company could have constructed so much mileage, and the whole colony has greatly benefited from the transport facilities. . . . Were the annual capital charges of the railway to be set alongside the aggregate income of the population which it serves, it would be clear that, short of a *valuable bulk mineral discovery*, the main direction in which the annual capital charges could be met year by year from railway earnings must be the carriage by it of a very large volume of agricultural products, and the whole of that volume wherever the railway can reach it. A sufficient volume of export products does not now exist.

Nigeria is one of the most prosperous of the colonies, and this chiefly because it has a large native peasantry. The railways reports from the French Congo and Belgian Congo *say exactly the same*, only they say it in French and with more despair, because the native peasantry is absent from both these huge colonies. Frankel concludes:

> In general, African railways have been constructed on the basis of a too optimistic view of the rate of economic development in the territories

they serve. . . . Failing the development of new mineral resources, considerable further railway construction in the near future will not be warranted from an economic point of view.

In other words, good-bye to railways.

THE MINING MERRY-GO-ROUND

In 1935 the export of gold was 47.6 percent of the total export of Africa. Most of this gold has been produced in the Union of South Africa. This fabulously "wealthy" African state, with 90 percent of the white population of colonial Africa, and the envy of all other African colonies, is in reality one of the most unstable economies in the world, and none knows it better than the South Africans themselves. Until the discovery of diamonds in 1857, the economic development of South Africa had been almost exclusively agricultural, and South Africa was of no importance. With the development of the diamond fields and afterwards of gold, the whole economy gradually grew dependent upon the income from these industries. For twenty-five years the legislature and the electorate have declared that the country must, for its own future salvation, find some ways and means of gaining income other than from mining. They have failed completely. With the exception of wool, today, in that vast country, there is not one important agricultural commodity which does not depend on protection or on the maintenance of an artificial price structure based on direct subsidy.

Exactly the same situation exists in industry, half of which would collapse but for the mining industry. Upon this unhealthy basis is grafted another vicious economic malformation. In 1934 and 1935, 41 percent of the workers employed in private industrial undertakings were Europeans. They took 74 percent of the wages and salaries paid, equivalent to $1,010 per head. The remaining 59 percent of the workers were non-Europeans, who obtained 26 percent of the wages and salaries, equivalent to $245 per head. In government undertakings, Europeans, consisting of 66.3 percent of the employees, took 91 percent of the total wages and salaries paid. The remaining 9 percent of the wages was divided among the 33.7 percent of non-Europeans employed.

The organized labor movement, i.e., the aristocracy of labor, shortly after World War I, forced through the Color Bar Act, which prohibited skilled labor to Africans. It is joined by the reactionary South African farmers, who keep the majority of natives on their farms in a state of peonage and slavery. Thus, the distinguishing characteristics of South African labor are 1) a low average productivity, 2) an artificial wage structure based on revenue from gold and diamonds, and 3) the literal pauperization

and degradation of 6 million blacks by less than one-half of the white
population of 2 million; less than one-half because there is a huge poor
white population. In the mining industry itself the ratio reaches incredible
proportions. The average pay of the European employee in the mines is in
round figures $155 a month. That of the native is about $20. The official
title for this discrimination is the "civilized labor" policy.

A RUINOUS POLICY

Lord Hailey sees that this is a ruinous business. He knows that both in
industry and agriculture, ultimately the equally efficient and less costly
producer would be the liberated African. As he states it, "the accumulating
weight of evidence would seem to inspire doubts" as to whether European
agriculture could ever do more than make a very modest living as a return
for hard work even in good times and be a constant recurrent charge upon
the revenues of governments in bad. He admits that "though there may be
both political and theoretical justification for the adoption of a 'civilized
labor' policy, its necessity must nevertheless be regretted." Hailey should
be given the task of explaining to the labor aristocrats and Boer farmers
exactly how beneficial a change would be. No amount of understatement
would save him from being lynched.

The significance of South Africa is this: Most of the other colonies in
Africa are either built on the same model or wish to heaven they could be.
That is why they sigh for the discovery of some bulk mineral. They could
then pay the interest on the railways and live on the rest, while the native
does the work in the mines. Where there are no unions to subsidize him, the
European is staring in the face the fact that he cannot compete with the
native African. He can prevent the African from cultivating coffee, as in
Kenya ("owing to physical and mental capability") but the world market,
such as it is, refuses to pay both the African for doing the work and the
European farmer for living like a gentleman, drinking whiskey, and playing
polo. "Everywhere, therefore," says Hailey, "the progress of the European
system of economy is likely in the future to be linked up with the exploitation of mines, with commerce, and with certain specialized forms of agricultural production generally requiring capital for their development."
Everywhere, in Rhodesia, French and Belgian Congo, French and British
West Africa, everywhere except in South Africa (and Southern Rhodesia).
We have seen upon what these areas depend. Their "ideal" is the ruthless
suppression of the native.

Hailey murmurs deprecatingly that the "possibility of a complete fulfillment of this ideal depends on economic factors (such, for instance, as the
continuation of gold production) which may themselves be subject to

modification." It certainly looks today, three years after Hailey wrote, as if South African gold export may soon be "subjected to modification." For the other nonmining communities, their "future economic prosperity . . . depends more upon the general development of native economic activity than on the results of European enterprise." Most important of all for British imperialism, he says flatly that there is no further field for capital export except for mining. After a little over fifty years, and the degradation of a population without parallel in the history of modern capitalism, this is where the imperialists have reached.

CONDITION OF THE WORKERS

Hailey had to be careful. Frankel had no cause to be. In his work, packed with statistical tables, Frankel has one theme. He states it on page 7. The task is "to broaden the ideas and heighten the creative possibilities of the citizen in a wider society. To realize this is the key to colonial states-manship." In South Africa, and all over East Africa, the African is bound by a series of pass-laws to particular employers, virtual slavery. Says Frankel,

> . . . it is no exaggeration to say that a basic cause of the low average income of the inhabitants of the Union is the lack of "economic mobil-ity" of its workers, both black and white. We are back again at the starting point of this study—progress involves change: inhibit change and inhibit progress.

Unlike Hailey, he calls for capital investment, if even not immediately profit producing; but on the condition:

> In the last resort, however, the future of capital investment, like the future of all African economic progress, will depend on freeing the African peoples from the factors which have checked their progress in the past, and the artificial restrictions which in some territories still prevent the unfolding of their abilities. . . .
> If twentieth century experience in Africa has proved anything at all, it is that the wealth of Africa has, as yet, hardly been discovered, simply because it lies deep in the soil of Africa itself. Only by the co-operant efforts of Africans and Europeans will it be unearthed. . . . The curtain has only just risen on the African scene. . . .
> Indeed the twentieth century opens the era of constructive and creative activity by western powers in Africa.

Frankel has stumbled on a tremendous conclusion here. He does not talk about "raising the standard of living," and such like primitive panaceas for the contradictions of capitalism. He has left the field of distribution and tackled the problem at its root—at the point of production.

MARXISM AND THE COLONIES

What is happening in Africa and what the British imperialists think about it, concerns every American worker, not only Negroes. The contradictions of capitalist production express themselves in a concentration of wealth at one end of society and of misery at the other. Every thinking American worker knows the fact. But these contradictions also express themselves in the concentration of wealth in rich nations like America, Britain, France, and Belgium, and the concentration of misery in poor ones like India, China, and Africa. There are 100 million Africans living in destitution; over 400 million Chinese, nearly 400 million Indians. Roosevelt talks about a third of a nation. These people constitute half of the world. It is capitalism which is destroying them as it is destroying the world. It has now confessed that in Africa it is bankrupt. They must therefore rid themselves of capitalism—for the same reason that the worker in the Western world must rid himself of capitalism, to use "capital" and not be used by it.

Frankel has hit upon a discovery but he has made a profound mistake in calling what Africa needs "capital." Nearly a hundred years ago, in *Wage-Labor and Capital*, Marx defined capital. It is accumulated labor. And land, not accumulated labor, was the chief means of material production in all societies previous to capitalist society. Capital, however, is accumulated labor in a definite social relation. "It is only the domination of past accumulated materialized labor over immediate living labor that stamps the accumulated labor with the character of capital."

"Capital does not consist in the fact that accumulated labor serves living labor as a means for new production. It consists in the fact that living labor serves accumulated labor as the means of preserving and multiplying its exchange value." As Marx expresses it in *The Communist Manifesto*, "In bourgeois society living labor is but a means to increase accumulated labor. In communist society accumulated labor is but a means to widen, to enrich, to promote the existence of the laborer." Frankel wants to promote, widen, and enrich the existence of the Africans, not to save his immortal soul but to save the African economy. Thus, what Frankel is really calling for is not capital, but communism. Hailey, however, merely observes: for that, no more accumulated labor. As usual, it is the Marxist and the bourgeois who face realities.

The inherent unworkability of the capital relation is seen very starkly in Africa. This is due to the advanced stage of European capital development when capitalism began to penetrate into Africa, the primitive character of African labor, and the added sharpness of race differentiation. What Frankel does not know is that what he sees so clearly in Africa was seen by Marx three generations ago in relation not to Africa, but to all of capitalist society.

Marx had little to say about socialist society, particularly about its basis, the socialist organization of labor. That new organization of labor would be accomplished by the proletariat and, as Lenin said most emphatically, the proletariat alone could accomplish it. But, for Marx, Africa's problem was the problem of capitalist society and only socialism could solve it. "The actual wealth of society, and the possibility of continual expansion of its processes of reproduction, do not depend upon the surplus labor, but upon its productivity and upon the more or less fertile conditions of production under which it is performed" (*Capital*, Volume II). He rarely spoke of socialism without coming back to this, and perhaps his most emphatic statement to the same effect is found in his chapter on "Machinery and Modern Industry":

> Modern industry . . . through its catastrophes imposes the necessity of recognizing, as a fundamental law of production, variation of work, consequently fitness of the laborer for varied work, consequently the greatest possible development of his varied aptitudes. It becomes a question of life and death for society to adapt the mode of production to the normal functioning of this law. Modern industry, indeed, compels society, under penalty of death, to replace the detail-worker of today, crippled by lifelong repetition of one and the same trivial operation, and thus reduced to the mere fragment of a man, by the fully developed individual, fit for a variety of labors, ready to face any change of production, and to whom the different social functions he performs are but so many modes of giving free scope to his own natural and acquired powers. (*Capital*, Volume I)

THE ONLY SOLUTION

It is the only solution to the permanent crisis. Marx did not use phrases like "life and death" lightly. Let living labor use accumulated labor to develop itself. The problem of expansion will be solved. Let accumulated labor use living labor only for the sake of expanding accumulated labor and it automatically ruins its capacity to expand. No need to point out here the monumental researches and scientific exactness with which Marx demonstrated the inevitability of his conclusions. It is to Frankel's credit that he came to the same conclusion after the most thorough examination ever made of capitalist investment in Africa. His mistake is to believe that this accumulated labor can ever be at the disposal of the African unless by means of the socialist revolution in Africa and in Europe.

One more word remains to be said. All the great communists have known that man is the greatest of all productive forces. In the general collapse of revolutionary ideology which has kept pace with the degeneration of the Russian Revolution, there has grown up a pseudo-Marxist or "economic" analysis which sees all sorts of possibilities in the technical and institutional reorganization of society, without the slightest consideration for the role of labor. The most recent is Mr. Burnham, who informs us that the managerial society will solve the problems of expansion of colonial countries which "capitalism" could not solve. How? He does not say. Hitler, however, tells us that "The free choice of trades and professions by the Negroes leads to social assimilation, which in turn produces racial assimilation. The occupations of the Black colonial peoples and their function in the labor process of the 'new order' will therefore be entirely determined by the Germans." And again, "[Negroes] will have no active or passive electoral rights in the German colonial empire; [they] are forbidden access to railways, street cars, restaurants, motion pictures and all public establishments." In other words, Hitler proposes to expand African economy by continuing to degrade African labor, the same old bankrupt policy of British imperialism. It is a contradiction that can be solved by socialism and not by Hitler's Panzer divisions, the race propaganda of Goebbels, nor the theoretical evasions of Burnham.

JUNE 1941

9

To and From the Finland Station: A Review of *To the Finland Station* by Edmund Wilson

Edmund Wilson found his way to the Finland Station in the wake of the proletarian revolution, but the revolution is now in eclipse and Wilson has lost his way. But Wilson is to be taken seriously for he has studied history and grappled with the Marxist material. Wilson rejects the dialectic. The Marxist movement is in a dilemma here. Engels said that the test of dialectic is Nature. Lenin, too, knew that Engels's illustrations about seeds were merely popularizations, that the demonstration of the dialectic lay in the study and analysis of science. Nobody has done any of the necessary work. It is as if Marx had written nothing about capitalist production except *The Communist Manifesto*. Wilson rejects also the labor theory of value, which is another story. Marx dealt beautifully with a Wilson of his day. In his letter to Kugelmann, July 1868, Marx showed himself rather short-tempered with the objection.

> The nonsense about the necessity of proving the concept of value arises from complete ignorance, both of the subjects dealt with and of the method of science. Every child knows that a country which ceased to work, I will not say for a year, but for a few weeks, would die. Every child knows, too, that the mass of products corresponding to the different needs require different and quantitatively determined masses of the total labor of society. That this necessity of distributing social labor in definite proportions cannot be done away with by the *particular form* of social production, but can only change the *form it assumes*, is self-evident. . . .
> The science consists precisely in working out *how* the law of value operates. So that if one wanted at the very beginning to "explain" all the

141

phenomena which apparently contradict that law, one would have to give the science before the science. It is precisely Ricardo's mistake. . . . [etc.]

Now compare Wilson. "Nor was it necessary to accept the metaphysics of the Labor Theory of Value and to argue from it *a priori.*"

Metaphysics! Marx thinks that every child can see it. And starting from that he solves, as Wilson admits, the future of capitalism. Most of Wilson's other objections are answered already by Marx himself.

Wilson believes Marx to have demonstrated that capitalism must have an end and demonstrated also "the necessity for socialism." Marx demonstrated not necessity but inevitability. But let that pass for the moment. Where does Wilson stand, for after all that is what matters? The capitalist world as we see it—it couldn't be worse. What is his attitude? And here Wilson breaks down. The British workers, through long subordination to machines and meager lives, have become "unfitted for class politics and class action." The British ruling class knows that this is nonsense. On America he is worse. Marx, he says, did not foresee that the absence of feudalism made possible in America a "genuine social democratization."

American people more nearly share "the same criteria than anywhere else in the civilized world." In America "money is always changing hands so rapidly that the class lines cannot get very deep . . . we have the class quarrel out as we go along." What blindness is this! Even Roosevelt, the grand panjandrum of baloney, talks about a "third of the nation" [in poverty] and "economic royalists." The National Industrial Relations Board reported to Roosevelt in 1939: "The opportunity for a higher standard of living is so great, the social frustration from the failure to obtain it is so real, that other means will undoubtedly be sought if a democratic solution is not worked out. The time for finding such a solution is not unlimited." And while Rome burns, Wilson sings fiddle-diddle-dee. Why is this intelligent and scholarly man so foolish on this issue of all issues? His book tells why.

It is a long study of the decline of the revolutionary tradition in French literature and the origins and development of revolutionary socialism in Europe and America, told chiefly through personal studies of key figures. Wilson plays about with psychoanalysis in an unpardonably light-minded manner, but his biographical work is interesting, his historical studies are valuable, and his essays on Michelet are splendid. He sees how, after the revolution of 1848 and the Commune of 1871, the French bourgeoisie could not write robust history any longer. Renan's portrait of Marcus Aurelius he sees as a projection of the personality of the French bourgeoisie after the Franco-German War and the Commune.

The book is full of many such judgments, large and small; not blatant, but acute and sensitive, never superficial and sometimes profound. I think

Wilson underestimates how savagely Taine, after the Commune, turned on himself and raged at the French Revolution like a maniac. But all this is a badly needed contribution to the historical materialist elucidation of history. In all history writing, all, the influence of the class struggle stands out like a big nose on a small face. Thiers, for instance, in his history of the revolutionary and Napoleonic period, was democrat in those parts written before 1848, Bonapartist in the parts written during the Second Republic, and when Bonaparte's nephew nearly put him in jail, ended the history with attacks on Bonapartism; while Mitford, the English historian, published an innocuous first volume of a history of Greece in 1784, but the French Revolution taking place in 1789, Mitford devoted the rest of his work to a fanatical attack on Greek democracy. Some day when a materialist history of history is written, it will be a marvelous verification of the Marxist approach and one of the most comic books ever published.

Wilson is a beautiful example of the same process he analyzes so well. Despite his disagreements he was swept along by Marx and the proletariat, and at the Finland station he is as excited as any of those who traveled in the sealed train. He writes a brilliant and, for him, enthusiastic essay on Lenin's revolutionary personality. But the proletariat since then knows only defeats. Hence Wilson's continued fascination by Marxism, his abstract belief in the necessity for socialism, but his opium dreams about American democracy.

The intellectual loves to show the class struggle acting on other people. He hates like hell for it to be applied to himself. There is only one way to overcome this and that is to accept it. Identify yourself with a fundamental class and go where it goes, mount with it when it mounts and fall with it when it falls. On this basis you will commit some blunders. But you are always in a position to judge and intellectually command the contending forces of society. You can do this as a person identified with the revolutionary struggle of the proletariat, or the struggle for the preservation of the bourgeoisie. But once you stand in the middle looking from one side to the other, all the knowledge and intellectual honesty in the world will not save you from futility and folly. And even worse may befall. For Wilson in this book constantly lays stress upon Marx's Jewish "blood," and he shows a truly Olympian calm in his remarks on Nazi Germany. Both are bad signs, especially in a man who nourishes such illusions about American bourgeois democracy.

JUNE 1941

10

In the American Tradition: The Working-Class Movement in Perspective

> But I consider this certain: the purely bourgeois basis with no pre-bourgeois swindle behind it, the corresponding colossal energy of the development . . . will one day bring about a change which will astound the whole world. Once the Americans get started it will be with an energy and violence compared with which we in Europe shall be mere children.

Thus on the 30th of March 1892, Engels wrote from London to a friend in America. Marx and Engels knew that in every country, in whatever continent, the socialist revolution denoted the seizure of power by the working class under circumstances dictated by the law of uneven development and the historical peculiarities of each country. But they were sensitive to the subjective qualities of different sections of the international proletariat. Thus they looked upon the German proletariat as the most theoretical in Europe; the English workers were somewhat slow but once they had gained some advantage, they did not let it go lightly, etc. In his last years, Engels always wrote about the American proletariat in such terms as the above. It is therefore important to see what Engels thought, why he thought it, to examine the historical development since his death, and to see how far his analysis and expectations have been justified. This, useful at all times, is particularly necessary today because Engels was stirred to write about America at the time when it seemed to him that a national labor party was at last on its way.

Engels based his views on two fundamental facts. The country in 1886 is *"rich, vast, expanding."* That is its special economic characteristic. Its special historic characteristic is that its political institutions are "purely *bourgeois* . . . unleavened by feudal remnants." These combined give to the economy a tremendous power of development and this national characteristic is of necessity imbued in the proletariat. Yet at the same time "in every young country" where the development is of a predominantly material nature, there is a "certain backwardness of thought, a clinging to traditions connected with the foundations of the new nationality." The "exigencies" of practical labor and the concentrating of capital "have produced a contempt for all theory" and in such a country the people must become conscious of their own social interests by making "blunder upon blunder." But always he insists that when the workers begin their political development it will be like nothing ever seen before. They will go fast, "faster than anywhere else, even though on a singular road, which seems from the theoretical standpoint, to be almost an insane road."

It would be perhaps most fruitful to begin with a comparison between the economic and political development of the working-class movement in America with the working-class movement in Great Britain. For Marx and Engels, England was the model capitalist country and in their day the most fully developed. It is the easier to do so because in his observations on America, Engels constantly referred to earlier parallels and future developments in Britain.

THE NATIONAL TRADITION

The "traditions connected with the foundations of the new nationality" date back to before the American Revolution. But just as the French Revolution is the foundation of the modern French nation and the English Revolution in the seventeenth century is the foundation of modern Britain, just so the modern American nation finds its roots in 1776. This revolution differs sharply from the other two. A hundred and fifty years before, in Britain, the Cromwellian revolution produced a powerful combination of petty-bourgeois and neo-proletarian elements. They raised a program for political democracy which was not realized in Britain until over two hundred years afterward. Though they raised the question of property openly in debate with Cromwell, they were not communists. The real communists, the Levellers and the Diggers, were a small minority to the left of this movement which was so large and well organized that it almost drove Cromwell and his associates into the arms of the monarchy. He had to suppress these formidable revolutionaries by force. Carlyle calls them "*sansculottes* before their time." The real *sansculottes* were the driving force and the mainstay of the French Revolution. From that day to this the French bourgeoisie has lived in terror of revolutionary Paris.

No such conflicts took place in the American Revolution. Whereas the other two nationalities were born out of civil war, the American nation was born in a national struggle against foreign rule. Despite the very real class differences among the American revolutionaries and the struggle against the Loyalists, the bourgeoisie, farmers, artisans, and mechanics were a more or less homogeneous whole against British imperialism. Their ancestors had left European tyranny behind. Now they were clearing it out of the magnificent new country for good. The economic opportunities of this rich and vast new world prevented the extreme sharpening of class relations which characterized the old, but the consequent absence of sharp class political differentiation had powerful subjective reinforcement in the very circumstances under which the American people first felt themselves a nation.

It is this which Engels refers to fifty years ago, and today, despite the unprecedented development during the last twenty-five years, this sense of America being a free country, inherently different from the rest of the world, is still enormously powerful among all sections of the people. It has its drawbacks, but it has its virtues also.

But if, except for Shays' Rebellion, the American masses did not assert themselves with the vigor and independence of the English petty bourgeoisie and the French *sansculottes*, they ran far, far ahead of Europe politically in the years immediately following their revolution. By 1825 the battle for manhood suffrage had been won. The vote of the farmers and the masses in the towns exercised an influence upon the ruling class, upon legislative machinery and upon the "money power" which today might seem more illusory than real. For it to be appreciated it should be seen in comparison with conditions in Britain, reputedly the classic country of bourgeois democracy.

POLITICS AND THE BRITISH WORKERS

If 1776 saw the Declaration of Independence of the American commercial bourgeoisie, the same year appeared *The Wealth of Nations*, the declaration of independence of the *British industrial bourgeoisie*. Britain entered upon a period of dazzling economic development. Politically, however, the country was a hundred years behind the United States. Feudal remnants had Britain by the throat. G. K. Chesterton has summed up the situation perfectly when he contrasted the Commons with a capital C and the commons with a small c. The English aristocracy ruled in the House of Lords and their sons, brothers, and sons-in-law sat in the House of Commons, in close alliance with the financial and commercial magnates. Not only the masses of the people but even the rising industrial bourgeoisie were excluded. It took nearly fifty years to break this political stranglehold of the feudal remnants. Britain reached the verge of revolution in 1832 before the aristocracy gave way. Yet the Great Reform Bill of 1832 enfranchised only some 200,000 people. The masses, whose revolutionary agitation and direct action were the main causes of the bill being passed, were entirely excluded. The political advance was so eminently satisfactory to Lord John Russell, who pioneered the bill, that he became known afterward as "Finality John."

We shall understand America better if we continue with Britain. The masses, disappointed with the results of the Reform Bill, started the Chartist agitation. It lasted from 1839 to 1848 and embraced millions of British workers. Its demands were a curious mixture of political and social aspirations which we shall meet again forty years later in the Knights of Labor in the United States. Politics, however, predominated. The Chartists demanded universal suffrage, equal electoral areas, payment of members of Parliament, no property qualifications, vote by ballot, and annual Parliaments. But they aimed also at "social equality." A worker needed a good house, good clothes, and "plenty of good food and drink to make him look and *feel* happy." They were not quite sure how to achieve all this and wavered between petitions and direct action which on one occasion reached the stage of a halfhearted general strike and on another a planned insurrection.

The movement suddenly collapsed in 1848. In 1846 the Corn Laws, by which the British landlords had kept up the price of corn, were abolished. The British industrialists, on the basis of cheap food, began that economic development by which Britain dominated the world market for forty years. The Chartist movement faded away. In 1851 the workers' movement took the form of slow and solid craft unionism, which dominated the British labor movement for forty years, the same period of time that Britain dominated the world market. It took the same forty years before Britain achieved manhood suffrage. The workers in the town got the vote only in 1867 and the workers in the country only in 1888.

THE AMERICAN "CHARTISTS"

In America between 1825 and 1850 industries are at a far lower stage of development than they are in Britain. But we have the beginnings of a labor movement, and the utopian socialism of Fourier and Owen flourishes not only in theory but in practice. Between 1850 and 1860 the growth of industry brings numerous strikes, fought out with the customary vigor of the American working class. But the political development of the country is overshadowed by the necessity of crushing the slave power. Astonishing development! Such is the territorial extent of America that the crushing of the plantation owners is a regional struggle. The industrial bourgeoisie wins its victory in civil conflict so gigantic that it is the first great modern war.

Yet it manages this without a single serious clash with the workers. (The draft riots only lasted a few days.) The leader of the bourgeoisie is a national hero who fights "to save the Union" and later to abolish slavery.

Yet the signs of a mass labor movement with political aspirations were ominously clear. This movement, however, was deflected by the richness and the vastness of the country and the absence of feudal relations. In the average European country there would have been no land. If there had been any it would have been owned by some noblemen. The Homestead Act of 1862, which opened up free land to the more dissatisfied and adventurous of the proletariat, diluted the independent political aspirations of the working class. America enters upon a period of industrial development comparable to that of Britain between 1784 and 1848. It took fifty years in Britain to produce Chartism. In America, where the energy of development is so colossal, the movement corresponding to Chartism appeared within less than ten years.

The Knights of Labor was organized in 1869 as a secret society. By 1879 the secrecy was discarded and between 1878 and 1886 it developed in much the same way and on much the same scale that Chartism had developed forty years before. The Knights wished "to secure to the workers the full enjoyment of the wealth they create, sufficient leisure in which to develop their intellectual, moral and social faculties, all of the benefits, recreations, and pleasures of association." The similarity to the ideas of the Chartists is very striking. Like the Chartists, the Knights aimed at a new social order, but they were not socialists in the European sense. Their main demands were not political because, being Americans, they already had political freedom. But in accordance with their country and their time, they demanded the reserving of public lands for actual settlers, the abolition of the contract system of labor and public works, the eight-hour day, etc. Like the Chartists, the movement aimed at helping all workers in all fields. Suddenly in 1886, the year of the "Great Upheaval," the Knights of Labor claimed international attention.

Late in 1885 and early in 1886 a huge strike movement, based on their struggle for the eight-hour day, swept over the United States. A number of labor parties sprang into being. In November 1886, candidates of the newly formed labor parties were successful in the municipal elections. In New York City, where a united Labor party had been formed only in July, it put forward Henry George as candidate. The Democrat got 90,000 votes. George came in next with 68,000, beating Theodore Roosevelt, the Republican candidate, by 8,000 votes. The Chartists had aimed at more but done much less.

Engels in London greeted the upheaval as the dawn of a new age. On June 3 he writes to America: "Six months ago nobody suspected anything, and now they appear all of a sudden in such organized masses as to strike terror into the whole capitalist class. I only wish Marx could have lived to see it." The old man was sixty-six, but he reacted with the exuberance of someone who had just joined the movement.

In November after the electoral successes he writes again and takes up the question of the National Labor party.

The first great step of importance for every country entering the movement is always the organization of the workers as an independent political party, no matter how, so long as it is a distinct workers' party. And this step has been taken far more rapidly than we had a right to hope, and that is the main thing. That the first program of the party is still confused and highly deficient, that it has set up the banner of Henry George, these are inevitable evils, but also only transitory ones. The masses must have time and opportunity to develop, and they can only have the opportunity when they have their own movement—no matter in what form, so far as it is only *their own* movement—in which they are driven further by their own mistakes and learn wisdom by hurting themselves. The movement in America is in the same condition as it was with us before 1848.

That the movement had attained such electoral successes after only eight months of existence was "absolutely unheard of."

Engels warned the German emigres working in the movement not to be doctrinaire. "A million or two of working men's votes next November for a bona fide workingmen's party is worth infinitely more at present than a hundred thousand votes for a doctrinally perfect platform."

These ideas Engels repeated formally in this introduction to the American edition of *The Conditions of the Working Class in England.* The passage is worth ample quotation.

In February 1885, American public opinion was almost unanimous on this one point: that there was no working class in the European sense of the word in America; that, secondly, no class struggle between workmen and capitalists such as tore European society to pieces was possible in the American Republic, and that therefore socialism was a thing of foreign importation which could never take root in American soil. And yet at that moment the coming class struggle was casting its gigantic shadow before it in the strikes of the Pennsylvania coal miners and of many other trades and especially in the preparations all over the country for the great eight-hour movement which was to come off and did come off in the May following. That I duly appreciated these symptoms, that I anticipated the working class movement on a national scale, my Appendix shows; but no one could then foresee that in such a short time the movement would burst out with such irresistible force, would spread with the rapidity of a prairie fire, would shake American society to its foundations.

The spontaneous and instinctive movements of these vast masses of working people, over a vast extent of country, the simultaneous outburst of their common discontent with the miserable social conditions, the same and due to the same causes, made them conscious of the fact that they formed the new and distinct class of American society . . . and with true American instinct this consciousness led them at once to take the next step toward their deliverance: the formation of the political workingmen's party, on a platform of its own and with the conquest of the Capitol and the White House for its goal.

A passage which followed is even more significant. For Engels the working-class movement developed in two stages, the mass trade union movement acting on a national scale and the independent labor party, also on a national scale. Usually there is a lengthy period between both of these. But history can develop very rapidly and Engels writes:

> On the more favored soil of America, where no medieval ruins bar the way, where history begins with the elements of modern bourgeois society, as evolved in the seventeenth century, the working class passed through these two stages of its development within ten months.

Engels really thought that the moment had come in America. In November 1886, he had written that the American bourgeoisie was persecuting the movement so "shamelessly and tyrannically" that it would bring matters rapidly to a decision "and if we in Europe do not hurry up, the Americans will soon be ahead of us." That was on November 29. Three weeks before, in his preface to the first English translation of *Capital*, he had shown that he was expecting social revolution in Britain. The number of unemployed in Britain was swelling from year to year "and we can almost calculate the moment when the unemployed, losing patience, will take their own fate into their own hands."

In both instances, the expectation was not realized.* In Britain the British bourgeoisie solved the problem by the export of finance capital, thus ushering in the age of imperialism. In the United States once more the vastness and richness of the country came to the rescue of the bourgeoisie.

THE TURN OF THE CENTURY

Let us once more take rapid survey of British development.

It was only three years after Engels's preface to the English edition of

---

* It is easy to point out the numerous occasions when Marx and Engels made predictions about revolution which did not come true and which seemed indeed to be wide of the mark. In their early days some of this was due to youthful enthusiasm. Later it was different. Whenever the possibility of revolution appeared, they threw themselves into it, hoping to make the best of the opportunities. In 1891 Bebel asked Engels if he had prophesied the collapse of bourgeois society in 1898. Engels replied: "All I said was we might possibly come to power in 1898. . . . An old casing like this can survive its inner essential death for a few decades, if the atmosphere is undisturbed."

Capital that Britain found itself in turmoil. The year 1889 was the year of two famous strikes in Britain: the dock strike and the match-girls' strike. There was none of the violence associated with similar large-scale actions in the United States. The strikes, in fact, evoked great popular sympathy. They were triumphant and they marked the beginning of the organization of the unskilled workers in Britain. Let us note that this took place precisely at the moment when Britain was beginning to lose its almost exclusive domination of the world market and just a few years after the working class in the agricultural areas had got the vote. But the long lag behind the political activity of the American masses was now rapidly overcome. Hitherto the British working class had on the whole supported the liberals. In 1892, however, Keir Hardie, a Scottish miner, and an avowed socialist, founded the first independent labor party. Then (as now) there was the usual lamentation that the formation of an independent labor party would weaken the "progressive" vote and so let in the reactionaries. For many years there had been working-class members in Parliament elected from predominantly working-class constituencies. They had supported the labor-liberal combination almost exclusively. But the work of Marx and Engels and their associates on the First International now bore fruit. By 1899 a joint committee of the Trade Union Congress, the Independent Labour party, and some socialist societies, was organized. The British Labour party was on its way.

In 1906 out of fifty candidates, twenty-nine were successful. In 1918 there were sixty-one members in Parliament; in 1922, 142 members; in 1923, 191, and the first Labour government took office in 1924.

Even for Britain this development was extraordinary, taking into consideration the long years that the British workers had to fight in order to gain manhood suffrage toward the end of the century. One reason for the success lay in the strength of the trade union movement which is the base of the Labour party in Britain. And the strength of the trade union movement lay not only in the cohesiveness of the British people but in the fact that between 1848 and the end of the century Britain became industrialized to a degree far surpassing that of any other European country. Britain imported food and raw materials and exported manufactured goods. The population was proletarianized until, by 1914, Britain was between 60 percent and 70 percent "proletarian." On this basis and the political pressure of a declining economy, the British workers pushed ahead in the representation of their interests by a national Labour party.*

Exactly the opposite is the development in America. After 1886 the Knights of Labor rapidly declined. American labor historians have blamed

---

* We do not propose here to go into the history of its failures. The history of the social democracy in Europe, its rise and decline, is well known to the readers of *The New International*.

the failure upon the weakness of the bureaucracy, etc. There is no need to go into these questions here. It is sufficient that immediately after the failure of the Knights, the American Federation of Labor emerged to prominence and took much the same place in the American labor movement that the craft unions in Britain had taken after the Chartist fiasco in 1848.

Engels visited America in 1888. He saw firsthand the immigrant problem and other subjective difficulties from which the American working class suffered. In 1892 he put his finger on the fundamental weakness behind its slow political development.

> *Land* is the basis of speculation, and the American speculative mania and speculative opportunity are the chief levers that hold the native-born worker in bondage to the bourgeoisie. Only when there is a generation of native-born workers that cannot expect *anything* from speculation *any more* will we have a solid foothold in America.

Yet so strong was his belief that the national characteristic would find powerful expression in the American proletariat that it was in that very 1892, after the failure of the Knights was patent, that he penned the confident words which head this article.

History slowly but nevertheless surely is justifying his concept of American development. Between 1880 and 1914 American industry developed with the colossal American energy, and the American proletariat reacted with equal vigor. The Homestead strike in 1892, the Pullman strike of 1894, the anthracite coal miners' strike in 1902, these were working-class actions which astonished the world and, in Engels's words, struck terror into the hearts of the American bourgeoisie. But whereas in Britain industry overwhelmingly outdistanced agriculture, in the United States, American industry developed not only itself but American agriculture as well. The total population of the United States in 1860 was not 30 million. In 1910 there were more than 50 million people living on farms or in villages dependent upon agriculture. The AFL grew steadily and a Socialist party appeared toward the end of the century. By 1908, however, the Socialist party could boast of only one member of Congress. In 1914 the national party of labor was pretty much where it had been after the failure of the Knights of Labor.

Yet the colossal energy of the development was perfectly visible, though Engels was not there to trace it after 1895. The later development of agriculture was thoroughly capitalistic. The disruption which capitalism carries into the countryside and financial swindling raised the wrath of the farmers and they replied with a Populist movement which repeatedly rocked the whole political life of the country. Though the rapid penetration of industry into the West prevented the organized extension of trade unions such as characterized countries with a more peaceful development like

Britain and Germany, yet even to these unstable conditions, the American working class reacted with an organization unique in the history of organized labor.

In the years just previous to World War I, the work of the IWW among the textile workers in Massachusetts, in the Western Federation of Miners and among nomadic workers, such as lumbermen and longshoremen, gave them a reputation which spread over the whole world and earned them the ferocious hatred of the American bourgeoisie. Their strikes for "free speech" and the fearless energies with which they threw themselves into all their industrial struggles made them internationally famous. Their songs and slogans have traveled all over the world. This is particularly remarkable because only for a few years in Australia did the movement ever take hold in any other country. It was a characteristic American phenomenon.

The end of World War I saw the United States pass rapidly through a period of the export of finance-capital. By 1929, however, the world crisis put an end to capitalist expansion on a world scale. Whereupon this most capitalistic of all countries experienced a crisis of a scope and depth far exceeding all other previous crises and greater than that of all the other countries of the world put together. America had now reached the stage that Britain had reached in 1889. The American proletariat, true to the national tradition, replied in kind. History will record that between 1935 and 1943 the American proletariat, in the organization of the CIO, did exactly what Engels fifty years before had prophesied. "Once the Americans get started, it will be with an energy and violence compared with which we in Europe shall be mere children."

The land boom is now over, the immigrant elements are being kneaded into a whole. The organization of labor and the struggles on the industrial field have given the American worker that class consciousness which has been so absent in his past. The American proletariat now faces the organization of an independent national party of labor. We need have no doubt that when the moment comes it will be true to its traditions.

NOVEMBER 1943

11

In the International Tradition: Tasks Ahead for American Labor

> We believe that the years immediately ahead are the most critical we
> have faced—"the years of decision," when new patterns will be formed.
> In man's long years there come short periods of time which profoundly
> influence his way of life for centuries thereafter. We are living in such a
> period today.
>
> —Philip Murray in *The American Magazine*,
> February 1944

The statements quoted above come from an article recently published by
Philip Murray and widely advertised in the bourgeois press. It is a sign of
the times. There is obviously going on in all thinking heads an examination
of the present in preparation for the pregnant future which lies ahead. In
the *New International* of November 1943, some attempt was made in an
article entitled "In the American Tradition" to outline the special national
characteristics of the American proletariat as evinced in its history up to the
organization of the CIO. The following article proposes to continue the
analysis. It will attempt 1) to trace the growth of social and class consciousness in the American proletariat from 1929 to the present day; 2) to observe
the manifestations of this growth in the programs and pronouncements of
the leadership; 3) to place this relationship and its probable development in
its historical and international setting; 4) to reaffirm some practical conclusions in the light of the above.

The most striking development of the Great Depression of 1929 is a
profound skepticism of the future of contemporary society among large
sections of the American people. It is most easily recognized in the widespread fear, if not conviction, of a tremendous and inevitable depression

154

after the present war. The most concrete reaction of the proletariat to the breakdown in 1929 was the organization of the CIO, one of the greatest and most significant chapters in the history of labor anywhere at any period. Any estimate of the American working class in action during the coming period must base itself upon that "colossal energy" of the American masses which was the driving force of the CIO.

LABOR IN EUROPE AND IN THE UNITED STATES

The late development of mass industrial organization in the United States has both stimulated and retarded the political development of the American working class. In foreign countries the rights of labor, social legislation, etc., were the obvious result of mass pressure organized by labor leaders. In the United States, the Roosevelt government cleverly presented itself as the originator, initiator, and organizer of these developments. Thus, whereas in Europe the winning of these advantages fortified the class consciousness learned in the industrial struggle, in the United States all these gains seemed to fortify the ascendancy of one political organization of the bourgeoisie over the working class. In reality this is only half the truth, and the lesser half. Organized labor in America, in so far as it supported (and still supports) Roosevelt, did so in a manner far more class-conscious than otherwise. *It considered the New Deal as essentially a New Deal for the working people.* To the great masses of the people, Rockefeller, Morgan, and Wall Street, the "rich," did not need any New Deal. They were getting on well enough. It was the starving third of the nation that wanted it, and however niggardly the New Deal administration might have been in fact, it handed out copiously to the workers in words.

While this inhibited the emergence of a national political party of organized labor, it has had inevitable and profound consequences in the working class. It has developed a conviction that unemployment and social suffering are no longer questions between the industrial worker and the private capitalist. The working class by and large believes that society is responsible. By society it means the government and it looks to the government to take whatever measures are necessary to repair what has become an intolerable state of affairs. How rapidly this sentiment has spread has its most eloquent testimony in the vigorous response of the bourgeoisie. The freshness, formidable militancy and confident expectations of the American proletariat gave it a power fully recognized by the state. In 1936 the highly developed political organizations and political experience of the French proletariat could force from the French bourgeoisie less than the purely industrial actions of the proletariat of America from the American bourgeoisie. The great wealth of the country, the national tradition of plenty, both of them complementary sides of the special American tradition, played and will continue to play a powerful role.

In 1939 the National Resources Board reported to the President as follows on the "basic characteristics" of the American economy:

> Moreover, as people become increasingly aware of the discrepancy between rich resources and poor results in living and as the ineffectiveness of the organization of resources becomes more clear, a sense of social frustration must develop and be reflected in justified social unrest and unavoidable friction. Individual frustration builds into social frustration. And social frustration is quite as likely to work itself out in socially destructive as in socially constructive ways. . . . The opportunity for a higher standard of living is so great, the social frustration from the failure to obtain it is so real, that other means will undoubtedly be sought if a democratic solution is not worked out. The time for finding such a solution is not unlimited.

Such was a brief but exact representation of the complex social relations in the United States of America in 1939. And all the more convincing because of the source and circumstances from which it comes.

THE INFLUENCE OF THE WAR

The influence of the war has merely accentuated these developments which were already so powerful in the decade before its outbreak. And if, as is inevitable in war, their full fruition has been retarded, the result must be their outburst with renewed force at some stage in the coming period. To begin with, the war has prepared the population for a social crisis to a degree that was impossible to avoid except by the state organization of the economy. By the millions, men have been torn from their homes and passed through the military machine. By the millions, the more backward elements have been dragged from rural stagnation, women from their homes, and petty bourgeois from offices, and hurled into the discipline of large-scale capitalist production. Never has there been such an uprooting in American life. The country has undergone a profound social upheaval, the greatest the proletariat has ever known.

Not only has the war disrupted normal existence to this unprecedented degree. Side by side with this it has compelled a growing consciousness among all ranks of the proletariat that production is a social process in which labor has both rights and responsibilities. In 1929, in the minds of the workers, organized labor was a small section of the population, the capitalists were another, and government a third, three different entities. The breakdown of the system of "free enterprise" in 1929 resulted in a steady growth in social and class consciousness. By 1939, "free enterprise" had disguised itself as "management" in order to emphasize its social role in production. Organized labor now looked upon itself as entitled to a voice in the management of the productive process and looked to government as the responsible mediator of conflicting social claims. Already, however, by 1940, as was shown by the Reuther Plan, the UAW, one of labor's most advanced sections, opposed itself to "management" as a candidate for the organization of production in the interests of society as a whole. The last three years have seen a truly astonishing development of the social consciousness of organized labor. This development of social consciousness has been as powerful as it is because of the special role of the state. Directly and indirectly the government has interfered in and controlled every aspect of economic and social life, from wages, working conditions, food and clothes, to the date of the conception of children and, in the army, even the right to marry.

After World War I the resentment of the working class against all that it had to suffer was directed more against Morgan, Wall Street, and private capital than the government. In World War II the hostility and the exasperation resulting from the stratification of the economy and the strain of the war have been directed as much against the government as against private capital. The course of the miners' strike, undertaken against the full power of bourgeois society and its state during wartime, shows how deep is the current dissatisfaction among the workers with the existing state of affairs and their consciousness of the center of responsibility. The government recognized this early and has not spared its efforts to counteract the deep anti-war feeling, the skepticism which was the aftermath of World War I, and the sufferings of the people during the depression. Through its highest officials, the president and the vice president, it has stimulated the masses by vague but constantly reiterated promises of repayment for the sacrifices of the war by the abolition of what the workers endured in the prewar period.

The culminating feature of the whole experience, however, while it permeates the consciousness of the great masses of the people, is as yet being held, as it were, in solution. But it will break forth with irresistible force as soon as the masses feel upon them the inevitable pressure of capitalist bankruptcy.

To the many-millioned mass already skeptical of "free enterprise," the war effort of the state indicates that a government by planned use of the American productive system can create a society of full employment and plenty for all.

At the present moment the proletariat is in a state of sullen suspiciousness toward the capitalist class in general and the Roosevelt government in particular. Like the bourgeoisie, it confidently expects that the war, at least in Europe, is near enough to its conclusion to justify intensive preparations for the postwar period. The end of this phase of the war can be the signal for the outbreak of the sharpest class struggles. It may even be impossible for the bourgeoisie to suppress them before the actual end of hostilities in Europe. It is not impossible that a break with Roosevelt may come before the 1944 elections. Such events are quite unpredictable. The decisive question, however, is that, although contradictory currents move among the working class, yet, as a whole, it knows what it wants and in millions, in its advanced groups, is determined to have it. It is conscious of great changes ahead in society both at home and abroad. It knows that labor is destined to play a great part in these changes. Such at least is the opinion of the present writer.

THE LABOR LEADERSHIP

One of the surest signs of the estimated changes in the consciousness of the American proletariat is to be found in the character of the demands now being put forward by the leadership. Let us take three of them.

William Green of the AFL has frequently expressed himself as being hostile to government interference in industry. He accepts it as a war measure but, fundamental class-collaborationist that he is, he claims that "free" political institutions must be based upon "free" enterprise. Permanent government control of industry, according to Green, means permanent government control of labor. There, Mr. Green is perfectly right within his own limitations, which are the limitations of capitalist society. If the capitalist government organizes industry, then, modern production being what it is, it is compelled to organize labor as well. And for capitalists, the organization of labor is merely a phrase for the control, the limitation, and the ultimate suppression of the rights of organized labor. The solution, obviously, is the organization of industry by the working class itself.

However, even a Green cannot be blind to the inexorable tendencies which are working themselves out in the process of production today. And on December 3, 1943, in an interview in Washington, Green recognized that the postwar reconversion program will inevitably be guided by the government. Green has discovered a new "friend of labor," no less a person than the discredited Donald Nelson. He proposed Nelson as leader of a "top policy council" in which Congress, management, labor and farmers would be represented. Thus, even in the mind of this most backward-minded labor leader, it is perfectly clear that the old days of free enterprise are gone, for the time being: that production is a social process for which government is responsible. More important, however, is the frank recognition that labor must actually be represented in the production councils of the nation. The old maneuvering, the intrigue and the barter in the corridors of Washington which go under the name of lobbying, this is no longer sufficient. Labor must take its own place in the councils of government.

The second example that we propose to take is the postwar program of the UAW. This program bases itself on international cooperation.

Organized labor of all United Nations must cooperate to assure the application of the principles of the Atlantic Charter and to establish a world-wide system of collective security, eliminating trade barriers and establishing minimum labor standards in all lands. *

The immediate question is that of reconversion.

Speediest reconversion for peacetime production must be carried out with maintenance of labor standards and job protection for workers who have transferred to war work. Returning members of the armed services must be guaranteed jobs, bonuses, education, and protection for dependents. The aim is:

Full Production and Full Employment—The government must operate monopolies and regulate other industries to guarantee full employment and production in the public interest. Small business must be rehabilitated. A gigantic construction program must be inaugurated by the federal government. Farm production must be geared to an economy of abundance, with elimination of absentee control and market insecurity.

Health, Education, and Security—A nation-wide program must eradicate disease and malnutrition; education must be equally available to all; and full social security must be guaranteed from cradle to grave.

The means is the necessary climax to such a program. "Democratic planning for peacetime economy is only possible with full participation of organized labor at all levels."

MURRAY'S MANIFESTO

Infinitely more important, however, is the pronouncement recently made by Philip Murray, extracts from which stand at the head of this article. It is obviously a kind of New Year Manifesto and we reprint some of its more important passages:

. . . Events have convinced us that labor must become a more influential factor in the future than it has been in the past.

For the first time in American history, the forces of labor are now setting up a nation-wide organization to protect the rights of the working man, as well as the rights of the returning soldier, the farmer, the small business man, and the so-called "common man."

---

* All quotations are from the summary printed in *Ammunition*, September 1943, the educational journal of the UAW.

This is not a "Labor Party" or a "Third Party." There is no present intention to form such a party.

This is something new in American politics. . . . We were impelled to action by the happenings of the last year or two, by a growing reactionary trend, and by the critical prospects raised by the elections in 1944 and the eventual reversion to a peacetime economy.

. . . When public apathy allows ignorant, selfish, and short-sighted men to get into Congress . . . it makes us dread to think what might happen if such men should be in control when the terrific problems of the war's end arise.

It was bad enough last time. This time, with a far greater war on our hands, and consequently with far greater problems of converting back to peace, such reckless courses might shake the foundations of the very democratic system we have been fighting for.

We believe that the years immediately ahead are the most critical we have ever faced—"the years of decision"—when new patterns will be formed.

Having helped to conquer tyranny abroad, the United States in peace must conquer unemployment and poverty at home. We have proved in war that this nation can produce a Niagara of armaments and materials.

Disaster comes by accident, but prosperity today comes only by planning.

In man's long history there come short periods of time which profoundly influence his way of life for centuries thereafter. We are living in such a period today.

No one knows to what extent a democracy can plan its future in advance.

We shall draw up and present to the American people a specific set of principles for the general welfare.

One thing immediately stands out. Murray is under no illusion whatever as to the easy transition in the United States to the world of the Four Freedoms and the Century of the Common Man. He is aware, on the one hand, of the tremendous capacity for planned production in America which has been demonstrated to the masses. He is equally aware of the determination of the bourgeoisie to wreck the democratic system, if need be, and to maintain its power and privileges at whatever cost to the nation. A deep fear for the future can be discerned in this serious analysis addressed to the American people as a whole. Yet this labor leader omits what everyone knows to be one of the fundamental constituents of the "years of decision." He omits all reference to the independent action of the working masses. He omits it because, like all his kind, he is afraid of it.

The ideological fig leaf of reformism of this type is that even if the labor leadership is aware of the perils ahead, the workers are so backward that it is impossible to take the drastic measures necessary for a radical working-class resolution of the crisis. As we follow Murray and look into the future, the first thing to do is to destroy this illusion of "advanced" labor leaders and "backward" workers.

Now estimates as to the particular stage of development reached by a working class will always differ widely. Precision on such a question, difficult at all times, is particularly difficult when the working class in question has no independent political organization of its own, carrying on a specific political education and in turn acting as a barometer of working-class development. But even where, as formerly for years in Europe, that difficulty did not exist, the extent to which social ideas or programs have penetrated into the minds of the workers cannot possibly be told until the workers take action, and mass action in which they feel their united strength. When the French proletariat moved into the factories in May–June 1936, only the events themselves showed how far the workers were consciously permeated with distrust of the ruling regime, and a deep determination to insure that their demands were carried out. Yet on the surface it could appear that if only the workers saw as clearly into the future as Murray and the leaders of the UAW, then it would be possible for labor to begin, *now*, to make great efforts and achieve great progress on its own behalf. This is "proved" by the fact that the American working class has not yet felt the necessity of an independent political organization of its own. Until then we must wait until the workers are more educated. In reality, such an estimate, true on the surface, is fundamentally false. The whole course of the development of labor in Europe and Asia, the history of the CIO in America shows that the labor leadership at the decisive moment is always lagging behind the working class. We have to see this to the end.

To see into the future, however, and visualize trends of social classes and groups requires first and foremost a clear concept of the past. The American proletariat has its own national characteristics. In the previous article we tried to indicate these by a rough comparison with the development of the proletariat in Great Britain. But the American proletariat is a part of the international working class. We can see best into its future by some comparison with the growth and distinct stages of the developing proletarian struggle.

STAGES OF PROLETARIAN STRUGGLE

The international proletariat first appeared on the scene in the early 1830s, and its first great action was the French Revolution of 1848. Since that time every great individual action of the proletariat has marked a stage in the development of the proletariat as a whole. Engels has outlined this movement for us. In his introduction to Marx's *Civil War in France*, he notes that the workers in 1848 themselves designated the Republic which followed Louis Philippe as the "Social Republic." Yet, "as to what was to be understood by this 'Social Republic,' nobody was quite clear, not even the workmen themselves." In 1871 came the Paris Commune. There we had much of the confusion which existed in 1848. Lenin, who followed Marx and Engels very closely, notes that "there was no workers party, *there was no preparedness and no long training of the working class*, which, in the mass, did not even clearly visualize its tasks and the methods of fulfilling them. There were no serious political organizations of the proletariat, no strong trade unions and cooperative societies." On another occasion, speaking to the Seventh Congress of the Russian Communist party, he gave a belligerent interpretation to the original idea expressed by Engels in the above-mentioned introduction: "The Commune was not understood by those who had created it. They created with the instinctive genius of the awakened masses, and not a single fraction of the French socialists realized what they were doing."

Was the immediate object of the Commune a complete socialist revolution? "We can cherish no such illusions." Lenin says that when Engels called the Commune a dictatorship of the proletariat, he had in view "only the participation, and moreover the *ideological leading* participation, of the representatives of the proletariat in the revolutionary government of Paris." This lack of consciousness in its revolutionary leadership helped to ruin the Commune, apart from the objective difficulties. Yet the progress from 1848 was immense.

Europe was then quiet for nearly thirty-five years. In 1905 the Russian proletariat took the advanced position. It established the general political strike as one of the great weapons of the proletariat in its struggle against capital. From out of its own instinctive response to the objective development of capitalist production, it organized the soviets. The international significance of this for the proletariat was soon seen. When the end of World War I brought to the head the gathering crisis of capitalism all over Europe, the general political strike and the organization of the soviets became fundamental weapons of the proletariat in revolutionary struggle. In backward China in 1925–1927, we see the same phenomena. The year 1936 is a very important one in the history of proletarian struggle. The workers developed a new weapon corresponding to the high stage of the struggle with the capitalist class. In France they go into the factories and threaten to stay there until their demands are satisfied. In Spain, in Catalonia, the *first* thing the workers do is to take hold of the property of the bourgeoisie. Never was a proletarian revolution so violent and decisive in this respect as was the revolution in this most important province of Spain *in the first seventy-two hours*. Had there existed in Spain anything like a revolutionary party the proletariat would have been able to consolidate itself over large areas in Spain even more rapidly than the extraordinarily rapid revolution in Russia between February and October 1917. *What we have to note is that in America the proletariat, though far less conscious politically and far less aroused than the proletariat either in France or in Spain, used precisely the same basic method of struggle.* It went into the factories. John L. Lewis, the militant labor leader, fought splendidly for the CIO. But the American working class, once it was aroused, showed itself ready to adopt the most advanced methods of proletarian struggle current at the time. At the decisive moment these apparently backward workers were far in advance of their most advanced leaders.

The lesson to be drawn from this is plain. When the American proletariat, as we confidently expect it will, does move into action, it will take steps which will correspond to the general stage of development of proletarian class struggle at the time. The Murrays, the Thomases, and the Reuthers will be found at the tail of the mass movement. So it always has been. So it always will be. We agree entirely with Murray as to the fateful character of the years ahead. We only add our confidence that the American proletariat will show in the moment of action that all of its present leaders are bumbling behind it.

REAFFIRMATIONS OF PRACTICAL CONCLUSIONS

Certain practical conclusions* can now be reaffirmed:

1. The propaganda and agitation for a Labor party which revolutionists will advance must serve first and foremost as a means of educating the working class to the perils of the hour, the fatefulness of the days ahead, and the need of drastic solutions to the social problems presented. Wherever the workers wish to form an independent Labor party, the revolutionists today support them and actively cooperate. But the revolutionary program for a Labor party goes far beyond what appears to be the immediate political consciousness of millions of workers. If our previous experience proves anything, it is that the explosive forces which are gathering in the working-class movement during the past ten years will drive it forward at the moment of decision far beyond the imagination of Murray and his brother bureaucrats. It can conceivably happen that the workers may face a very sharp stage of the class struggle even before an independent Labor party is formed. A genuine mass Labor party may be stifled, as Murray obviously intends to stifle it for 1944. The crisis may unloose a torrential movement

---

*See Workers party resolution on "The Struggle for the Labor Party," *New International*, December 1943.

for an independent Labor party. Such things do not concern us here and in any case are unpredictable. But the revolutionists under all circumstances hold before the workers a program for the reconstruction of society. *The American working class has not suffered the destruction of the American economy by war. It is outside the international complications of the European proletariat. It has had hammered into its head from all sides the corrupt origins and fundamental bankruptcy of fascism. It has learned a great deal both on a national and international scale from the intensive political education which war brings and the fortunate position in which it has been placed in relation to the actual conflict. It has suffered none of the drastic blows which have fallen upon the European proletariat during recent years. It is conscious that its great battles are before it.* Any kind of political analysis which thinks that a bold political program is too "advanced" for the "backward" workers completely misunderstands that sharp transposition of roles between masses and the labor bureaucrats at the moment that the masses move in action. And, in the United States in 1944, to talk about "years of decision" without visualizing mass action is the escapist fantasy of a frightened bureaucrat.

2. The second practical conclusion is the recognition of the necessity of the revolutionary Marxian party *today*. A Marxian party is always necessary but a frank recognition of struggle for the organization of an independent Labor party does not in the least mean subordination of the struggle for a revolutionary party. Exactly the opposite is the case. It is clear from Murray's article that the labor bureaucracy which he represents does not see labor's participation in the "years of decision" except as giving its votes to be used at the dictates of its "leaders." Any illusions about the labor bureaucracy on this score will be paid for at heavy cost. The labor bureaucracy is a social phenomenon with certain social and political characteristics. That it does not wish a Labor party is not in any way surprising. Tomorrow it may or may not be of the same opinion. But even if a dynamic development should push the caste of Murray, Green, and the rest of them, or others of their type, into the leadership of an independent Labor party, then these gentlemen will do substantially what all their colleagues in Europe have been doing for the past fifty years. They will try to use the party as an instrument of class collaboration and suppression of working-class militancy. The more powerful is the urge of the masses to come to grips with their oppressors, the more certainly will our labor "statesmen" maneuver to suppress the workers. The struggle, therefore, for the as-yet unborn Labor party and the struggle to make the Labor party, if and when formed, an instrument for the organization and education of the workers, that is a task that will have to be performed *against* the labor bureaucracy. In other words, it is a task of the revolutionary party.

Finally, when we watch the horizons of Europe, Asia, and Africa and see the vast explosions of the class struggles which impend, it becomes clear that the American working class needs its revolutionary party not only to assist it in its struggles with the quaking bureaucrats who lead it only to stifle its growing aspirations for independence. It needs such a party to help it draw the lessons of the great international class battles ahead so that these lessons can be applied to the national field.

JANUARY 1944

12

The American People in "One World": An Essay in Dialectical Materialism

America has entered upon a new phase of relationship with the rest of the world. Its armies tramp and roll over the most remote corners of the globe; its navies scour the five oceans; every day its airmen blaze new "Santa Fe" trails over African jungles and the China Sea. American military and political leaders lay down the law in Casablanca, London, Chungking, and Rome, and partition continents in Cairo and Teheran. Arabs, Hindus and Koreans, seeking the bread of independence, jostle one another along the stone corridors of Constitution Avenue. All the world has been converted and Washington is the modern Mecca. Within the White House, Roosevelt arrogates the right to O.K. rulers of empires as a merchant O.K.'s prospective salesmen. Augustan Rome, the Pope sitting crowned upon the grave thereof, even imperial Britain, seem to have been merely successive anticipations of this monstrous, this incredible concentration of power. The American people are grappling with the change. The sales of Willkie's *One World*, the greatest publishing success in history, is a political and not a literary phenomenon. Yet the true nature of the new relation remains obscure for the great masses of the people. How could it be otherwise? Day after day, year after year, it has heard American history past and present discussed in the following terms:

> It is not a coincidence . . . that the United States and Russia, under the czars and under the Soviets, have always in vital matters been on the same side; that for more than 100 years Britain and America have in the end always found that against the moral enemy of either, they would support one another, and that France, which did so much to liberate America, has twice in her mortal peril found us at last beside her. (Walter Lippman, *Herald Tribune*, July 8, 1944)

166

We propose to expose the falsity of this interpretation of American history in its international relations. It is not the truth about American history and can be factually exposed. Left unexposed, it affords too fertile a soil for the organized deception of the people as to the true character of America's foreign relations of today and still more, of tomorrow. We propose, however, to make a preliminary statement of our own principles, first because of the vastness of the subject and the danger of becoming lost in it; secondly, owing to the necessity of constantly counterposing Marxism to the bourgeois* ignorance and superficiality of Lippman's method, which in bourgeois society seems as natural as the air we breathe; finally, owing to the reinforcement of this nationalistic empiricism, now being provided by the Stalinists in the name of Marx. This inexhaustible source of corruption celebrated the latest July 4 as follows:

> The fact that our country was able to rally from the unclear national policy and the dark days of division of Munichism to play the tremendous part it has in the great anti-Hitler war of liberation is in large measure due to the democratic content which for 168 years, despite many vicissitudes, has continued to characterize our national existence. (F. J. Meyers, "How America Got That Way," *New Masses*, July 4, 1944)

What are these but the historical method and the ideas of Lippman dressed in a pink sweater? This deliberate and criminal falsification has a clear purpose. The political struggle of the proletariat in international relations now becomes a struggle as to whether "our country," i.e., Roosevelt, will continue to play the role it has played "for 168 years," i.e., in 1944 support Stalinist Russia. Under this potent but poisonous fertilizer, the advocacy of incentive pay, of the no-strike pledge becomes the continuation of the great traditions of the Declaration of Independence, not only at home but abroad.

Yet, in reality, the history of the United States, properly understood, is a clarion call to the masses of the people everywhere to raise the concept of the nation to a higher plane by inseminating it with the concept of class. Dialectically handled, this history is a weapon to be used by and for the people and not against them.

THE METHOD OF INVESTIGATION

1. Marx has stated that "as in the eighteenth century the American War of Independence sounded the tocsin for the European middle class, so in the

---

*We say bourgeois advisedly. Lippman is intelligent, well informed, and conscientious—but bourgeois.

nineteenth century the American Civil War sounded it for the European working class." All Marx's method is contained in that sentence. Not America in general, but the *class struggle* in America, the American Revolution and the American Civil War. Not Britain or France or Germany in general, but the progression from the European middle classes in the eighteenth century to the European proletariat in the nineteenth. The method of dialectical materialism at one stroke clears its skirt from the hereditary stupidities of the bourgeois publicist and the criminal huckstering of his Stalinist hack. We today must bear in mind that logical class movement from the eighteenth to the nineteenth century and by projecting it, disentangle from complicated historical phenomena the class relations and international perspectives of the twentieth. It is precisely this logical connection we wish to establish and precisely this that the Stalinists wish to destroy, because it is this more than anything else that the American people need.

2. This is no mere academic exercise. We can orient for the future only by comprehension of the present in the light of the past. This apparent truism, with the bourgeoisie mere "common sense" or sententiousness, for the Marxist has an entirely different significance, both logical and historical. Marx taught us that the very categories by which we distinguish the various phases of the social movement are fully developed and therefore fully comprehensible only in the maturity of bourgeois society. Today it can go no further. It is in the decay of bourgeois society as it falls to pieces that concepts centuries old shed all social and traditional disguise and stand naked. When Jesse Jones, after Pearl Harbor, heard that stockpiles of rubber had been destroyed by fire in Boston and asked if they had been insured, half the country laughed at him. The fetishism of commodities stood exposed as an idol of the marketplace. In every sphere of social knowledge contemporary developments reveal the past in truer perspective and show us our own great contradictions as merely the logical climax of embryonic movements maturing through the centuries.

The history of Bolshevism etches in sharper and clearer perspective the apparent hair-splitting of the early Christians and the Puritans and thus gives historical discrimination to the conflicts of today in the light of tomorrow. Only the October Revolution could extend our knowledge of the British and French revolutions, and the three in sequence together constitute a new statue of liberty that illuminates the whole contemporary darkness. This extension of American power to the remotest reaches is a dramatic climax to the role this country has played in international relations, lighting up the past of the whole of Western civilization and projecting its present contradictions into their future resolution.

Today, in American imperialism, the commodity has reached its most grandiose historical manifestation. All people are entangled in the net of the world market. We have only to examine the historical development to see concretely posed the revolutionary socialist solution which Marx distilled by logical abstraction. It is necessary to do this so as not to be misled by the apparent ignorance and bewilderment of the great masses of the people. The masses do not learn history, they make it. More accurately, they learn it only when they make it. Even Washington had little conception of what tocsin he was sounding, and Lincoln had less. So, today the American proletariat, as it went into the factories to protect the birth of the CIO and now girds itself for the postwar struggle against unemployment, is, unawaredly, preparing international and economic transformations and social realignments on a scale comparable only to the elevation of American capitalism to its position as dominant world power. This for us is the objective movement of history which we attempt, by precept and example, subjectively to clarify and advance. Not forgetting, however, that the subjective movement, whatever its accidental chances, is in its totality the complement of objective necessity and cannot be separated from it.

THE FIRST TOCSIN

In the last quarter of the eighteenth century bourgeois Europe needed to emancipate itself from that combination of feudalism and commercial capitalism which we know as mercantilism. Yet the protagonists of the new industrial capitalism, in Britain as well as in France, had been nourished on the famous "triangular trade" of mercantilism—Africa, America, and the West Indies. After the end of the Seven Years' War in 1763, the up and coming industrial bourgeoisie began to find itself in conflict with the mercantilist commercial and political domination. Each class sought to solve its difficulties at the expense of the periphery—the thirteen colonies. But in the thirteen colonies the resulting economic and political crisis soon brought on to the political stage the artisans and mechanics of the towns. Says Beard: "They broke out in rioting in Boston, New York, Philadelphia and Charleston. . . . In fact, the agitation, *contrary to the intent of the merchants and lawyers*, got quite beyond the bounds of law and order" (emphasis mine). Well might Gouverneur Morris remark: "The heads of the mobility grew dangerous to the gentry, and how to keep them down is the question."

In the border areas the farmers, checked in the first agitation against the British, broke out into furious revolt against the American ruling class. A conservative historian (Miller, *Origins of the American Revolution*, 1943, p. 319) sums up his research thus:

But this Eastern ruling class was at no time disposed to sacrifice any of its privileges in order to bring the Western farmers wholeheartedly into the revolutionary movement. Instead the aristocracy urged Americans to center their attention wholly upon British tyranny and not to seek to apply revolutionary principles to conditions at home.

The "no-strike pledge" and "incentive pay" have a long ancestry.

When the victory was won, the bottom had been torn out of the "triangular trade" and the British industrial bourgeoisie came immediately into its own. The Treaty of Versailles which ratified the independence of America was signed in 1783. One year later, 1784, is the traditional date set as the "beginning" of the Industrial Revolution in Britain. In a surprisingly few years the trade with America on a new basis rivaled the old mercantilist prosperity to the confutation of the prophets of evil. Not only in the internal affairs of Europe did the loss of America create a revolution. Colonial relations underwent a radical transformation. One year after the loss of America came the first of the great India Bills which marked the beginning of the change from the old-fashioned robbery and plunder of India to the more systematic economic exploitation based on the developing textile industry. Three years after Versailles, Pitt personally asked Wilberforce to undertake the agitation for the abolition of the slave trade. This was accomplished in 1806 and marked the beginning of a new relationship between Great Britain and Africa. Mercantilist Britain, for a century the undying foe of colonial independence, by 1820 had become the champion of the freedom of the Latin American colonies. Where George III had said of the struggle with the thirteen colonies, "Blows will decide," Canning, with his eye on British trade in Latin America, declared: "We have called a new world into existence to redress the balance of the old."

George Washington might preach isolationism and nonintervention. The revolution had set in motion great class struggles in Europe and given a new direction to international trade and colonial relations. Today we can estimate the relative values of the Declaration of Independence and the essential *political* document of the time, *Wealth of Nations*. Adam Smith had worked on it for ten years when it appeared in 1776. He wrote that the present system of management, i.e., mercantilism, procured advantage "only to a single order of men," i.e., one class. Great Britain (and Europe as well) "derives nothing but loss from the dominion which she has assumed over her colonies." The problem was how to achieve the death of this system. In the opinion of this bourgeois, to propose that Britain "give up all the authority over her colonies . . . would be to propose such a measure as never was and never will be adopted by any nation in the world." The American revolutionary leaders for years had been in close contact with the radical opposition in Britain. But all these politicians were, like Smith, unable to visualize the radical and compete break. It was the artisans, the mechanics, and farmers who started the ball a-rolling and converted Smith's theories into reality. Thus Washington's "isolationism" was merely the appearance of things. Their essence was far different. We shall see this difference between the appearance and the essence constantly repeated on an ever more extensive scale until it reaches truly gigantic proportions in the contradiction between the apparent power of Washington today and the underlying economic and social movement.

THE SECOND TOCSIN

Technological discoveries are the spermatozoa of social change. The cotton gin not only created the historical patterns of American capitalism. It laid an indelible impress on European development as well. In 1847 Marx, engaged in the congenial task of exposing the misuse of the Hegelian dialectic by Proudhon, took as one of his illustrations slavery:

> Without slavery you have no cotton, without cotton you have no modern industry. It is slavery which has given their value to the colonies, it is the colonies which have created the commerce of the world, it is the commerce of the world which is the essential condition of the great industry. . . . Without slavery North America, the most progressive country, would have been transformed into a patriarchal country. Efface North America from the map of the world and you would have the anarchy, the complete decadence of modern commerce and civilization. Cause slavery to disappear and you will have effaced America from the map of nations. (*Poverty of Philosophy*)

By 1847, however, this was the summation of an age which was dying. Its death was to change the social structure of America and signalize the coming of age of a new force in Europe.

Just one year before Marx's book, the British bourgeoisie won its final victory over the landlords by the abolition of the "corn laws," which brought the cheap wheat of the New World into Britain and lowered the value of the laborer. The South had calculated all along that the loss of its cotton would inevitably bring intervention by the European powers, particularly Britain. It miscalculated the interest of the industrialists in cheap wheat from the wheat belt, which was one of the most powerful weapons of the North. But the role of cheap wheat was a testimony to the fact that the special claims of the textile industry, always the first to mature in a nascent capitalist development, had already been superseded by the interests of the bourgeoisie as a whole. The varied and expanded accumulation of capital had brought with it a varied and expanded proletariat. In 1848 this proletariat appeared on the scene in France in the first proletarian revolution. Europe trembled, but in Washington, the White House, the government, and the people rejoiced at the downfall of the monarchy. The ruling classes of Europe therefore hated the political system of America with its scorn of aristocracy and monarchy, its emphasis on equality, manhood suffrage, and popular government.

But in the United States, by 1848, forces were at work converting the bourgeoisie from the ally to the foe of popular aspirations abroad. In 1850, a desperate attempt was made to compromise the differences between North and South. But the economic conflict was irrepressible. The fugitive slaves and the abolitionists would not let the question be forgotten for a moment. In 1858 economic crisis shook not only the United States but the whole of the now vastly extended world market. From then on the sequence of international events came thick and fast.

First, between 1857 and 1859, a series of great strikes and class conflicts broke out all over Europe, Britain included. In 1860 came Lincoln's election. The South expected that the commercial capitalists of the North would as usual capitulate. But independent farmers of the Northwest could not for a moment tolerate the idea of a hostile power holding the mouth of the Mississippi and they were among the chief supporters of Lincoln. But even more important, *the victory of the Republican party was due more than anything else to the support of labor.* (The neglect of this fact is one of the strangest features of radical propaganda and agitation in the United States.) And labor, though no lover of Negroes, was by 1860 conscious enough of the stake which free labor had in the struggle with slave labor. *Thus labor and the independent farmers were the most powerful forces in the North while the general unrest and minor but repeated insurrection among the slaves* completed the forces which pushed the unwilling rulers of the North and South to the final settlement by arms. *The mechanics, the artisans, the frontiersmen of 1776 and the Negroes* who had fought with Washington had now developed into the powerful force on whom Lincoln had ultimately to depend for political support and military victory.*

But political activity, the concrete expression of social consciousness, though sometimes accelerated, sometimes retarded, must keep pace with social development. Even before 1848 the abolitionists not only led an incomparable agitation in the United States. Garrison and Negroes who had escaped from slavery placed the case of the slaves before vast numbers of European workers. They enrolled supporters by the hundreds of thousands. One Negro alone enrolled 70,000 in Germany.

When war actually began, the European ruling classes were on the alert for an opportunity to intervene. Everything hinged on Britain. The British

---

*They had also joined the British in large numbers, listening to their promises of freedom.

government was hesitant and hoped for an encouraging signal from the Lancashire cotton operatives, who were in great distress over the cessation of cotton exports from the South. The British textile operatives, however, denounced the intervention plans of the government and what took place in Britain was repeated on a lesser scale all over Europe. The British bourgeoisie was sneering at Lincoln's repeated declarations that the war was not a war for the abolition of slavery. The European workers shouted across the ocean that it was, and called on Lincoln to say so. Lincoln, with the North in great danger, finally penned the Emancipation Proclamation, to take effect on January 1, 1863. The European proletariat celebrated a great victory. It came just in time. Marx tells us (Schlueter, *Lincoln, Labor, and Slavery*, p. 187; see also Marx and Engels's *Correspondence*) that in April 1863, "a monster meeting . . . prevented Palmerston from declaring war against the United States when he was on the point of doing it."

In 1861, the Tsar, fearful of rebellion from below, had emancipated the serfs. In 1862 had come the rebellion of the Poles. A great international mass meeting took place in London in July 1863 on behalf of Polish independence. These two events, the American Civil War and the Polish rebellion, brought to a conclusion the tentative negotiations long in progress and on September 28, 1864, the First International was founded. On November 1 the executive committee adopted the inaugural address by Marx. Nothing so contributed to the final consummation as the Civil War.

At the beginning of that same November, Lincoln was reelected president. Marx, on the Council of the International, initiated a series of mass meetings in Britain protesting against the hostile attitude of the English ruling class and government to the Union. On the 29th, Marx presented to the Council the address to Lincoln. The International became the terror of the European governments. If in the eighteenth century the American Revolution had initiated the struggle for bourgeois democracy, the Civil War had set on foot the movement which ended its first phase in the Paris Commune—the dictatorship of the proletariat.

ORIENTAL INTERLUDE

It is in revolutionary periods that the culmination of previous trends and the beginning of new ones appear. That is why they are so important.

Before we draw together the developing historical tendencies which meet in the colossal power of the United States today, we have to note briefly the temporary but symptomatic Far Eastern colonial adventure which spurted during the revolutionary crisis of 1850–1860.

In that critical decade the Northern industrial capitalists, unwilling to challenge seriously the combination of plantation owners and financial and commercial interests, seriously sought an outlet in the Far East. The low tariffs imposed by the mainly agrarian Democratic party brought European goods into the United States, and already by 1844, American merchants in Canton had extracted a commercial treaty from the Chinese, granting them, among other things, "extraterritoriality." Ten years later, Daniel Webster, Whig mouthpiece, sent Commodore Perry to open Japan, chiefly as a port of call on the long journey to China. The hapless Japanese had seen what Britain had done and was doing to China and knew, moreover, that British and Russian battleships were waiting to do likewise to Japan. They accepted the "gentle coercion." American agents seized the Bonin Islands and Formosa. The United States was already ankle-deep in the bloody mud of the imperialist scramble. *But the class struggle at home checked the adventure.* The Southern agrarians had their own idea of imperialism—conquest of land for plantations in Cuba and Mexico. The Pacific islands were far and could not be defended except by heavy expenditure of a navy. The neo-imperialists began a dog-in-the-manger policy which they canonized as the defense of the "territorial integrity" of China.

Imperialist enterprise draws political consequences. By 1850 European industry and European plunder had thrown the subsistence economies of India and China into disorder. In that tumultuous decade the first of the great series of Oriental revolutions burst upon the world. The Taiping rebellion against the Manchu dynasty began in 1850, and it has been described as mass movement of the propertyless against the corruption, inefficiency, and capitulation to Britain of the old Chinese ruling class. By 1856 this revolution was at its height. In 1857 followed what the British call the Indian Mutiny but which Indians call the First War of Independence. *The American representatives in China played their part side by side with the British and other imperialists in suppressing the Taiping rebellion.* From that beginning to this day American imperialism has never wavered in its unrelenting hostility to the democratic aspirations of the Oriental peoples. When, in the seventies, radical elements in Japan established a republic in one part of the islands, and again in 1894, when the Japanese Parliament was leading popular hostility against the throne and the bureaucracy, the administration in Washington gave every assistance, military, political, and diplomatic, to save the monarchy and the militarists.

THE CONTEMPORARY GRANDEUR

As the industrial bourgeoisie felt the struggle of the proletariat at home, so they became its enemy abroad. At the end of World War I, American food and diplomatic power had to be used to stifle the socialist revolutions in Europe. Today, American capital has had to take upon itself the defense of

European capital and the defense of European interests in Africa and the Far East against their incorporation by Germany and the new contender, Japan. Hence its far-flung armies, navies, and air force. But this war has brought with it an unprecedented disintegration of capitalist society in Europe and Asia. Never was there such destruction, such misery, such barbarism; never such disillusionment by the masses of the people in every continent with the old order. American imperialism therefore becomes the chief bulwark of the capitalist system as a whole. At the same time, ten years of the New Deal have shown the impossibility of solving the great economic depression. Therefore the United States hopes to restore its own shattered prosperity by substituting its own imperialism for the imperialism of Britain and France, its "allies." It even prepares to "liberate" India in the interests of the "open door" and the "territorial integrity" of India. The Gandhis and Nehrus, however, seek the protection of this new patron to pacify the masses, satisfy their hatred of Japan and Britain and divert them from social revolution. The United States is the friend and ally of every reactionary government and class in Latin America except insofar as these for the moment assist the Axis.

This, in 1944, is "our country." The colossal power of American imperialism is the apex of a process—the rise, maturity and decline of the capitalist world market. In the eighteenth century, "our country," in the triumph of its industrial bourgeoisie, released the great political potentialities of the European proletariat, the mortal enemy of the European bourgeoisie. Today "our country" can release nothing. Driven by the contradictions of its own capitalistic development and of capitalism as a whole, it is now the enemy of hundreds of millions of people everywhere. The appearance of liberator of peoples is a necessary disguise for the essential reality of American imperialism, epitome of decadent capitalism, mobilized for the defense of privilege and property against a world crying to be free.

The laws of dialectics are to be traced not in metaphysical abstractions such as 168 years of "our country," but in economic development and the rise, maturity, and decline of different social classes within the expansion and constriction of the capitalist world market. The greatest progressive force in the eighteenth century, the nationalism of "our country," is in the twentieth century the greatest of obstacles to social progress. In accordance with a fundamental dialectical law, the progressive "nationalism" of eighteenth-century America is transformed into its opposite, the reactionary "internationalism" of American imperialism. The liberating "isolationism" of Washington is transformed into the reactionary "interventionism" of Roosevelt. The essence underlying each social order is exactly the opposite of its appearance on the surface. The power of Washington as capital of the world rests on no sound foundation. Except to those for whom a logical development of historical forces has ceased, or has never existed, the imperialist American grandeur is the mark of imperialist American doom. Imperial Washington, like imperial Rome, is destined to be cursed and execrated by the embittered millions. The liberating international tradition can and will have a new birth in this nation but, today, in accordance with historical logic, only in the service of the American proletariat, consciously using the great American tradition of the past and its present economic power as the pivot and arsenal of international socialism.

"MODERN INTERNATIONAL SOCIETY"

The stage is set. "There are unmistakable indications that there is rapidly rising a truly popular demand for a cleaning of the Augean stable of modern international society and that it will not admit defeat." The author of that is no Marxist but a man who for years directed the international policy of American imperialism, Sumner Welles. But history has proved again and again since 1917 that the agrarian revolution on which hangs the salvation of India, of China, and of Latin America cannot be achieved without the conscious aid of the working class in each country. In our compact world, successful revolt in any area will sound the tocsin for the center more violently than the American revolutions of the eighteenth and nineteenth century shook metropolitan Europe. And the social crisis in America must bring onto the scene the American proletariat.

Yet it would be a grave error to mistake the twentieth for the nineteenth century and to believe that the American proletariat is dependent upon the tocsin from abroad to engage in relentless class struggles with American capital. Whatever may be incidental occasion, that struggle is rooted in the inability of American capital to solve the problem of the industrial reserve army of labor. Significant action of any kind by the American proletariat will reverberate in every corner of our "One World." Every Chinese knows that it is impossible to have great class struggles in China without provoking the intervention of American imperialism. The whole tendency of the modern economy shows that foreign trade will be increasingly a transaction under the aegis of governments. American imperialism cannot escape its entanglements in foreign class struggles even if it would. Revolutionary movement anywhere can release only the international proletariat and the hundreds of millions dependent upon it. And that too is a law of the dialectic, proving the ripeness of the organism for transformational change.

The American proletariat itself may view the tangled skein of world politics with faint interest or even with indifference. To judge the future of contemporary history by these subjective appraisals is to make an irreparable error, to forget that being determines consciousness and not vice versa. In our "One World" the first serious and prolonged struggle upon which the American proletariat embarks with its own bourgeoisie will rapidly educate it in the realities of international politics.

This must be the theoretical basis of action. The masses who comprised the Sons of Liberty had little understanding of the fact that they were sounding tocsins for the European middle classes. Lincoln, the leader, did not even know that he would have to emancipate the slaves, far less sound the tocsin for the organization of the first Workers' International. The farmers, mechanics and artisans, the workers and Negro slaves, pursued strictly immediate and concrete aims and made world history.

The premises of international proletarian organization are here. The individual productive unit of early competitive capitalism found its political complement in bourgeois democracy where individual units of the bourgeoisie fought out its collective problems. The maturity of capitalist production drove the proletariat to international organization in the nineteenth century. By the twentieth century the size of the productive units had linked the national units of production so closely that imperialist war marked the final decline of capitalism. From the large-scale productive unit came the new political form of the future—the soviet. For the soviets are *not* merely organs of struggle but the political framework of the new society. To the soviets [which constitute an] instinctive rejection by the masses of the organs of bourgeois democracy, the bourgeoisie responded with the totalitarian state. The most glaring sign of the degeneration of the role of the workers in Stalinist Russia is the destruction of the soviets by the constitution of 1936. Stalinist totalitarianism, the historical result of the first proletarian revolution, its growing collaboration with American imperialism, the mischievous power of its satellites abroad, have disoriented those whose Marxism, based on emotion and superficial reading, rejects the dialectic in history. They work from Stalinist Russia and American imperialism back toward the possibilities of socialism. They see the absence of international organization, the acquiescence and indifference of the workers, the organizational power of the Stalinist corruption inside the working class and draw the gloomiest prospects for international revolutionary action. Such was never the theory or the practice of Marx. Let us end this theoretical study with one of his most mature and pregnant sayings:

> The international activity of the working class does not by any means depend on the existence of the International Workingmen's Association. This was only the first attempt to create a central organ for that activity: an attempt which from the impulse it gave is an abiding success that was no longer practicable in its first historical form after the fall of the Paris Commune.

It was in that reasoned faith that Lenin and his band of Bolsheviks worked and created the Third International. We who have seen the determination of the contemporary masses to cleanse the Augean stables of modern international society are not in any way dismayed by the power of Washington or of Moscow. In the contradictions and barbarism of world economy we see the soil from which, at whatever remove, and through whatever corruption from without or within, must ultimately rise the Fourth International.

JULY 1944

13

The Revolutionary Answer to the Negro Problem in the United States*

The decay of capitalism on a world scale, the rise of the CIO in the United States, and the struggle of the Negro people have precipitated a tremendous battle for the minds of the Negro people and for the minds of the population in the United States as a whole over the Negro question. During the last few years certain sections of the bourgeoisie, recognizing the importance of this question, have made a powerful theoretical demonstration of their position, which has appeared in *The American Dilemma* by Gunnar Myrdal, a publication that took a quarter of a million dollars to produce. Certain sections of the sentimental petty bourgeoisie have produced their spokesmen, one of whom is Lillian Smith. That has produced some very strange fruit, which however has resulted in a book which has sold some half a million copies over the last year or two. The Negro petty bourgeoisie, radical and concerned with communism, has also made its bid in the person of Richard Wright, whose books have sold over a million copies. When books on such a controversial question as the Negro question reach the stage of selling half a million copies it means that they have left the sphere of literature and have now reached the sphere of politics. . . .

We can compare what we have to say that is new by comparing it to previous positions on the Negro question in the socialist movement. The proletariat, as we know, must lead the struggles of all the oppressed and all those who are persecuted by capitalism. But this has been interpreted in the past—and by some very good socialists too—in the following sense: the independent struggles of the Negro people have not got much more than an episodic value and, as a matter of fact, can constitute a great danger not only to the Negroes themselves, but to the organized labor movement. The real leadership of the Negro struggle must rest in the hands of organized labor and of the Marxist party. Without that the Negro struggle is not only weak,

179

but is likely to cause difficulties for the Negroes and dangers to organized labor. This, as I say, is the position held by many socialists in the past. Some great socialists in the United States have been associated with this attitude. We, on the other hand, say something entirely different.

We say, number one, that the Negro struggle, the independent Negro struggle, has a vitality and a validity of its own; that it has deep historic roots in the past of America and in present struggles; it has an organic political perspective, along which it is traveling, to one degree or another, and everything shows that at the present time it is traveling with great speed and vigor.

We say, number two, that this independent Negro movement is able to intervene with terrific force upon the general social and political life of the nation, despite the fact that it is waged under the banner of democratic rights, and is not led necessarily either by the organized labor movement or the Marxist party. We say, number three, and this is the most important, that it is able to exercise a powerful influence upon the revolutionary proletariat, that it has got a great contribution to make to the development of the proletariat in the United States, and that it is in itself a constituent part of the struggle for socialism. In this way we challenge directly any attempt to subordinate or to push to the rear the social and political significance of the independent Negro struggle for democratic rights. That is our position. It was the position of Lenin thirty years ago. It was the position of Trotsky which he fought for during many years. It has been concretized by the general class struggle in the United States, and the tremendous struggles of the Negro people. It has been sharpened and refined by political controversy in our movement, and best of all it has had the benefit of three or four years of practical application in the Negro struggle and in the class struggle by the Socialist Workers party during the past few years.

Now if this position has reached the stage where we can put it forward in the shape that we propose, that means that to understand it should be by now simpler than before; and by merely observing the Negro question, the Negro people, rather, the struggles they have carried on, their ideas, we are able to see the roots of this position in a way that was difficult to see ten or even fifteen years ago. The Negro people, we say, on the basis of their own experiences, approach the conclusions of Marxism. And I will have briefly to illustrate this as has been shown in the Resolution.

First of all, on the question of imperialist war. The Negro people do not believe that the last two wars, and the one that may overtake us, are a result of the need to struggle for democracy, for freedom of the persecuted peoples by the American bourgeoisie. They cannot believe that.

On the question of the state, what Negro, particularly below the Mason-Dixon line, believes that the bourgeois state is a state above all classes, serving the needs of all the people? They may not formulate their belief in Marxist terms, but their experience drives them to reject this shibboleth of bourgeois democracy.

On the question of what is called the democratic process, the Negroes do not believe that grievances, difficulties of sections of the population, are solved by discussions, by voting, by telegrams to Congress, by what is known as the "American way."

Finally, on the question of political action, the American bourgeoisie preaches that Providence in its divine wisdom has decreed that there should be two political parties in the United States, not one, not three, not four, just two; and also in its kindness, Providence has shown that these two parties should be one, the Democratic party and the other, the Republican, to last from now until the end of time.

That is being challenged by increasing numbers of people in the United States. But the Negroes more than ever have shown it—and any knowledge of their press and their activities tells us that they—are willing to make the break completely with that conception. . . .

As Bolsheviks we are jealous, not only theoretically but practically, of the primary role of the organized labor movement in all fundamental struggles against capitalism. That is why for many years in the past this position on the Negro question has had some difficulty in finding itself thoroughly accepted, particularly in the revolutionary movement, because there is this difficulty—what is the relation between this movement and the primary role of the proletariat—particularly because so many Negroes, and most disciplined, hardened, trained, highly developed sections of the Negroes, are today in the organized labor movement.

First, the Negro struggles in the South are not merely a question of struggles of Negroes, important as those are. It is a question of the reorganization of the whole agricultural system in the United States, and therefore a matter for the proletarian revolution and the reorganization of society on socialist foundations.

Secondly, we say in the South that although the embryonic unity of whites and Negroes in the labor movement may seem small and there are difficulties in the unions, yet such is the decay of Southern society and such the fundamental significance of the proletariat, particularly when organized in labor unions, that this small movement is bound to play the decisive part in the revolutionary struggles that are inevitable.

Thirdly, there are one and a quarter million Negroes, at least, in the organized labor movement.

On these fundamental positions we do not move one inch. Not only do we not move, we strengthen them. But there still remains in question: what is the relationship of the independent Negro mass movement to the organized labor movement? And here we come immediately to what has been and will be a very puzzling feature unless we have our basic position clear.

Those who believed that the Negro question is in reality, purely and simply, or to a decisive extent, merely a class question, pointed with glee to the tremendous growth of the Negro personnel in the organized labor movement. It grew in a few years from 300,000 to 1 million; it is now one and a half million. But to their surprise, instead of this lessening and weakening the struggle of the independent Negro movement, *the more the Negroes went into the labor movement, the more capitalism incorporated them into industry, the more they were accepted in the union movement. It is during that period, since 1940, that the independent mass movement has broken out with a force greater than it has ever shown before.*

That is the problem that we have to face, that we have to grasp. We cannot move forward and we cannot explain ourselves unless we have it clearly. And I know there is difficulty with it. I intend to spend some time on it, because if that is settled, all is settled. The other difficulties are incidental. If, however, this one is not clear, then we shall continually be facing difficulties which we shall doubtless solve in time.

Now Lenin has handled this problem and in the Resolution we have quoted him. He says that the dialectic of history is such that small independent nations, small nationalities, which are powerless—get the word, please—*powerless*, in the struggle against imperialism *nevertheless* can act as one of the ferments, one of the bacilli, which can bring onto the scene the real power against imperialism—the socialist proletariat.

Let me repeat it please. Small groups, nations, nationalities, themselves powerless against imperialism, nevertheless can act as one of the ferments, one of the bacilli which will bring onto the scene the real fundamental force against capitalism—the socialist proletariat.

In other words, as so often happens from the Marxist point of view from the point of view of the dialectic, this question of the *leadership* is very complicated.

What Lenin is saying is that although the fundamental force is the proletariat, although these groups are powerless, although the proletariat has got to lead them, it does not by any means follow that they cannot do anything until the proletariat actually comes forward to lead them. *He says exactly the opposite is the case.*

They, by their agitation, resistance and the political developments that they can initiate, can be the means whereby the proletariat is brought onto the scene.

Not always, and every time, not the sole means, but one of the means. That is what we have to get clear.

Now it is very well to see it from the point of view of Marxism which developed these ideas upon the basis of European and Oriental experiences. Lenin and Trotsky applied this principle to the Negro question in the United States. What *we* have to do is to make it concrete, and one of the best means of doing so is to dig into the history of the Negro people in the United States, and to see the relationship that has developed between them and revolutionary elements in past revolutionary struggles.

For us the center must be the Civil War in the United States and I intend briefly now to make some sharp conclusions and see if they can help us arrive at a clearer perspective. Not for historical knowledge, but to watch the movement as it develops before us, helping us to arrive at a clearer perspective as to this difficult relationship between the independent Negro movement and the revolutionary proletariat. The Civil War was a conflict between the revolutionary bourgeoisie and the Southern plantocracy. That we know. That conflict was inevitable. But for twenty to twenty-five years before the Civil War actually broke out, the masses of the Negroes in the South, through the underground railroad, through revolts, as Aptheker has told us, and by the tremendous support and impetus that they gave to the revolutionary elements among the abolitionists, absolutely prevented the reactionary bourgeoisie—revolutionary later—absolutely prevented the bourgeoisie and the plantocracy from coming to terms as they wanted to do. In 1850 these two made a great attempt at a compromise. What broke that compromise? It was the Fugitive Slave Act. They could prevent every-thing else for the time being, but they could not prevent the slaves from coming, and the revolutionaries in the North from assisting them. So that we find that here in the history of the United States such is the situation of the masses of the Negro people and their readiness to revolt at the slightest opportunity, that as far back as the Civil War, in relation to the American bourgeoisie, they formed a force which *initiated* and *stimulated* and *acted as a ferment*.

That is point number one.

Point number two. The Civil War takes its course as it is bound to do. Many Negroes and their leaders make an attempt to get incorporated into the Republican party and to get their cause embraced by the bourgeoisie. And what happens? The bourgeoisie refuses. It doesn't want to have Ne-groes emancipated. Point number three. As the struggle develops, such is the situation of the Negroes in the United States, that the emancipation of the slaves becomes *an absolute necessity*, politically, organizationally, and from a military point of view.

The Negroes are incorporated into the battle against the South. Not only are they incorporated here, but later they are incorporated also into the military government which smashes down the remnants of resistance in the Southern states. But, when this is done, the Negroes are deserted by the bourgeoisie, *and there falls upon them a very terrible repression.* That is the course of development in the central episode of American history.

Now if it is so in the Civil War, we have the right to look to see what happened in the War of Independence. It is likely—it is not always certain—but it is *likely* that we shall see there some *anticipations* of the logical development which appeared in the Civil War. They are there. The Negroes begin by demanding their rights. They say if you are asking that the British free you, then we should have our rights, and furthermore, slavery should be abolished. The American bourgeoisie didn't react very well to that. The Negroes insisted—those Negroes who were in the North—insisted that they should be allowed to join the Army of Independence. They were refused.

But later Washington found that it was imperative to have them, and 4,000 of them fought among the 30,000 soldiers of Washington. They gained certain rights after independence was achieved. Then sections of the bourgeoisie who were with them deserted them. And the Negro movement collapsed. We see exactly the same thing but more intensified in the Populist movement. There was a powerful movement of one and one quarter of a million Negroes in the South (the Southern Tenant Farmers' Association). They joined the Populist movement and were in the extreme left wing of this movement, when populism was discussing whether it should go on with the Democratic party or make the campaign as a third party. The Negroes voted for the third party and for all the most radical planks in the platform. They fought with the Populist movement. But when populism was defeated, there fell upon the Negroes between 1896 and about 1910 the desperate, legalized repression and persecution of the Southern states.

Some of us think it is fairly clear that the Garvey movement came and looked to Africa because there was no proletarian movement in the United States to give it a lead, to do for this great eruption of the Negroes what the Civil War and the Populist movement had done for the insurgent Negroes of those days. And now what can we see today? Today the Negroes in the United States are organized as never before. There are more than half a million in the NAACP, and in addition to that, there are all sorts of Negro groups and organizations—the churches in particular—*every single one of which is dominated by the idea that each organization must in some manner or another contribute to the emancipation of the Negroes from capitalist humiliation and from capitalist oppression.* So that the independent Negro movement that we see today and which we see growing before our eyes is nothing strange. It is nothing new. *It is something that has always appeared in the American movement at the first sign of social crisis.*

It represents a climax to the Negro movements that we have seen in the past. From what we have seen in the past, we would expect it to have its head turned towards the labor movement. And not only from a historical point of view but today concrete experience tells us that the masses of the Negro people today look upon the CIO with a respect and consideration that they give to no other social or political force in the country. To anyone who knows the Negro people, who reads their press—and I am not speaking here specially of the Negro workers—if you watch the Negro petty bourgeoisie—reactionary, reformist types as some of them are in all their propaganda, in all their agitation—whenever they are in any difficulties, you can see them leaning toward the labor movement. As for the masses of Negroes, they are increasingly pro-labor every day. So that it is not only Marxist ideas; it is not only a question of Bolshevik-Marxist analysis. It is not only a question of the history of Negroes in the United States.

The actual concrete facts before us show us, and anyone who wants to see, this important conclusion, that the Negro movement logically and historically and concretely is headed for the proletariat. That is the road it has always taken in the past, the road to the revolutionary forces. Today the proletariat is that force. And if these ideas that we have traced in American revolutionary crises have shown some power in the past, such is the state of the class stuggle today, such the antagonisms between bourgeoisie and proletariat, such, too, the impetus of the Negro *movement toward the revolutionary forces*, which we have traced in the past, is stronger today than ever before. So that we can look upon this Negro movement not only for what it has been and what it has been able to do—we are able to know as Marxists by our own theory and our examination of American history that it is headed for the proletarian movement, that it must go there. There is nowhere else for it to go. And further we can see that if it doesn't go there, the difficulties that the Negroes have suffered in the past when they were deserted by the revolutionary forces, those will be ten, one hundred, ten thousand times as great as in the past. The independent Negro movement, which is boiling and moving, must find its way to the proletariat. If the proletariat is not able to support it, the repression of past times when the revolutionary forces failed the Negroes will be infinitely, I repeat infinitely, more terrible today.

Therefore our consideration of the independent Negro movement does not lessen the significance of the proletarian—the essentially proletarian—leadership. Not at all. It includes it. We are able to see that the mere existence of the CIO, its mere existence, despite the fakery of the labor leadership on the Negro question, as on all other questions, is a protection and a stimulus to the Negroes. We are able to see and I will show in a minute that the Negroes are able by their activity to draw the revolutionary elements and more powerful elements in the proletariat to their side. We are coming to that. But we have to draw and emphasize again and again this important conclusion. If—and we have to take these theoretical questions into consideration—if the proletariat is defeated, if the CIO is destroyed, then there will fall upon the Negro people in the United States such a repression, such persecution, comparable to nothing that they have seen in the past. We have seen in Germany and elsewhere the barbarism that capitalism is capable of in its death agony. The Negro people in the United States offer a similar opportunity to the American bourgeoisie. The American bourgeoisie have shown their understanding of the opportunity the Negro question gives them to disrupt and to attempt to corrupt and destroy the labor movement.

But the development of capitalism itself has not only given the independent Negro movement this fundamental and sharp relation with the proletariat. It has created Negro proletarians and placed them as proletarians in what were once the most oppressed and exploited masses. But in auto, steel, and coal, for example, these proletarians have now become the vanguard of the workers' struggle and have brought a substantial number of Negroes to a position of primacy in the stuggle against capitalism. The backwardness and humiliation of the Negroes that shoved them into these industries is the very thing which today is bringing them forward, and they are in the very vanguard of the proletarian movement from the very nature of the proletarian struggle itself. Now, how does this complicated interrelationship, the Leninist interrelationship express itself? Henry Ford could write a very good thesis on that if he were so inclined.

The Negroes in the Ford plant were incorporated by Ford: first of all he wanted them for the hard, rough work. I am also informed by the comrades from Detroit he was very anxious to play a paternalistic role with the Negro petty bourgeoisie. He wanted to show them that he was not the person that these people said he was—Look! he was giving Negroes opportunities in his plant. Number three, he was able thus to create divisions between whites and Negroes that allowed him to pursue his anti-union, reactionary way.

What has happened within the last few years that is changed? The mass of the Negroes in the River Rouge plant, I am told, are one of the most powerful sections of the Detroit proletariat. They are leaders in the proletarian struggle, not the stooges Ford intended them to be.

Not only that, they act as leaders not only in the labor movement as a whole but in the Negro community. It is what they say that is decisive there. Which is very sad for Henry. And the Negro petty bourgeois have followed the proletariat. They are now going along with the labor movement: they have left Ford too. It is said that he has recognized it at last and that he is not going to employ any more Negroes. He thinks he will do better with women. But they will disappoint him too. . . .

Let us not forget that in the Negro people, there sleep and are now awakening passions of a violence exceeding, perhaps, as far as these things can be compared, anything among the tremendous forces that capitalism has created. Anyone who knows them, who knows their history, is able to talk to them intimately, watches them at their own theaters, watches them at their dances, watches them in their churches, reads their press with a discerning eye, must recognize that although their social force may not be able to compare with the social force of a corresponding number of organized workers, the hatred of bourgeois society and the readiness to destroy it when the opportunity should present itself, rests among them to a degree greater than in any other section of the population in the United States. . . .

DECEMBER 1948

Note

*This article consists of substantial excerpts from a report with which James presented a resolution on "the Negro question" to the 1948 Convention of the Socialist Workers Party—ED.

__14__

Stalinism and Negro History

PART ONE

The policy of Stalinism in regard to the working masses everywhere is universally recognized as a policy of *manipulation*. From the Kremlin comes the line. The workers are supposed to obey, sometimes, as in June 1924, without an hour's notice. This, of course, is based upon an enormous contempt of the masses who are seen as political cannon fodder and nothing else. But as the self-professed party of the working class, Stalinism must present itself as guardian of the immediate and historic rights of the workers who are the initiators of a new free society. To be aware of this reality, which the Stalinists need to manipulate and to disguise, is to gain an invaluable insight into their theory, propaganda, and political practice. Nowhere is this dual attitude more strikingly illustrated than in their attitude to American Negroes.

In 1937, two years after the inauguration of the popular front policy, American Stalinism invaded with fanfare the history of the Civil War. To the winter 1937 issue of *Science and Society*, Richard Enmale contributed "Interpretations of the American Civil War." "The time has come," he proclaimed, "for American Marxist historians to complete the unfinished tasks of the liberal bourgeois historical school." He denounced the Bourbon historians but he omitted the entire school of Negro historians whose thirty years of serious work on the Civil War, though in form limited to Negroes, in reality had already provided the indispensable groundwork for any comprehensive analysis of the period. In his analysis of the social forces of the Civil War, Enmale omitted Negroes altogether.

This was a serious tactical error. The essay was used as the introduction to *The Civil War in the United States* by Marx and Engels and there the Negroes were "included." The way in which they were "included" became, as time passed, highly instructive. Enmale gives full statistics of the number of Negroes who fought and the number who died. He praises their "heroism," "their caliber as fighting men," and "their eagerness to enlist and fight for freedom"; some rose from the ranks to become officers; a great

188

number rendered valuable services as cooks, laborers, etc. That is all. Here, naked and as yet unadorned, is the summation of Stalinist policy, theoretical, historical, strategic and tactical on Negroes and therefore on the Civil War. There are many Negroes (manpower), heroic and ready to die (shock troops); they have men of ability who are fit for leadership (recognition).

Enmale again ignored the Negro historians. Thus the contemporary Negroes were kept in the background, theoretically and politically, in the role reserved for their ancestors in the actual conflicts of the Civil War. In this apparently slight but pregnant episode was embodied the general Stalinist conception of history and its particular application to Negroes in the United States. It has been refurbished, embellished, disguised, but it remains in all essentials the same wherever the Stalinists touch the Negro question.

In 1937 there also appeared James Allen's *Reconstruction*. This book bore traces of the period when Roosevelt was being called a Fascist by the Stalinists. But whatever it had of value, it owed to W. E. B. Du Bois's magnificent *Black Reconstruction* which had appeared in 1935. Du Bois is solemnly reproved by Allen for "failing to grasp the fundamental bourgeois character of the revolution." Here again the Stalinists revealed themselves. Du Bois did indeed make the mistake of calling the Reconstruction government a sort of dictatorship of the proletariat. Far from doing harm, the conception that lay behind the mistaken formula was the strength of Du Bois's book: he recognized that the Negroes *in particular* had tried to carry out ideas that went beyond the prevailing conceptions of bourgeois democracy. Precisely this was aimed at the heart of the whole Stalinist popular front conception. Hence their hostility to Du Bois. Du Bois is praised, however, both by Enmale and by Allen for his "spirited defense" of the Reconstruction—both use the same phrase.

FAITHFUL DISCIPLE OF STALINISM

Thus, in 1937, Stalinism prepared 1) to place itself before the Negroes as the vindicator and guardian of their historical rights; 2) to show not merely liberal historians but liberal politicians how valuable was the Negro and precisely what he had to contribute; 3) to whip up the Negroes themselves for the necessary heroism and martyrdom; and 4) to see to it that the Negroes, historically and politically, were kept in their place.

The man who carried out the line in regard to Negro history was Herbert Aptheker. In popular pamphlets Aptheker demonstrated many of the elementary facts, to a large degree suppressed, of Negro revolutionary struggle in the United States. Aptheker has also published a book and a collection of articles where the same subjects have been treated with a more scholarly apparatus. Altogether his writings have been the most effective weapons in the Stalinist propaganda armory among radicals, Negroes and Negro intellectuals in particular. Presumably among all intellectuals, the two books pass as Marxism. Yet in the work of a dozen years, Aptheker has never once stepped outside the bounds of the limits prescribed by Stalinism for Negroes—as manpower, as shock troops, and as deserving of "recognition." So organic to present-day Stalinism is this attitude and so Stalinized is Aptheker that he can find in his quite extensive explorations only what fits this pattern, infinitesimal as it may be; and he is blind to everything else, though it shouts for notice without benefit of research. The pattern shapes the structure of his work and the very style of his writing.

The Negro intellectuals and historians are indirectly and directly aware that something is wrong with the method and results of Aptheker's "Marxism." (See for example the article by Ernest Kaiser in *Phylon*, No. 4, 1948.) But they will need to grapple seriously with Marxism to penetrate to the corruption behind the facade of class struggle, conflicts of social systems, panegyrics to Negro heroism, etc., with which Aptheker generously sprinkles his writing. We propose to begin here by contrasting side by side the method of Marxism and the method of Aptheker. We shall begin with the subject which Aptheker has, so to speak, made his own, the question of slave insurrections.

SLAVE INSURRECTIONS

Negro slavery was more or less patriarchal so long as consumption was directed to immediate local needs. But in proportion as the export of cotton became of interest to the United States, patriarchal slavery was, in the words of Marx, "drawn into the whirlpool of an international market dominated by the capitalistic mode of production." The structure of production relations was thereby altered. By 1860 there were over 2,000 plantations each with over a hundred slaves. Division of labor increased. Slaves began to perform skilled labor, were hired out for wages. Slave production took on more and more the character of social labor. The slave revolts that began in 1800 were therefore of an entirely different character from those of the seventeenth and eighteenth century.

Gabriel's revolt in 1800 involved at least 1,000 and perhaps many thousands of slaves. Gabriel himself was a blacksmith. The insurrectionists had themselves made swords, bayonets, and cullets. So much for the new revolutionary forces. In a system of labor that is predominantly social, revolution and counter-revolution are closely intertwined. Though the revolt did *not* attract national attention, it impelled the slave owners to become declared enemies of the idea of gradual abolition, which had hitherto held sway among semi-liberal circles in the South.

Unrest grew with the economy and in 1817 the slave owners formed the

Colonization Society. Under the guise of philanthropy this powerful society aimed at creating and controlling all opinions about Negroes and slavery in the North. Its program was to deport all free Negroes to Africa. Free Negroes fought it undeviatingly from the start. Thus was the battle joined which was to end at Appomattox in 1865. The climax to this phase came in the next decade, 1820–1830.

This was one of the crucial decades in American history, the decade of transition from colonial America to nineteenth-century capitalism. Politically this took shape in the tumultuous democracy of Jackson. The first great slave revolt of the period is the revolt of Denmark Vesey. Most of Vesey's followers are urban artisans. They are determined never to "cringe to the whites." They are suspicious of the domestic slaves. The revolt failed, in 1824.

The sequence of dates from 1824 is very important. It is about this time that we have the first indication of an organized underground railroad. In 1826 is organized the Massachusetts General Colored Peoples Association. The free Negro had now entered definitively upon the political scene. Vesey had been a free Negro. The response of the slave owners was violent. Along with relentless persecution of the free Negroes in the South, they multiplied their efforts to expand the persecution to the North. They wished to silence the free Negro and to drive him out of the country altogether. In 1827 the Negroes published *Freedom's Journal*, the first Negro newspaper in the United States, and dedicated to the militant defense of Negro rights. The Colonization Society, determined to smash it, bought up John B. Russwurm, one of the junior editors of the paper; the paper had to suspend publication.

In 1828 David Walker laid his *Appeal* before the Massachusetts Association. The famous document called openly for slave insurrection. It was published in three editions and sold 50,000 copies in less than five years, some of which reached the South. Wrote a North Carolina newspaper:

> If Perkins' steam-gun had been charged with rattle snakes and shot into the midst of a flock of wild pigeons, the fluttering could not have been greater than has recently been felt in the eastern part of this state by a few copies of this perishable production. When an old Negro from Boston writes a book and sends it among us, the whole country is thrown into commotion.

Two states enacted laws prohibiting the circulation of incendiary publications and forbidding that slaves should be taught to read and write. For the second offense the penalty was death. For Walker dead $1,000 was offered, for Walker alive $10,000. The slave owners tried to extradite him from Boston. They failed. But they continued to terrorize free Negroes in the

South and instigated a terrible persecution of the free Negroes in the North, particularly in Cincinnati and other parts of Ohio, involving thousands.

The free Negroes published another paper called *The Rights of All* and the same leaders who had organized *Freedom's Journal* called together the first National Negro Convention in September 1830. William Lloyd Garrison's *Liberator* appeared in 1831. At that time the majority of white anti-slavery proponents were gradual abolitionists and supporters of the Colonization Society. Even Garrison supported the society. By their published arguments and by personal contact the free Negroes persuaded Garrison as to the true nature of the Colonization Society and Garrison began an international campaign of denunciation against this organization.

THE SIGNIFICANCE OF TURNER'S REVOLT

At this critical moment came the greatest of all Negro revolts, that of Nat Turner, a "mechanically gifted man." It failed, but it struck terror in all the South and startled the whole country. Walker's *Appeal* could be blamed but Walker was dead. Garrison, however, was alive. Overnight he and his obscure *Liberator* were made responsible for the uprising and became nationally famous. As Turner's was the last of the great revolts of the early nineteenth century, so it precipitated on a national scale an entirely new form of struggle.

This is no mere Negro history. It is the central line of the history of the United States. The Missouri Compromise took place in 1820. All sides, terrified by the abyss that had yawned over the Missouri struggle, decided to suppress all discussion of slavery (except along the poisonous lines of the Colonization Society). De Tocqueville and others noted the blight that had descended over free discussion *in the whole country*. It was this nationwide conspiracy of silence that the sequence of events from Vesey to Turner's revolt blasted wide open. The revolting slave, the persecuted free Negro, and the New England intellectual had got together and forced the nation to face the slavery question. When Garrison wrote "I will be heard," he was not being rhetorical. That was the first problem: to be heard. After Turner's revolt that problem was solved for Garrison.

A SUPERFICIAL TREATMENT

Now let us take Aptheker's treatment of this period in *The Negro in the Abolitionist Movement*, the section headed "Early Nineteenth Century." "The first generation of the nineteenth century witnessed a significant expansion in the anti-slavery activities of the Negro people which did much to prepare the ground for the tilling and harvesting that was to come from 1830 to the Civil War." We read on: "Among the individuals" was Peter Williams, Jr., a minister in New York City. He worked so hard that in 1834 he was appointed to the Board of Managers of the American Anti-Slavery Society, Garrison's organization. James Forton vigorously denounced slavery. "Negroes ever in the forefront" did "vital spadework" for the abolition movement. Reverend Nathanial Paul made "radical" speeches. Groups sprang up. David Walker published his *Appeal*. It was sent into the South and when discovered "caused great excitement." There were Negro newspapers which actually appeared before Garrison's *Liberator*. That is all there is to Aptheker's "Early Nineteenth Century."

But maybe in another pamphlet, *Negro Slave Revolts*, he deals seriously with the effects of the revolts? Not he. He finds that the year 1800 is the most important year in the history of American slave revolts. Why? "It is the year in which John Brown and Nat Turner were born, the year in which Vesey bought his freedom, and the year of Gabriel's conspiracy."

Between 1824 and 1831 there was the creation of a new movement in which Negroes and whites are in appearance separate but in essence unified. This was *not* the kind of unity of whites and Negroes which took place when Negroes joined Washington's army and became appendages to an already established revolutionary movement. The driving force in the formation of this new movement was the insurrectionary slave and the free Negro in opposition to the Southern slave owner.

In a lengthy chapter on the effects of these rebellions, Aptheker says: "At least one important effect of the slave rebellions is apparent. This is the added drive they directly gave to the abolitonist movement." But what he means is something far different from what we have described. For him, the revolts serve to "stimulate" the Northern abolitionists. Aptheker tells us that the slave owners were forever preaching of the docility and contentedness of the slave while "news of slaves conspiring and dying" *proved* the opposite. To this is added characteristically that John Brown was "inspired" and "influenced" by Nat Turner's revolt to strike his "noble and world-shaking blow against human bondage."

In *The Negro People in America* Aptheker attacks Gunnar Myrdal for not understanding the slave insurrections. He says that "above all" these rebellions "pricked the consciences" of Jefferson and Madison, "stimulated" anti-slavery feeling and served to "inspire" the abolitionists. He has a deep compulsion to play down the positive contributions of the Negroes in the developing events. Thus in "Buying Freedom," an article in the collection *To Be Free*, he says that the activities of the Negroes were "fundamental" to the abolition movement. But he immediately explains: "Each of these actions demonstrated the inequities of bondage and the deep desire of the Negro for liberation."

Aptheker sees the slaves, the mass, on the one side and the abolitionists on the other. He faithfully follows the Stalinist line of viewing the Negroes as manpower and shock troops. Cut away from seeing the binding revolutionary link, he is compelled to substitute inspiration as the tie. Hence the following: "And to this day, the selfless devotion of Gabriel's, Vesey's . . . bequeathed to lovers of liberty a memory that remains green . . . death of these was not in vain. No blow struck is ever wholly lost."

While it is legitimate and natural to derive inspiration from heroic martyrs, it becomes an absolutely false method when rhetoric is used as a substitute for the concrete role played by the Negroes in building the revolutionary movement. It has nothing in common with the Marxist method of theoretical analysis.

Turn now to Aptheker's more critical writings. In his book on *American Slave Revolts* he spends forty pages on what he calls "The Turner Cataclysm." You look in vain for any conception of what the Turner revolt meant to American revolutionary politics, of the close logical and historical connection between the revolutionary slaves and the revolutionary needs of American society.

MARXIST VIEW OF ABOLITION

Let us now sketch a Marxist analysis of the abolitionist movement. The abolitionist movement was an expression of revolutionary classes and groups. To the slaves, the free Negroes and the urban intelligentsia was added the Northwest farmers.

The concrete link and theoretical axis is the underground railroad. One road ran through the Ohio of the small farmers who could see across the river the effects of slavery. Another road ran though the Eastern seaboard states. In farming areas as well as in the towns of the Eastern states the free Negroes at various times lived in daily fear. They were beaten up and murdered; their houses, churches, and schools were burnt; escaped slaves were caught and returned; free Negroes were kidnapped and sold into slavery.

Slave owners and slaves battled for the support of the petty bourgeoisie in town and country. (The working class came in much later but when it did, its intervention was decisive.) Now that slavery was no longer a closed question, the slave owners worked through their innumerable and powerful Northern contacts to drive the free Negroes out of the United States. The slaves, learning from Turner's failure, sent a never-ending stream of representatives north to the free Negroes and through them to the abolition movement, supplying it with revolutionary personnel and revolutionary *politics*. This question of fugitive slaves was the rock on which all attempts at compromise between North and South were shattered.

The first crisis of radical abolitionism came from the farmers. In the 1830s a great revivalist movement came out of the West moving eastward to New York and Philadelphia. It embraced abolitionism. But unlike the drunkard, the prison inmate, the Sabbath-breaker, and the girl who had sinned, the slave was a member of a social class, a class which had signified that it stood for radical, i.e., revolutionary abolition.

Garrison and his radicalism now personified abolition. He beat off two attempts to supplant him by organizations with watered-down policy. His most precious support came from the free Negroes, attested repeatedly by Garrison himself and the efforts of his rivals to win them away.

The radicalism of Garrison was now a danger to social peace. The depression and the decline of the religious fervor gave conservative abolitionists their chance. They succeeded in decentralizing the movement. They proposed to tone down "immediate" emancipation; they sought to substitute for the New England intellectuals the leadership of the regular clergy; they sought to exclude women. The unutterably degraded status of Negro women in the South and the activities of free Negro women in the North had helped to bring into the movement numbers of white petty-bourgeois women, stirred also by their own grievances. On the question of women being allowed in the movement, Garrison, the New England intellectuals, the women, and the free Negroes kept abolitionism radical.

In 1840 James Birney split the movement. He "politicized" abolitionism, directing it toward New York philanthropists and other "sympathetic" bourgeois who detested radicalism. In 1840 this kind of politics was a foolhardy venture and the Liberty party was a total failure. Garrison and the New England intellectuals, for various abstract and utopian reasons, were militantly anti-political. In this crisis Garrison again owed his ideological and organizational victory to the support of free Negroes. They were not anti-political; many of them were actively engaged in state politics. But they rallied to the principled radical abolitionism of Garrison.

CONFLICTS AMONG ABOLITIONISTS

However after this victory Garrison declined and, to quote a sympathetic biographer, for years seemed to live "in a sort of waking trance." In the difficult early days his intransigence had been invaluable, and had saved the movement. Now that slavery was a national issue, he had neither program nor perspective. Feeling the need for a new orientation he now preached disunion with the slave South on the ground that the Constitution was a pro-slavery document.

Others beside Garrison came forward to lift abolitionism to a higher plane. The free Negroes began a counter-offensive to the slaveholders, raiding the South to help slaves escape. Henry Highland Garnett, a Negro who republished Walker's *Appeal*, in 1843 presented to a Negro convention a call for slave insurrection. It was defeated by only one vote. Wendell Phillips by degrees assumed the virtual leadership of the Garrisonians. He shared Garrison's theory of disunion, but was only formally in agreement with his pacifism. He preached abolitionism with such philosophical breadth, oratical power, and denunciation of slaveholders and their allies that the general effect was profoundly revolutionary.

But the greatest figure in this period was Frederick Douglass. In 1843 at the Negro convention he had opposed Garnett's call for insurrection, being still a Garrisonian. But he split with the Garrisonians and later joined the new Free Soil party. With fierce and devastating polemic he repudiated Garrison's disunionism and defended the revolutionary and anti-slavery implications of the Constitution at a time when that document and with it the American revolutionary tradition was under fire both North and South. In 1850 came the Fugitive Slave Act over which the country seemed to explode. The fighting over Kansas, John Brown's raid, and the other revolutionary events of that period were supported by the continuous undercurrents of revolt in the South. The above is a rigidly stylized account of a highly complex movement. But this much is certain. What we are watching here is the growth of the revolutionary movement from 1800 to 1860.

From Gabriel through Turner to militant abolitionism we have one road for the abolition of slavery. The parliamentarians, the compromisers, the gradual abolitionists, the maneuvers in Washington pointed to another road. Marxist history consists always in contrasting these two and showing how a great social conflict is finally resolved along the lines of the despised, rejected, persecuted movement and not along the line of parliamentarians and petty-bourgeois reformists. In any history of 1830–1860 the role of the Negro for purely objective and social reasons is paramount.

Now for Aptheker. Does he mention in his pamphlet on Negro abolitionists the crisis with Birney? No. Does he mention Henry Highland Garnett? He does, once—to say that he was "present" at a convention. Does he mention the resounding split between Garrison and Douglass? Not a line, not a word. There is not the slightest hint that the Negro was anything more than an appendage, a very valuable appendage, to what Aptheker considers the abolitionist movement to have been. His whole conception is that the abolitionist movement was predominately white, and Negroes joined it. In fact if you could imagine a writer being given an assignment to write about Negroes in the abolition movement and to *exclude* every example of their *political* activity, then the result could easily be Aptheker's pamphlet.

It is possible to say that Aptheker is writing a popular account of Negro abolitionists. But he has also written an essay "Militant Abolitionism" in his volume *To Be Free*. It is the only essay in all his writings on these subjects where he does not treat Negroes specifically. It is thirty-three pages long and has appended to it eleven pages of notes in fine print, taking up 105 references from the text.

What does it deal with? Practically the whole essay treats of discussions by abolitionist figures about the abstract question of resistance or nonresistance. At a meeting in Boston in April 1835, the question is submitted for discussion. Sides are taken. By 1841 Garrit Smith has moved to the point of urging slaves to flee. One Spooner had a plan for slave rebellion, sent it to leading abolitionists, and received and preserved nine replies. Such-and-such a Negro advocated insurrection, such-and-such a white abolitionist did or did not. So page after page.

We shall understand this evasive emptiness best by examining a speech of Wendell Phillips at an abolitionist meeting on April 12, 1852. The question was: What should fugitive slaves do when threatened with arrest? Wendell Phillips proposed: 1) that unless fugitives were prepared to take the lives of any officer who tried to arrest them, they should leave the United States; 2) that in every town vigilance committees should be formed which "would avail themselves fearlessly, according to their best judgement, of all the means God and Nature have put into their hands, to see that substantial justice be done." Note the "fearlessly" and "all the means." The quoted section, as Phillips's speech showed, was a direct call to action.

Garrison proposed an amendment. It must be quoted in full:

> *Resolved*, That if "resistance to tyrants," by bloody weapons "is obedience to God," and if our Revolutionary Fathers were justified in wading through blood to freedom and independence, then every fugitive slave is justified in arming himself for protection and defence, —in taking the life of every marshal, commissioner, or other person who attempts to reduce him to bondage; and the millions who are clanking their chains on our soil find ample warrant in rising en masse, and asserting their right to liberty; at whatever sacrifice of the life of their oppressors.
>
> *Resolved*, That the State in which no fugitive slave can remain in safety, and from which he must flee in order to secure his liberty in another land, is to be held responsible for all the crimes and horrors which cluster about the slave system and the slave trade, —and that state is the Commonwealth of Massachusetts.

Phillips, with gracious deference to Garrison—but with what Marx calls his "iron determination"—rejected the amendment and he said everything when he said that it "seems . . . too ambiguous; it contents itself with announcing an important principle, but suggests nothing, advises nothing."

What is the value of Aptheker's lengthy account of who was for resistance in principle and who against, except that he does not even understand the principled question. In that very speech Phillips said that he was an opponent of a slave revolution in the South only because he did not think it would succeed. If the hour should ever come—"God hasten it"—when a national crisis gave the slave an opportunity, he would say to every slave, "Strike now for freedom!" The applause was "long-continued and deafening." This attitude to revolution permeates the speeches of Phillips. Garrison's resolution showed how complicated a thing was this whole abolitionist pacifism. When he said "immediate unconditional emancipation on the soil," when his admitted aim was to goad the South into madness, slave owners and innumerable other people understood that this program was what mattered and not Garrison's nonresistance and "moral suasion." Furthermore "moral suasion" as Garrison practiced it meant such unbridled denunciation not only of slave owners but of all who were not for immediate emancipation that the effect was and could not have been otherwise than divisive and revolutionary. At a meeting after John Brown's death, Garrison in the course of his speech asked how many nonresistants were in the room. Among many thousands present only two or three stood up.

Wendell Phillips said of the abolition movement that it was the first genuine American movement and the first that spoke with a native voice— all previous American politics had borne the stamp of Europe. It was one of the most profound observations this great revolutionary habitually made. It is fascinating to see how even while some abolitionists theoretically enunciated and advocated "moral suasion" *empirically* the movement met every obstacle with a determination that stopped at nothing; and with casuistry and at other times with no respect for principle or logic, continually exceeded the bounds of the accepted theory.

This is one of the most difficult but one of the most important aspects of the movement. Aptheker, except for a characteristically academic footnote in *American Slave Revolts*, has no understanding of this and he cannot even begin to probe this vital question because the most uncompromising advocates and practitioners of direct action and rebellion were free Negroes and fugitive slaves.

THE NEGRO MOVEMENT

Aptheker knows very well that to speak of militant abolitionism is to pose immediately the question of Negro abolitionism. But the inescapable superficiality of his treatment is evidenced by the fact that nowhere does he treat of the great split between Douglass on one side, and Phillips and Garrison on the other. He omits the continuous conflicts between whites and Negroes. There is no word about the fact that Garrison opposed all formation of Negro organizations and objected even to Negroes publishing a paper.

Aptheker gives no hint that the Negro conventions were political conventions always, where the participants were aligned for and against "moral suasion," for and against the Liberty party, the Free Soil party, etc. In the early days the richer Negroes opposed special Negro demands and the treating of Negro problems as a Negro question; they wanted Negroes to demand equal rights as citizens. They were overwhelmingly defeated. It is these Negro organizations which, as organizations, passed the most revolutionary resolutions about resistance and rebellion, reprinted the revolutionary writings of Walker, etc.

Aptheker knows this too. But apart from a reference to the convention at which Garnett spoke (and this could not be avoided), Aptheker finds no room for this in his text. It appears only in a reference note on page 205 of *To Be Free*. This cannot be accidental.

Aptheker cannot break through the theoretical vise in which he is enclosed. He sees the Negro organizations essentially as early versions of the Stalinist Negro Congress, Southern Welfare Association, etc., which have no politics of their own but exist to corral Negroes and bring them into the popular front coalition in which the Stalinists are at the moment interested.

What *does* Aptheker write about in his *The Negro in the Abolitionist Movement* and why? This we shall take up in the next article.

NOVEMBER 1949

PART TWO

In the last article, we showed: 1) that from 1826 to 1831 the Negro people, slave and free, being locked in mortal combat with the slave owners, were the driving force of what became the political movement of abolitionism; 2) that Herbert Aptheker's whole account shows that he sees the historical role of Negroes essentially as predecessors of the National Negro Congress and other Stalinist Negro organizations, that is to say, as groups whose sole function was to organize Negroes as appendages to the anti-slavery coalition. Thus Aptheker reverses completely the political relation of the Negro slaves and free Negroes to the other revolutionary classes.

This becomes absolutely clear when he touches what he calls "The Pre-Civil War Generation" (*The Negro in the Abolitionist Movement*). He lists conventions, meetings, articles, speeches, etc., that occupy three pages (pp. 36–39). Never once is there the slightest reference to the political perspectives or political line of any one of these organizations, groups or individuals. Just as the Stalinists view the function of the Negroes (and the proletariat) today as being one of abandoning all independent political activity and being simply "anti-Fascist," following docilely behind the CP, so it is sufficient that the Negroes in those days were "anti-slavery," following docilely behind the abolitionists.

We must follow Aptheker's account closely. First, the Negroes meet and organize Negro resistance. Then, in addition to this, they organize "encouragement and assistance for progressive forces." Thus we are told that certain Philadelphia Negroes, only two months after the launching of the *Liberator*, met and pledged their support to it, to which is added: "Such gatherings were common in various cities throughout the paper's life." The *Liberator* and the abolitionists over here; the Negroes over there, pledging support. Under the heading of "United Struggles," we read that Negroes "did not, of course, restrict themselves to independent work but struggled side by side with white people in the common effort."

How did the Negroes struggle side by side? These Negroes "wrote many letters to Garrison, giving not only moral stimulation but also . . . money and subscriptions." We are informed that "contributions by Negroes in that paper and other abolitionist publications were exceedingly common." Again we can see here the sharp division between the *Liberator*, abolitionism, and the Negroes.

Now Aptheker takes a leap. He gives us examples of what the Negroes wrote. "The *Liberator* for February 12, 1831, gave a third of its space to articles by two Philadelphia Negroes, a call to an anti-Colonization mass meeting in Boston." Aptheker notes an account of a similar meeting held earlier in New York. He then informs us that these contributions of Negroes to the paper are "fairly typical of the entire thirty-five volumes of the paper."

The observant reader cannot help being startled and can very well ask himself: Is this all that the Negroes wrote about in a paper that lasted from 1831 to 1864? He need not be disturbed. Aptheker's account is an incredible falsification. But let us continue with more of it. He says that the record of the proceedings of the abolitionist organizations "is studded with accounts of, or contributions by, Negroes." Aptheker is always making statements of this kind. But the moment you examine what he says concretely, a different picture appears.

Here, for instance, are the examples chosen at random by Aptheker. The 1849 meeting of one of these organizations was opened by an invocation by the Reverend Sam R. Wood and "the entertainment was furnished by four Luca boys, Negro youngsters, who sang an anti-slavery song called *Car of Emancipation*." Aptheker describes for us a Negro lady at a meeting who said that she had heard of the abolitionists as inciters to violence, knaves, fools, etc., but she had been sitting and listening and "she knew the Lord would bless them for they were good and righteous folk." It has been necessary to give almost word for word Aptheker's account. For it represents as vicious and subtle a piece of anti-Negro historical writing as it is possible to find and infinitely more dangerous than the chauvinism of the Bourbon historian.

THE REAL FACTS OF HISTORY

Any unbiased person who spends a few hours looking through the *Liberator* and other abolitionist papers, and the accounts of abolitionist societies, will see that they are studded with innumerable political contributions by Negroes to some of the greatest political conflicts that have ever taken place in the United States.

Here are only a few taken at random.

On June 8, 1849, Frederick Douglass made the open call for a slave insurrection in the South. Garrison, the pacifist, was sitting on the platform. The whole speech appeared in the *Liberator*. At the World Convention against Slavery held in London in June 1840, among the delegates representing the United States were Garrison and Charles Lenox Remond, a Negro. The World Convention objected to women being seated and Remond with three other American delegates sat amongst the rejected women and fought the issue through to the end.

During the intense excitement generated by the 1850 Compromise, the anniversary meeting of the American Anti-Slavery Society fell due. The notorious Captain Isaiah Rynders, with a band of hoodlums who had the backing of the metropolitan papers and official society, sat in the gallery determined to break up the convention. Garrison's incendiary speech started the disturbance. Rynders shouted from the organ loft and then marched down the aisle, followed by his band. But as Garrison's biographer tells us, on that day, Rynders and his men were "quite vanquished by the wit, repartee, and eloquence of Frederick Douglass, Dr. Furness, and Reverend Samuel R. Ward whom Wendell Phillips described as so Black that 'when he shut his eyes you could not see him.'"

In the *Liberator* and other abolitionist papers and in abolitionist proceedings, you will find the great debates upon the U.S. Constitution, the reports of tours at home and abroad by Douglass, Remond, Wells Brown, Douglass's defense of having purchased his freedom, the question of political action versus "moral suasion."

At the May 1855 meeting of the American Anti-Slavery Society, Douglass attacked Garrison's theory of the U.S. Constitution. The New York *Daily News* reports the meeting as follows: "A grand and terrific set-to came off between Abby Kelly Foster, Garrison, and Frederick Douglass, who defended the Union while claiming rights for his people. He was insulted, interrupted and denounced by the Garrison Cabinet, but stood amid them and overtopped them like a giant among pigmies."

At the end of the Civil War, when Garrison wanted to disband his society, Douglass, Remond, and Wendell Phillips led the attack against him and insisted that the Society should continue until at least the Negroes got the vote.

We cannot go here into the history of the abolition movement. But enough has been said to show the political mentality of a writer who in this mass of material selects a call for a meeting as typical of thirty-five years of Negro contributions to the *Liberator* and finds that Negro parsons giving invocations, Negro boys singing, and old Negro women blessing abolitionists are the most characteristic aspects of Negro contributions to the struggle.

SUBTLE FORMS OF PREJUDICE

This is no ordinary racial prejudice. It is something far worse. It is political method which *compels* the writer to place the Negroes in a subordinate category and at whatever sacrifice of historical fact *keep them there*. Whatever does not fit into this scheme must go out. Aptheker cannot escape the consequences of his political ideas. Any history of the Civil War which does not base itself upon the Negroes, slave and free, as the *subject* and *not the object* of politics, is ipso facto a Jim Crow history. That is why even the Negro writers, with all the good work that they have done and their subjective desire to elevate the Negro's past, seldom escape paternalism or apologies—both of them forms of white chauvinism; paternalism, an inflation, and apologetics a deflation of the subtle chauvinistic poison. But these and the carelessness or traditional ignorance of liberals can be fought and corrected. You cannot correct Stalinist history without destroying Stalinism.

To keep his history within the confines of his politics, Aptheker must not only omit, he must falsify. We cannot pursue *all* his falsifications. What we have to do, however, is to show the thoroughly reactionary anti-Negro, anti-proletarian, and even anti-liberal ideas which stage by stage emerge from the encomiums to the Negroes with which he plasters his writings.

One of the greatest lessons of the abolitionist movement is the way in which (despite constant accusations of racial chauvinism) the political representatives of the classes, while in perpetual conflict with each other, achieved a racial unity, cooperation and solidarity unknown in the United States up to that time and afterwards, until the formation of the CIO. While it is possible formally and for special purposes to separate Negroes from whites, any account of whites or Negroes in the abolitionist struggle is totally false unless it shows this integration. Aptheker, while perpetually talking about the "united struggles" of Negroes and whites, destroys this precious heritage.

When Douglass toured in England, he made a vast number of friends for the movement and for himself as a representative of it. Money was subscribed to pay for his freedom, and a substantial sum was given him for the purpose of starting a paper of his own. He finally did so, but the expense was great, he had to mortgage his house, and he got heavily into debt.

At this time one of his English friends, Miss Julia Griffiths, and her sister came to the United States, and settled down in Rochester, taking over the management of Douglass's paper to leave him free to write and carry on his general political activities. A woman of literary ability and great energy, she not only made a success of the management of the paper but in her spare time edited *Autographs for Freedom*. To characterize Douglass's article in this publication as an example of how Negroes contribute to "the progressive forces" is to show how alien to the actual struggle is the mentality which Stalinism brings to this striking but characteristic episode in the history of abolitionism.

DOUGLASS IN THE FOREFRONT

Let us continue with this aspect of Douglass's career, for Aptheker's treatment of Douglass more than anything else betrays his conception of the role of the Negro in politics. In the struggle for women's emancipation as in all the causes of the day, Douglass was in the forefront. His paper, *Frederick Douglass' Paper*, was the official organ of the Free Soil party in New York State. At the second convention of that party he was elected secretary by acclamation. At the National Loyalist Convention after the Civil War, sponsored by the Republican party, Douglass represented the city of Rochester. The people of Rochester asked him to stand for Congress as a Republican and Theodore Weld made a special visit to Rochester to persuade him. But he refused. Here obviously was no "mere" Negro appendage to the abolitionist movement.

Now to return to Aptheker. Undoubtedly conscious of the fact that this account so far had been terribly lacking, Aptheker pulls out all his stops when he comes to the Negro propagandists of abolitionism. This, he says, is "the most vital part" of the story, and he is correct, it is the most vital part of *his* story. Again he tosses in one of his misleading phrases about the "decisive role of the Negroes." Close examination, however, shows that as usual here where the phrasing is most radical, the political content is correspondingly reactionary. To see this we must transfer ourselves to the abolition period and try to catch some of its social atmosphere.

In the middle of the nineteenth century the slave owners sought to prove that the Negroes loved slavery, and in any case that Negroes were no men. Therefore when escaped slaves denounced the institution with eloquence and logic, they had tremendous effect. Aptheker quotes Garrison on this. But there was another side to this question. Escaped slaves who gained some education, insofar as they formed a group apart from others, carried on their own political activity. As we have repeated, the fundamental struggle within abolitionism was the struggle represented by these against the humanitarian tendency of the New England intellectuals.

"Give us the facts—and leave the philosophy to us," said a Garrisonian to the aspiring young Douglass. Douglass was to say later that these white abolitionists thought that they "owned him." Later Garrison fought Douglass with extreme ferocity, not only on his politics but on the very idea that Douglass should have a paper of his own. There were all kinds of conflicts in the abolition movement on the chauvinist issue. Yet it must be remembered that Douglass, who stood no nonsense on any slights upon him as a Negro, revered Garrison to the end; to the extent that the accusations of chauvinism were true, they were essentially political; and Garrison's character, reputation, and achievements were such that they could stand the charges, not only today but then.

Aptheker cannot claim similar consideration. The pernicious character of Stalinist politics is revealed by the fact that in the middle of the twentieth century, when even some of the reactionary Southern senators have dropped the argument of organic Negro inferiority, Aptheker's whole argumentation remains within the confines of the nineteenth-century debate. That is why for him, the Negro propagandists are "the most vital part" of the story. Like the Garrisonian who spoke to Douglass, Aptheker has no use for Negro philosophy, i.e., Negro politics. The escaped Negroes by "their bearing, courage and intelligence" were the most "devastating anti-slavery forces." This is the politics which sees the sharecropper's contribution essentially as a recital of his wrongs.

Aptheker does not merely mention the suitability of the ex-slaves as propagandists and then pass on. This is his main theme. "Had none of these people existed but one, his existence and participation in the Abolitionist movement would justify the assertion that the Negro's role therein was decisive. That man is Frederick Douglass. . . ." This is what Aptheker means by the role of the Negroes—not their politics, but their heroic deaths, the contributions of money, songs, and stray articles to the *Liberator*, and abolitionist agitation. Thus he no sooner touches Douglass than he defiles him. He says that Douglass "from his first public speech in 1841 to his organizing and recruiting activities during the war against the slavocracy was the voice of America's millions of slaves." Completely one-sided and therefore totally wrong.

From 1841 to his recruiting for the Northern army, Douglass was the voice of the American Revolution. Stage by stage he embodied its development until in 1860 he gave critical support to the Republican party while defiantly proclaiming he was still a radical abolitionist. It was precisely when the bourgeoisie took over that Douglass became primarily a leader of the Negroes. (And at this same time also, Wendell Phillips, who had been for a time eclipsed by Douglass, rose to his greatest heights and spoke superbly for a revolutionary conduct of the war and for a revolutionary settlement of the Southern question.)

QUESTION OF RACIAL EQUALITY

Had that been all Aptheker had to say, it would have been bad enough. But Aptheker then spends almost a page on Douglass as follows: He was a magnificent figure of a man, impregnable, incorruptible, scars on his back, African prince, majestic in his wrath, grand in his physical proportions. A tailor who heard him in England had never been so moved in his life, etc., etc. Why all this? Why, when there has not been a word about Douglass's politics?

Aptheker gives the show away when he quotes a famous incident in Douglass's career. Captain Rynders once baited Douglass with the taunt that Negroes were monkeys. Douglass turned to him and asked him: "Am I a man?" Aptheker relates: "the effect was nothing short of stupendous." No doubt it was. The reader, however, cannot help noting, after all these "African prince" paragraphs, that the effect on Aptheker in 1940 is still stupendous.

American racial prejudice is usually crude but at the same time can be a very subtle thing. To understand how unhealthy is Aptheker's ignoring of Douglass's politics and his excitement at the Rynders episode, we must see how Douglass himself treated the question.

Douglass personally fought race prejudice wherever he met it. But in discussion he treated the purely racial attacks of his enemies not only with counter-arguments but with a certain humorous contempt. Thus in this very debate he switched the problem aside by saying if he was a monkey, his father was a white man, and therefore Rynders was his half-brother. Twice he called Rynders his half-brother. On another occasion, after speaking very movingly in England on this question of Negroes being considered monkeys in the United States, he broke the tension by relating that a few days before a big dog had come up to him and stared him in the face and, said Douglass, I could see in his eyes that he recognized humanity.

He used to relate how when sleeping space was limited on the benches aboard ship, he would simply show his face and say to newcomers, "I am a Negro," hoping they would go along. But one man said to him: "Negro be damned, you move down." So concluded Douglass, my being black is no longer of any use to me.

Some hecklers who asked him if it was true that his wife was a white woman were treated to a long discourse as to the irrelevance of the question, what business was it of theirs, etc., and were constantly led up to the point where they expected him to make the admission. He never admitted anything but soon went on with his speech, leaving them to find out afterwards that his wife (his first wife) was Negro.

This sort of thing occurs in many speeches and was obviously habitual with him. The reason is not far to seek. Douglass was not only a sensitive

Negro, but a highly political person. And despite the powerful social pressure, he would not allow *this* question to occupy any status more than was absolutely necessary. He dealt with it, brushed it aside often with a smile, and then went on to politics.

Exactly the opposite is Aptheker's Stalinist method. The politics he ignores, and therefore reaches the most genuine pitch of enthusiasm when he is proving that Negroes were not only men but some Negro slaves were marvelous men and did wonderful work side by side with "the progressive forces." This was not merely popular writing. A portion of this pamphlet appeared in the Stalinist theoretical journal *Science and Society*, replete with footnotes and references.

ANTI-FASCIST NOT ANTI-CAPITALIST

Aptheker's politics not only in relation to Negroes but in relation to the American workers is pitched at the same lowest level. He is busy proving to the American proletariat, to labor bureaucrats and liberals that the Negro is a man and a brother, will struggle hard, and can produce many brilliant men who will speak *for the Negro* far more effectively than any white man can. At the same time he is offering to the Negro leaders place at the table of the anti-Fascist coalition. Aptheker by the way does not hide this. Here is the conclusion of his *Negro Slave Revolts*:

> An awareness of its history should give the modern Negro added confidence and courage in his heroic present-day battle for complete and perfect equality with all other American citizens. And it should make those other Americans eager and proud to grasp the hands of the Negro and march forward with him against their common oppressors—against the industrial and financial overlords and the plantation oligarchs who today stand in the way of liberty, equality, and prosperity.
>
> That unity between the white and Negro masses was necessary to overthrow nineteenth century slavery. That same unity is necessary now to defeat twentieth-century slavery—to defeat Fascism.

See how swiftly in the last paragraph capitalism is pushed aside and fascism substituted for it. This is vital to the whole scheme. To talk about the overthrow of *capitalism* would destroy the concept of the anti-Fascist coalition, it would bring onto the scene independent proletarian politics and independent Negro politics. Aptheker maintains an unrelenting hostility to any such manifestation among Negroes either today or in the Civil War.

Aptheker, writing on "Militant Abolitionism" in the *Journal of Negro History* (Vol. 26, p. 463) had to refer to Douglass's call for slave insurrection. That a Negro should consciously call for insurrection! God forbid! Aptheker writes that Douglass *"found himself saying . . ."* The magnificent African prince could do much, but that he could stand on a platform and out of his own head consciously speak of insurrection, that Aptheker simply could not stand. He makes it into a visitation from on high. Douglass just "found himself saying" it. In *To Be Free*, where the article reappears, the damning phrase is omitted, but Aptheker cannot get rid of his whole reactionary conception of Negroes in American history which this phrase embodies without withdrawing every line he has written.

STALINIST SLEIGHT-OF-HAND

Stalinism tries to manipulate history as a sleight-of-hand man manipulates cards. But unlike the conjurer, a stern logic pushes Stalinism in an ever more reactionary direction. For five years Aptheker covered up his anti-Negro concepts with constant broad statements about the "decisive character" of slave insurrections, Negro agitators, etc., in the Civil War and the period preceding it. In 1946, however, in *The Negro People in America*, Aptheker broke new ground. He put forward a new theory that at one stroke made a wreck of all that he had said before. Let his own words speak.

> It was the development of increased agitation on the part of non-slaveholding whites prior to the Civil War for the realization of the American creed that played a major part in provoking the desperation that led the slaveholders to take up arms.

Upon the flimsiest scraps of evidence, the theory is elaborated that it was the withholding of democracy from nonslaveholding whites that pushed the South to the Civil War:

> In terms of practice, as concerns the mass of the white people of the South, this anti-democratic philosophy was everywhere implemented. The property qualifications for voting and office-holding, the weighing of the legislature to favor slaveholding against non-slaveholding counties, the inequitable taxation system falling most heavily on mechanics' tools and least heavily on slaves, the whole system of economic, social and educational preferment for the possessors of slaves, and the organized, energetic, and partially successful struggles carried on against this system by the non-slaveholding whites form—outside of the response of the Negroes to enslavement—the actual content of the South's internal history for the generation preceding the Civil War.

It is clear that only at the last minute Aptheker remembered the slaves and threw in the phrase about their "response." Historically this is a crime. The nonslaveholding whites who supposedly pushed the South into the Civil War were not in any way democrats. They were small planters and city people who formed a rebellious but reactionary social force, hostile to the big planters, the slaves, and the democratically minded farmers in the nonplantation regions.

What particular purpose this new development is to serve does not concern us here. What is important, however, is its logical identity with the hostility to Negro radicalism and independent Negro politics which has appeared in Aptheker's work from the very beginning up to this climax—pushing the Negroes aside for the sake of nonslaveholding whites in the South.

However fair may be the outside of Stalinist history and politics, however skillful may be the means by which its internal corruption is disguised, inevitably its real significance appears. There is no excuse for those who allow themselves to be deceived by it. For all interested in this sphere, it is a common duty, whatever differences may exist between us, to see to it that the whole Stalinist fakery on Negro history be thoroughly exposed for what it really is.

DECEMBER 1949

Afterword

American Civilization and World Revolution: C. L. R. James in the United States, 1938–1953 and Beyond

If there is any period one would desire to be born in, is it not the age of Revolution; when the old and the new stand side by side and admit of being compared; when the energies of all are searched by fear and hope; when the historic glories of the old can be compensated by the rich possibilities of the new era? This time, like all times, is a very good one, if we but know what to do with it.

—Ralph Waldo Emerson,
"The American Scholar" (1837)

Shakespeare and Lenin, cricket and Victorian literature, Hegel's *Science of Logic* and wildcat auto strikes, Pan-Africanism and the democratic polis of Greek antiquity—a unique combination of interests unfolds across the decades of C. L. R. James's life and work. From book to book—sometimes even from page to page—the perspective shifts among widely separated regions of experience and activity. But this is no mere eclecticism. James's writings display something all too rare: a genuinely open and responsive intelligence, a cosmopolitan sensibility which, although intensely concerned with the past and with cultural traditions, also possesses an acute and visionary feeling for "the future in the present" as it emerges from the struggles of ordinary people around the globe for a better life. Over the course of more than half a century, C. L. R. James devoted his considerable gifts to carrying out what the young Karl Marx had called the "task" of the revolutionary intellectual: "to drag the old world into the full light of day and to give positive shape to the new one" in birth.[1]

It has become a commonplace of sorts to call James a Renaissance man. To appreciate just how fitting the appellation is, we have to look more closely at that age and the variety of personality it produced. In writing about the Renaissance, Frederich Engels said:

209

The heroes of that time had not yet come under the servitude of the division of labor, the restricting effects of which, with their production of one-sidedness, we so often notice in their successors. But what is especially characteristic of them is that they almost all pursue their lives and activities in the midst of the contemporary movements, in the practical struggle; they take sides and join in the fight, one by speaking and writing, another with the sword, many with both. Hence the fullness and force of character that makes them complete human beings.[2]

It was the birth time of capitalism. Engels calls it "the greatest progressive revolution that mankind had so far experienced." Every page of James's work reflects the conviction that a transformation on the scale of the Renaissance was under way in the twentieth century.

Born in 1901 on a small island at the margin of the British Empire (a vast colonial system long since dismantled when he died in 1989), C. L. R. James lived through the decline of one world order and the emergence, from its ruins, of another. He threw himself into "the midst of the contemporary movements, in the practical struggle." And his work as a historian and a theorist seeks to establish connections among the revolutionary traditions in those parts of the world—Africa, Europe, and America—linked by the slave trade during the earliest stages of the capitalist mode of production. For "the greatest progressive revolution that mankind had so far experienced" (the transition from feudalism to capitalism) had also been the greatest disaster in the history of Africa and the Americas. The conflicts and contradictions that structured the modern world at its birth returned, now, in the terminal phase of capitalist development. In his roles as activist and intellectual, James sought to recount that history of domination and (more importantly) of resistance, so that the logic of contemporary social movements could emerge with greater force and clarity.

It was difficult to take the measure of James's work during his lifetime. The first comprehensive study of his career, Paul Buhle's study of "the artist as revolutionary," appeared only shortly before his death.[3] Tributes published since then have emphasized the variety of James's accomplishments. They testify to the depth and range of his influence among diverse audiences throughout the Caribbean, Africa, Europe, and North America. But in spite of this posthumous acclaim, the full extent of his activity has by no means been recognized or appreciated. One may refer to book after book on African-diaspora politics, or the history of the Left in the United States during the twentieth century, without ever coming across a reference to James. And a significant number of his writings remain completely unknown, even to those most concerned with the fields James explores.

Consider, for instance, the essays assembled in this volume, originally published during James's first stay in the United States (1938–1953). Except for "The Revolutionary Answer to the Negro Problem in the United States," none has ever been reprinted.[4] Several are overlooked in even the most comprehensive bibliographies of his work.[5] These writings have not so much been ignored, as simply disappeared from view. Taken together, they reveal dimensions of James's work seldom known even to his enthusiasts: James as revolutionary journalist, as popularizer of history and theory, as Marxist organization man. The editors hope that the present collection may win James new audiences—especially among readers concerned with the history of African-American revolutionary traditions and those interested in the anti-Stalinist legacy of democratic-communist thought and politics.

The experience of reading these political essays may prove jolting for someone trained to the cadences and protocols of contemporary Marxist discourse—so much of it produced and circulated largely within the academy. James writes clearly and even simply. There is no finely modulated equivocation, no subtle pursuit of nuances. Footnotes do appear, but not many. Arguments are presented in a forthright and often very polemical fashion. Some of James's most ambitious projects are sketched, or alluded to, in the course of his journalistic activity. Occasionally, the style does reach for a rhetorical grace note. Many of those who heard James lecture recount his gifts as a speaker; and there is at times in his prose, as with Trotsky's, something oratorical about the phrasing. (The final paragraph of "The Revolutionary Answer" is, I think, exemplary in this respect.) His main priority was to be accessible. Each text was meant as an intervention in the immediate political conjuncture, which James considered to be one of immanent and radical social transformation.

But if the writing itself is clear, the circumstances in which James wrote are not. Until recently, the reader looking for information on the context of James's work during this period could find little help from scholarly publications.[6] The Introduction by Paul Le Blanc supplies the first accurate and thoroughly documented account of James's political and organizational trajectory through the U.S. Trotskyist movement. Also of value is Kent Worcester's comparative study of the development of James's political ideas amid the various national contexts in which he was active.[7] A manuscript James drafted in 1950, *American Civilization*, will be published at about the same time as the present volume.[8] All of this material serves to enhance the suggestiveness of his political essays. In the following pages, I want to approach them with an eye to some implications not readily visible, but which acquire more significance as one reads James's American writings against the grain of their previous obscurity.

I

When he arrived in the United States during the final weeks of 1938—for a lecture tour, before the recommencing of the cricket season the following May—C. L. R. James might well have expected he would return to England once his visa expired at the end of six months. He had marked out a small but distinguished place as a literary and political figure in the years since leaving the West Indies to establish himself as a writer in the metropolitan center of the empire. James drew recognition for a pamphlet arguing *The Case for West Indian Self-Government* (1933), published under the imprint of Virginia and Leonard Woolf's press, as well as for his novel *Minty Alley* (1936). A larger public knew his graceful writing on cricket for the *Manchester Guardian* and the *Glasgow Herald*. In 1936, he made a first venture as playwright. Although *Toussaint-Louverture* was a fairly "talky" drama (worked up, rather too directly, from material gathered during his research into the Haitian slave revolt), nonetheless public interest in it was heightened by the appearance on stage of both the author and the American actor Paul Robeson.[9] A role for a black performer in serious drama was quite rare.

In addition to his writing, James was active in politics. He served as a prominent spokesman for the British Trotskyists and became involved as well with the French section of the movement. In 1938, he attended the founding conference of the Fourth International as a delegate. James also served as the coordinator for a network of independence-minded Africans and West Indians, some of whom later took a prominent place in the decolonization process. These political interventions seemed inextricably connected with the work of writing history. Before arriving in Britain in 1932, James had written a biography of the Trinidadian labor and political leader Captain Cipriani. With *World Revolution* (1937), he presented the most thorough overview in English of the Trotskyist critique of Stalin's policies. His extraordinary study of the Haitian revolution, *The Black Jacobins* (1938), appeared shortly before he left for the United States, as did the much shorter *History of Negro Revolt*. And James's translation of Boris Souvarine's *Stalin* was published in 1939.

The trip to the United States would broaden his political perspectives and contribute to the building of the new International. Although few in number and thinly dispersed, the Trotskyists—like Lenin's Bolsheviks, not so many years before—were nonetheless ready to respond to any opening for socialist initiative. Of that, James was certain. "We may well see," he had written in *World Revolution*, "especially after the universal ruin and destruction of the coming war, a revolutionary movement which, beginning in one of the great European cities, in the course of a few short months, will sweep the imperialist bourgeoisie out of power, not only in every country in Europe, but in India, China, Egypt, and South Africa."[10] Visiting the United States would give James the opportunity to work in the largest section of Trotsky's embryonic international movement.

Perhaps James also saw the trip to America as a new stage in his personal education and his development as a writer. It would offer him the chance to experience and study another way of life. Decades later, an interviewer asked if James had ever planned the move to be permanent. "No," he replied, "I went to the United States, but with the intention of coming back."[11] Yet at the end of six months James renewed his visa. Then, in the midst of the war, slipping through the bureaucratic net, James stayed on in the United States for as long as possible. During most of that time he lived in New York—in Greenwich Village, Harlem, and the Bronx. But in the course of his political work, he traveled frequently, lecturing and organizing in Detroit, New Orleans, Chicago, Los Angeles, Reno, St. Louis, and Washington, D.C. The sheer size of the country impressed him. "I remember my first journey from Chicago to Los Angeles by train," he later wrote, "the apparently endless miles, hour after hour, all day and all night and the next morning the same again, until the evening. I experienced a sense of expansion which has permanently altered my attitude to the world."[12] He observed the people, and read up on the nation's history and literature. In Herman Melville's *Moby Dick*—a novel which had not engaged his interest upon first reading it in Trinidad during the 1920s—he now found new resonances.

When James finally did leave, in 1953, it was under duress, after years of harassment and a spell of internment on Ellis Island. Forced back to England, James again had a place in the public eye, writing for the newspapers, lecturing in Paris, preparing a book on cricket. By the end of the 1950s, in the midst of decolonization, he returned to the West Indies, to greater prominence than ever before.

The period James spent in the United States remains enigmatic. Its contrast with the years before and after could not be more striking. "Writing under a half-dozen pseudonyms, living the somewhat shadowy life of the small Marxist group leader," as his first biographer puts it, James "firmly abandoned the semi-celebrity status he had achieved in Britain as a cricket journalist and prominent Trotskyist spokesman. It is a measure of seriousness that this personal eclipse disturbed him not in the least."[13] Years later, Kwame Nkrumah, in an intriguing passage of his autobiography, recalled being initiated by James into the techniques of working illegally, during the 1940s. And in 1956, following a split in James's small political organization in the United States, an embittered former comrade called James "the underground man." Perhaps this referred in part to James's fascination with the fiction of Dostoyevsky and other Russian literature of the nineteenth century. More directly, though, it was an allusion to his surreptitious manner while in America.[14]

James had reason to be stealthy. During the early 1940s, twenty-eight domestic Trotskyist leaders were arrested, and eighteen of them were convicted and jailed under the Smith Act—a forerunner of the repressive measures against dissent that later became the trademark of Senator McCarthy. In the early 1950s, Max Shachtman was denied a passport, although by then he was an unmistakably anti-Communist radical, leaning toward support of the United States in the Korean War.[15] And James's scathing account of the Communist International, *World Revolution*, published before his entry into the United States, was a major part of the government's case against him during the deportation proceedings.

(Even safely beyond the territorial limits of the United States, James's politics made the U.S. government uneasy. In 1955, his associates in the United States were placed on the list of subversive organizations. Later in the decade, an American consul general commented on James's role in the West Indies: "there is always the possibility that James is under international Communist discipline, and continues to use his Trotskyite identification as a cloak."[16] The notion of James as Soviet agent was preposterous, and by that time James had long since abandoned any "Trotskyite identification." But those searching out evidence of "un-American activities" did not make the precise distinctions that Marxists themselves often did.)

The need to evade notice by the government accounts only for some aspects of this period's obscurity, however. His creative production underwent a profound transformation. Like his life, James's writings during these years were for the most part "underground." One scholar has tallied the list of James's literary output in Britain from 1932 to 1938: besides editing two newspapers, translating one book, ghost-writing another, and staging a play, he published four books and two substantial, well-circulated pamphlets.[17] While in the United States, James was prolific, but most of what was published was ephemeral: newspaper columns, political commentary, a few book reviews. Little of his work reached the stage of detailed and finished presentation. James did plan and work on a number of extensive projects: a play about Harriet Tubman; an account of U.S. slave revolts and the abolitionist movement; and *Notes on American Civilization*, a study of American culture, history, and society that James began drafting in 1949–1950. But these were never completed. Some traces of the longer projects can be discerned in the political essays from *New International* and *Fourth International* published here.

If James's writings did not circulate widely during these years, that was not for want of contacts with prominent literary and intellectual figures who could have helped him. The poet and fiction writer Delmore Schwartz recalled meeting James at Dwight Macdonald's house in 1939. James might well have found his way into the *Partisan Review* or *Politics*, had he been so inclined. And his circle of friends included such prominent black writers as Richard Wright and Ralph Ellison, with whom he discussed launching a magazine to be called *American Pages*. Many an American radical literary or cultural figure sought to work out a viable middle way during these years — perhaps writing or editing or teaching in some nonsocialist institution, while penning articles for the radical press under a pseudonym.[18] Only during the final portion of his stay, it seems, did James seriously consider returning to the life of a man of letters, largely in an effort to mollify the authorities who were seeking to expel him.

Instead of working to advance his literary career, as he had upon arriving in England from Trinidad in 1932, James devoted his energies to socialist political activity. And the record suggests that James was very deliberate about this. He treated his abilities as being, in effect, requisitioned to meet the demands of the revolutionary movement. He published in a few American Marxist newspapers and journals, always under pseudonyms. Several more extensive writings — including works of book length — were distributed among the ranks of small Marxist organizations to which James belonged.[19] This orientation was not something he discovered only in America. Robert Hill has commented on the role of such organizational activity ("narrow," perhaps, but intense) throughout James's life. It began in England with his work in the International African Service Bureau (seven members) and the Marxist Group (the Trotskyist faction, of about fifty members, in the Independent Labour party):

> By 1937 . . . the conjunction of Pan-African agitation and organized Trotskyism was complete, for not only was James advocating both objectives simultaneously but he had become part in both cases of the type of organized activity which would characterize the rest of his entire political career, namely, *the small Marxist organization*. This is a distinct political formation with deep historical roots and deserves much greater scholarly attention than it has hitherto received.[20]

What such a group lacks in size, it can at times make up for in leverage. The bureau included such prominent figures as Jomo Kenyatta and George Padmore. And during World War II, the British Trotskyists came to have an influence in the labor movement vastly disproportionate to their small number. What distinguished James's small group in the United States (which came to be known as the Johnson-Forest Tendency)[21] was neither the later prominence of its members nor any direct impact on the social movements, but rather its great intensity and originality in exploring the fundamental questions of Marxist history and theory.[22] This included a profound re-orientation of Marxist perspectives on the role of African Americans in the dynamics of U.S. politics. In 1947, the Johnson-Forest Tendency published the first English translation of Marx's *Economic and Philosophical Manuscripts of 1844*. Raya Dunayevskaya translated a number of previously unavailable texts by Plekhanov, Luxemburg, Bukharin, and Lenin, including the note-books on Hegel's *Science of Logic* Lenin prepared in 1914. The group undertook studies of the English, French, and Russian revolutions, as well as the Civil War in the United States.

Correspondence within the intellectual leadership of the tendency—among James, Raya Dunayevskaya, and Grace Lee—at times resembles notes from an advanced seminar in Marxist theory.[23] But in a number of publications, beginning with *The American Worker* (1947), the tendency placed great emphasis on recording the lives and thoughts of industrial workers and other groups. This blend of journalism and social history reached its fruition with a series of pamphlets the group published after leaving the Trotskyist movement. It included a black auto worker's memories, a booklet on working women's changing attitudes toward housework, and an account of a strike among high school students.

After four or five decades, these theoretical and documentary writings still convey a sense of the group's excitement as new areas were being explored. Some years later, while describing the Johnson-Forest Tenden-cy's work to an audience of European Marxists in London, James sought most of all to convey the feeling of discovery:

> [W]hen a group of people . . . find something new, it is as if they have been living on a level with everybody else but by some chance they happen to get up on a great height. When you get to a certain height above the others it is as if you have discovered a new field, a new prairie, a new landscape, and all you have to have is the energy and the drive to go on and you immediately begin to pick up a whole lot of new things which others on the level below don't see, it never crosses their mind. Well we had managed . . . to make that move up, that leap, whereupon our various people began to move and find [things] out. Everybody who had any energy or anything was just going to go forward, discovering and developing in fields that had not been touched by Marxists for the previous hundred years.[24]

Here James engaged in some slight exaggeration. Work on dialectics had absorbed the energies of several brilliant European theorists. Antonio Gramsci, writing in his prison notebooks, had addressed some of the same problems about subaltern class consciousness that James and his co-thinkers tried to solve in practice. But in the American scene they were unique.

This was an intensive and collaborative effort. James was, without question, the one who set the agenda for the group's research but fully recognized how much he owed to the workers and intellectuals around him. Theoretical labor, like every other form of activity in modern society, was increasingly socialized. In a letter from 1945, James described a meeting during which a position paper was worked out, drawing on the ideas and knowledge of the different people attending. "One person writes," James said,

> but in the world in which we live all serious contributions have to be collective; the unification of all phases of life makes it impossible for the single mind to grasp it in all its aspects. Although one mind may unify, the contributory material and ideas must come from all sources and types of mind. . . . The best mind is the one so basically sound in analytical approach and capacity to absorb, imagination to fuse, that he makes a totality of all these diverse streams.[25]

The cooperative nature of this activity has often been neglected in the rush to celebrate James as a genius. Every major political statement by James published over the period of 1947 through 1967 was written in collaboration with others.[26] One might also stress the fact that his participation in the Fourth International gave James an audience beyond his immediate contacts. The two journals to which he contributed the essays gathered in the present volume, *New International* and *Fourth International*, were circulated throughout the International; likewise with the internal discussion bulletins of the WP and the SWP. Documents by James and his co-thinkers had international distribution.[27] Discussions of James's relation to Trotskyism usually begin and end on a single point: James disagreed with Trotsky and went on to develop his own interpretation of Marxism. The difficulty here is not strictly factual—a split did take place—but too much emphasis on the split can be distorting. James spent most of two decades in the international movement and continued to work in it long after his criticisms of its main theses had become profound. His writing found a small but very serious readership in the movement's ranks, not only in the United States but in dozens of countries around the world.

II

The writings collected in the present volume represent James's most public work from his years as a man underground. Until now, we have treated this period as a "turn" in James's career. It marks a profound shift in the coordinates of his personal identity: from Europe to America; from public intellectual to surreptitious emigré; from man of letters (on the model of William Hazlitt or Arnold Bennett) to professional revolutionist (with Lenin and Trotsky now being the chief influences). Yet deep continuities bridge the divide. And the changes that mattered the most to James, namely those involving his politics, unfolded at a pace having little to do with the dramatic shift in his personal circumstances.

A single link—an abiding concern or theme—connects James's British years with his American sojourn. That nexus is revolution. His work from the mid-1930s on is directed toward analysis of, and intervention within, the revolutionary process. He always treats it as fundamentally creative: the release of suppressed or previously unknown human powers, the institution of new social formations suited to the fuller development of people's abilities. In *The Black Jacobins* he contrasts the sullen, apathetic character of the slaves before the uprising with the surge of confidence, knowledge, and energy after they took up the republican demands for "liberty, equality, fraternity" and proceeded to overthrow the "aristocrats of the skin" who dominated them. James made the study of revolutions the center of his historical and philosophical work. And that concentration heightened throughout the period covered by the present volume. As he wrote in "The American People in 'One World'": "It is in revolutionary periods that the culmination of previous trends and the beginning of new ones appear. That is why they are so important."

It would be difficult to overemphasize James's belief, not only in the possibility or even the necessity of world socialist revolution, but in its immanence. "I live at present," James wrote privately during these years, "in daily expectation of the beginning of an upheaval . . . marking the beginning of the socialist revolution. I think of that many hours every day."[28] And yet, perhaps paradoxically, this simple urgency of purpose makes it more difficult to read his work with any sense of the full scope of its implications. For we now approach James's texts, so to speak, from the far side of the crisis they project. Today, the future James anticipated belongs to our past; the revolution he foresaw did not happen. Therefore (we may be prone to assume) it never could have. The prospect of radical social change was a mirage.

It now requires a sustained act of historical and political reconstruction for us to imagine the extent to which, beginning in 1929, the capitalist world seemed to many people to be in irreversible decline. At the very least it appeared to be mutating into some new kind of society. A host of crises suggested that capitalism and parliamentary democracy had reached their breaking points: the global economic depression; the rise of fascism; the transformation of Russia; two world wars in fewer than three decades; the growing political as well as economic demands of the labor movement; gathering forces for independence in nations long dominated by European and American capital. Since 1929, such growth or even stability in the economy as there had been came through state intervention. The beginnings of a centralized, rationalized control of the economy to meet the demands of the war had heightened productivity. "Free enterprise"—that is, private control of industry—no longer seemed a natural and self-evident order of things. The crises, and the search for a way beyond them, James took as indications of "the ripeness of the organism for transformational change."[29] While James's conviction regarding the short-term prospects for socialist revolution in the 1940s were not common (indeed, just such ideas were denounced by the Communist party), nevertheless, the horizon of expectations had changed.

The political essays collected here trace the shifting emphases within James's understanding of the possibilities and directions for revolutionary politics. We might divide the selection of writings in this volume into two groups or periods. The pieces first published in 1939–1941 mainly continue the work James began in England. These essays serve as condensations of, or extrapolations from, the books he wrote before coming to the United States. "Revolution and the Negro," for instance, is a much briefer treatment of the material presented in *The History of Negro Revolt* and *The Black Jacobins*; it also provided a historical background to his political documents on African-American politics, written the same year (1939). "Imperialism in Africa" reads as if it could have been a pamphlet for the International African Service Bureau. (By coincidence, it was published the same year James was introduced to Nkrumah.) The tribute to Leon Trotsky and the review of Edmund Wilson's now-classic book *To the Finland Station* both reflect the interest in European history (and the craft of history writing) that informed *World Revolution*. A second group of essays begins with "In the International Tradition" (1943) and continues through the polemic against Herbert Aptheker, "Stalinism and Negro History" (1949). In these writings, James begins the project of rethinking American history within the context of socialist politics (and vice versa). Overlapping in time with both sets of writings are the Johnson-Forest Tendency's studies in Marxist theory and dialectics. And in the Introduction, Paul Le Blanc has charted the organizational developments that concerned James as well. For present purposes, however, we might bracket out these contextual matters— important as they are—and focus instead on the essays themselves.

The first set of writings (1939–1941) drew on a store of information and arguments James had accumulated since joining the Trotskyist movement and writing *World Revolution*, *The Black Jacobins*, and *The History of Negro Revolt*. But there were already traces here of the ideas and concerns that came more and more to preoccupy James in his later work. He had come to the United States at least in part to organize the Trotskyists' work among African Americans. But in writing "Revolution and the Negro," he went beyond concrete details of political activity, or even of historical narration:

What we as Marxists have to see is the tremendous role played by Negroes in the transformation of Western civilization from feudalism to capitalism. It is only from this vantage-ground that we shall be able to appreciate (and prepare for) the still greater role they must of necessity play in the transition from capitalism to socialism.[30]

Here, in embryonic form, was the dialectical sense of change James later fleshed out with a full (and rather daunting) Hegelian vocabulary: the forces present at the start of a historical period or social formation reappear, with special intensity, at its close.[31] The reduction of a human being to a commodity and the unfolding resistance to enslavement throughout subsequent history were inscribed in the origins of capitalism and would reach a new height of development at its end. When discussing Bigger Thomas, the central character in Richard Wright's novel *Native Son*, James was no doubt also thinking back on Toussaint and the other "Black Jacobins" of San Domingo:

The great masses of Negroes carry in their hearts the heavy heritage of slavery, and their present degradation. Such has been their past, it is their present, and, as far as they can see, it is their future. It is the revolution which will lift these millions from their knees. Nobody can do it for them. Men, personalities, will be freed from the centuries of chains and shame, as Bigger's personality was freed, by violent action against their tyrants. It is on the evening after the battle, with smoking rifle and bloody bayonet, that the Negro will be able to look all white men in the face, will be able to respect himself and be respected.[32]

The memorial essay on Leon Trotsky—which took up most of an issue of *New International*—highlighted two aspects of the Russian Marxist's work that continued to influence James's perspectives long after he had broken all connection with the international movement Trotsky founded: 1) the theory of the permanent revolution; and, 2) the analysis of fascism and of the role the Stalinists had played in its rise and triumph. This understanding of the great potential of the colonial world as an agent in socialist transformation of the world (and the equal potential of the "advanced" countries for barbarism) is reflected in "Imperialism in Africa." But what emerges most forcefully from the long tribute essay of 1940 is James's sense of Trotsky as historian, and of his *History of the Russian Revolution* as the representative and culmination of the great tradition of historical writing. The review of Edmund Wilson's *To the Finland Station* repeats, more briefly, the point James insists upon in the sweeping essay on Trotsky: historiography is not "above" history, not a "value-neutral" form of social analysis, but is always caught up in the processes it describes. To write history is a mode of intervention *within* history.

These scattered insights from the political essays of 1939–1941 elucidate the second group of writings, beginning with "In the American Tradition" (1943). James's effort to write a historical study of the United States remains one of the least recognized aspects of his work during these years. It has been overshadowed, for instance, by his arguments that the Soviet Union was state capitalist. Even the rather esoteric writings on Hegel have been more widely discussed than James's concern with American history and culture. Within the Johnson-Forest Tendency, it was understood that Raya Dunayevskaya would write a book on the theory of state capitalism, to provide an interpretation of the Russian Revolution and its aftermath, while Grace Lee would prepare a study of dialectics and Marxist philosophy.[33] For his part, James was focused on the history of African-American resistance from slavery through the Civil War. He was also interested in the U.S. working class in its relation to the world labor movement. James's project was never completed, but indications of his intent can be found throughout his organizational documents, his letters, and the articles published in *New International* and *Fourth International*.

Because (as the essays from 1940–1941 claimed) history writing was a form of political activity, James conceived his work on American history as possessing specifically Marxist significance. In 1944, he stated:

> The present writer has found that precisely because of the absence of feudal remnants in modern America, many of the most abstract analyses of Marx find their most perfect exemplification in the United States. Today this is the model capitalist country. Here increasingly in the future the utmost implications of the theory will be practically demonstrated.[34]

But James was intensely concerned with the growing fissure between (as he might have put it) consciousness and being—or, to use Gramsci's more political term, the problem of hegemony, of the ideological leadership exercised by the capitalist class. Almost a decade after leaving the United States, James still addressed the question. In 1962, he summed it up:

> The American bourgeoisie has never been seriously challenged for the leadership of the nation. In the three great crises of American history, the War of Independence, the Civil War, and the Depression, the bourgeoisie was able either to maintain unchallenged its official control of the state, or, in 1776, to form a state and an army to carry out its war. All the objective causes that can be given for this are subordinate to the fact itself. And one continuing cause and effect is that the American bourgeoisie has been able to establish itself abroad and at home, in the national consciousness, as the originator and guardian of individual liberty, freedom, and equality. Marxists are inclined to forget that in social life and conduct these ideas are more firmly established in the United States than elsewhere.

The American bourgeoisie did establish something new in the world. All this inhibits the working class in independent class action and independent class thinking.[35]

The problem, as James saw it, was less one of persuading workers to accept the Marxist analysis of their situation than one of putting that analysis in terms appropriate to American history and culture. This idea was not unique to James. A radical intellectual, V. F. Calverton, had pursued much the same project in his journal *The Modern Quarterly* (1923–1940) and in several volumes of American literary and political history. In the early 1930s, Leon Trotsky had given qualified assent to this program:

> You are perfectly right in saying that the vanguard of the American proletariat must learn to base itself on the revolutionary traditions of its own country too. In a certain sense we can accept the slogan, "Americanize Marxism!" . . . To Americanize Marxism signifies to root it in American soil, to verify it against the events of American history, to elaborate by its methods the problems of American economy and politics, to assimilate the world revolutionary experience from the standpoint of the tasks of the American revolution.[36]

Even without direct evidence, it seems very likely that James knew of Calverton and his work. They may also have met, although Calverton died shortly after James's arrival in the United States. But where Calverton had been a freelance writer, a radical intellectual working for the most part independently of Marxist parties, James considered the project of articulating a socialist historical vision to be the responsibility of a revolutionary political organization.

He argued this at greatest length in an internal document of the Workers party, *Education, Propaganda, Agitation* (1944).[37] There, James expressed the idea in terms of "Americanizing Bolshevism"—just as Lenin had "Russified" Marxism in his studies of capitalist development in Russia. By no means did this imply revising Marx's categories or general theoretical principles. (This potential had bothered Trotsky about Calverton's slogan of "Americanizing Marxism.") "The principles have universal application," James wrote.

> But to the extent that the conditions from which they were drawn are not familiar to the Marxists, they remain to a greater or less degree abstract, with infinite potentialities for confusion and mischief. Either the would-be Marxist must have some serious knowledge of European history in its broadest sense, constantly renewed, amplified, and developed, or the principles of the doctrine must have been incorporated, worked over, and made to live again in a study of the economic structure, social develop-

ment, history, literature, and life of the country with which he has been many years familiar. Only then is he on the road to becoming a serious exponent and contributor to the doctrine. In fact and in truth [it is] only [when] one has dug the principles of Marxism for himself out of his own familiar surroundings and their historical past that the Marxism of Marx and Engels, Lenin or Trotsky, and the famous European Marxists truly stand out in their universal application.[38]

The crucial problem was cultural. "The classics of Marxism are European in origin and content," James argued. "They require more than an ordinary knowledge of European history and particularly by an American worker."[39] The writings of Marx, Engels, Lenin, and Trotsky, among others, responded to conditions and historical events familiar to Europeans. The German worker could read Engels on the peasant rebellions, or the French could read Marx's short book on *The Eighteenth Brumaire*, not only as classics but as clues to their national past and present. James had learned that this did not apply in the same fashion in the United States:

> For the average American worker these books as a beginning are alien. Doubtless if he reads one he is impressed with its power and brilliance and learns something. But what they cannot give to him in sufficient measure is that sense of reality of the development of his own country, that feeling that in addition to the daily class struggle, he is part of something beyond himself that is the beginning of theoretical Bolshevism and the rejection of bourgeois ideology. Such historical data, knowledge, general reading, social experiences as he has, the structure in which his theoretical experiences must grow, are American. We have to begin now, not to write a few pamphlets but to build up the American counterparts to *The Communist Manifesto*, *The Eighteenth Brumaire*, and perhaps even more important, the American counterpart to *What Is to Be Done?*[40]

He went on to comment: "Not only do raw workers need this Americanization. *The party members from the highest to the lowest need it also.* No one has any serious grasp of Marxism, can handle the doctrine or teach it, unless he is, *in accordance with his capabilities and opportunities*, an exponent of it in relation to the social life and development around him."[41]

This was a sharp (even strident) factional intervention. It bore a clear implication: the leaders of the Workers party were deficient in the "serious grasp of Marxism." James was offering an orientation to rectify this lamentable circumstance. One imagines this did little to endear him to the majority tendency. But the stakes of the dispute were not small. In the ranks of a party built on the Bolshevist model, theoretical clarity and a thorough command of Marxism were necessary and urgent: "Unless it is rooted in the American environment and in such terms as the American workers can grasp, we cannot lift them above the instinctive class struggle, sharp as that will inevitably become. Isn't this what Lenin meant by the socialist consciousness which the party carries to the working class?"[42]

With "In the American Tradition" (1943), James adduced passages showing the keen interest of Marx and Engels in American developments during the nineteenth century. But that would not be sufficient. The internal document of 1944 elaborated on the relation of this historical work to organizational prospects:

> We do not wait until we become a large party to do these things. This is the way to prepare ourselves and all our supporters for the gaining of forces and the building of the revolutionary party. If in time among our efforts, we can manage at last to get one such solid pamphlet that does for United States history or the development of the labor movement or any such topic what these pamphlets do for Europe, and catch some of their spirit, we have the possibility, not only of immediate response but, in time, of reaching an ever-widening circle of concrete rewards.[43]

And this "Americanization" project had implications going beyond the United States. Writing in the internal bulletin, James considered the matter in terms of the ideological dominance American capitalism would soon seek to exert elsewhere in the world:

> America occupies a peculiar place in international affairs today. Knowledge of this country has never formed more than a cursory part of European culture and education. In all probability the number of English universities in 1939 which gave a course in U.S. history and culture could be counted on the fingers of one hand or at most two. It is the last hope for imperialism and the old democracy. The American bourgeoisie is going to flood the world with accounts of this country, its history, its development, its politics, its ideals, etc. In the present writer's opinion substantial sections of the European bourgeoisie and certainly the Social Democrats and liberals have no hope of salvation except in actual American overlordship or the American "ideal." . . . The theoretical interpretation of the United States, its past, present, and future, becomes therefore a truly international task, a part of the international struggle for socialism and the national independence of oppressed peoples. And in this, the central issue of our times, we have an exhaustive role to play.[44]

In "The American People in 'One World,'" an essay for *New International*, James addressed the political implications of growing U.S. power. It required a counter-offensive by the American revolutionaries—with historiography being one crucial terrain.

To James, the dimension of American history of greatest contemporary importance was the Civil War. He was not interested so much in the war itself (although he saw in its territorial range and sheer destructiveness something like a foreshadowing of total war on the European continent during the twentieth century) as in its significance as a national process, which began with slave revolts and abolitionism and continued, beyond the war, into the period of Reconstruction. As "Stalinism and Negro History" shows, James saw the decisive issue in the analysis of the process to be the independent activity of the slaves: how they organized their struggle and sought, by every means they could devise, to accomplish their own emancipation. And if the military conflict was a dress rehearsal for world war, the Reconstruction period was analogous to the revolutionary opening in 1917–1920, with the postwar mass action of former slaves as something approaching Bolshevism. James had read *Black Reconstruction* by W. E. B. Du Bois not long after arriving in the United States, and it deeply influenced him. "Du Bois did indeed make the mistake of calling the Reconstruction government a sort of dictatorship of the proletariat. Far from doing harm, the conception that lay behind the mistaken formula was the strength of Du Bois's book: he recognized that the Negroes *in particular* had tried to carry out ideas that went beyond the prevailing conceptions of bourgeois democracy."[45] To continue the analogy, James saw the emergence of the Ku Klux Klan as a prototype of the Fascist bands in the 1920s and 1930s—their robes being a uniform like the black and brown shirts of Mussolini's and Hitler's followers.[46]

Aside from some sketches by James in magazine articles, plus an essay by the Johnson-Forest Tendency member William Gorman, the work on American history never reached the public eye.[47] In a document circulated to a few comrades of his tendency, James complained that he ought not to be doing such work anyway, that he was not the person to write on American matters. He considered it another instance of being compelled to do something because others in the Trotskyist movement hadn't troubled themselves to do the essential. It is difficult to know how seriously this should be taken. But the passage bears quoting, if only because it has escaped the notice of previous scholarship:

I got acquainted with Trotskyism, in fact with Leninism, in 1934. I wrote *World Revolution*. I maintain to this day that it was not *my* job. Max Shachtman and the others had *lived through the events*. I had to read them up. I come here [the United States] and have to take up dialectic. I am no philosopher. That was a job for a *trained academic* who had embraced Bolshevism. Luckily Grace [Lee, later Boggs] was there to help. I then found myself writing [like] hell about (1) American politics. That was not my job either. . . . But (2) I next find myself up to the eyes in the analysis of internal party politics in the U.S. That was not *my* job either. *This should have been the job of a trained dialectician*, to whom the experiences were familiar. . . . I *know* that where I could work most concretely would have been *British* politics; the literature, the politics, the traditions of Britain are in my bones. I grew up on them. This work forced upon me has been valuable. I have become a world citizen, and have worked through from the start the chief spheres of our movement's theory. Today also everything is knit tight. National politics *is* world politics. But the American comrades must realize that all this general training and thought and coordination must end in their becoming master of *American* revolutionary thought and revolutionary practice.[48]

James did write occasionally on British matters for the Trotskyist press — but at this point he sought a larger canvas than journalism could provide him. (Of course, he would later write his book on cricket, where he made a remarkable synthesis of "the literature, the politics, the traditions of Britain . . . in my bones.") His sense of political theory, world revolutionary traditions, and American society had an epic quality. That makes it particularly unfortunate that his writing on U.S. history was confined to a few intriguing miniatures.

III

By the mid-1940s, James felt a need to synthesize the work he had done while in the United States. He had not written a book since leaving England. The urge to pull the pieces together strengthened following a discussion in 1945 with Richard Wright, who had just publicly broken with the Communist party and was, at the time, correcting the proofs of *Black Boy*. "I have been wavering about writing a book," James noted in a letter. "But I shall hesitate no longer. By the time they have recovered from his autobiographical novel, I shall hit them across the eyes with a historical study."[49] His ambition was to write a book that would do for the understanding of American culture what *World Revolution* had done for the critique of Stalinism, what *The Black Jacobins* had done for the Haitian revolution, and what *Beyond a Boundary* was to do for cricket, some years later: a work at once comprehensive, definitive, and interesting to the average reader. But after years of research into the history of slave revolts and abolitionism, the study remained unfinished. Nor was the play he drafted about Harriet Tubman accepted for production. And early in 1950, he prepared a lengthy proposal for a book under the working title *Notes on American Civilization*. It would integrate his historical investigations, his appreciation of American literature, and thoughts about contemporary industrial society. This, too, remained only a rough sketch — the magnificent ruins of his cultural and historical conception. The manuscript alternated between brilliant passages and extensive quotations from primary sources but was never integrated into a finished book.

Only at the very end of the American sojourn, while being held on Ellis Island under the threat of deportation, did James finish a short volume, *Mariners, Renegades, and Castaways* (1953), a critical study of Herman Melville. It bears little discernible relation to his previous writings from the American period.[50] And that discontinuity was almost certainly intentional: it was published as part of his appeal for citizenship, and the autobiographical concluding statement emphasized his literary prominence, not his political activities. Perhaps James had hoped that a work of literary criticism might help him pass as an ordinary American intellectual. The book drew on the *American Civilization* draft. Yet *Mariners*, while much more polished, lacked the conceptual sweep of the earlier project, without gaining much from its concentration on Melville. It is perhaps the oddest volume James published—certainly the least exemplary of his profoundly historical imagination. At the same time, it was insufficiently formalist in its critical approach to find much of an audience among literary critics. It apparently got no reviews at the time of publication and has left no trace whatsoever in subsequent Melville commentary.[51]

What James wanted to write, throughout his American years, was historical narrative. For the most part, what he actually produced was Marxist theory. Until 1950, his most extensive work was "The Nevada Document," a tutorial guide of Hegel's *Science of Logic* with political applications, now published as *Notes on Dialectics*. And in 1950, the year he drafted *American Civilization*, James produced *State Capitalism and World Revolution*, in which his critique of Trotskyism reached its culmination, and a work he later referred to as his "masterpiece."[52]

Each document responded to what James saw as a stage of profound cultural crisis within capitalism. The unceasing drive for industrial concentration and centralization—ever larger units of manufacture, increasingly automated, striving for heightened productivity by intensifying the division of labor—made for an incredible growth in economic output. Yet it also wasted human abilities. It promised freedom and an end to want, while narrowing the exercise of individual development. The labor process remained outside the control of those who carried on the labor; there might be a democracy in politics, but none in production. Although the capitalist control of the conditions of production had been challenged by the industrial unionism of the 1930s and 1940s, the labor bureaucracy increasingly limited its demands to the sphere of consumption. This was what Marx had described as alienation in the *Economic and Philosophical Manuscripts of 1844*, which the Johnson-Forest group first published in English. And in James's vision of the prospects for socialist revolution, the demand for the abolition of alienation was growing, if not always voiced in explicitly socialist terms.

The process of capitalist accumulation and concentration was global; so, too, would be resistance to it. But in the course of his sojourn in the United States, James came to see the Americans as being especially fitted to grasp the potential for a new social order in which (as Marx had said of communism) the full development of all required the full development of each. Anna Grimshaw has brilliantly summed up this tendency in James's thinking, apropos of his *American Civilization* project:

> James found, in the New World, the conditions for a fundamental revolution in human relations, of a size and scope commensurate with changes in the organization of production. He believed that the movement of the modern world was towards integration, towards the reconstruction of the human subject or what he called "the creation of man as an integral human being." By this he meant that the search for new forms, the extension of artistic premises, was motivated by people's desire to found a new society in which they could bring into contact the separate elements of their lives. James anticipated that, in seeking to integrate lives fragmented by the division of labor, the mass of the American people, unburdened by Europe's past, would create new kinds of political association and expression. Politics would no longer be separate from everyday life.[53]

With this statement, Grimshaw cogently presents what is essential and definitive about James's political, historical, and theoretical efforts throughout the years he lived in the United States. It was also the conception shared by the Johnson-Forest Tendency. Hence it seems peculiar that she also remarks:

> Aside from the two conventional political documents James published on the American revolution in 1944, there were few hints of this enormous, but largely personal project [of studying American life and culture] in his voluminous journalistic contributions to the debates within the Trotskyist movement during the 1940s.[54]

The present collection (along with numerous other writings by James and his group) abundantly document that, far from being a "largely personal project," the work James attempted to synthesize in *American Civilization* had been at the center of his revolutionary activities and public concerns for more than a decade.

The social need for a sense of completeness or integration in the conduct of life extended beyond the point of production—although James, as a Marxist, always returned his focus to the labor process. Beyond his historical or strictly political efforts, there was in James's work during the American period a cultural dimension that Paul Buhle and Anna Grimshaw have sought to emphasize. Their accounts present this cultural concern as something emerging in the final years of his stay, in *American Civilization* (1950) and in *Mariners, Renegades, and Castaways* (1953). However, as early as the review of *Native Son* in 1940, he approaches the question of how aesthetic and social activity might be related:

The artist, by methods compounded of conscious logic and his own intuition, observes society and experiences life. He comes to his conclusions and embodies them in character, scene, and dramatic situation. According to the depth of his penetration and the sweep of his net, his capacity to integrate and reproduce, he writes his novel, paints his picture, or composes his symphony. Psychologist, historian, politician, or revolutionary, drawing on his own experience, sees symbols, parallelism, depth and perspective unsuspected by the creator. The artist can see the truth and nothing but the truth, but no one can expect him to see the whole truth.[55]

Following the period covered by the selections in the present volume, James's attention returned to cultural matters—considered now, not with regard to the mystery of creation, but in light of the political role art might have in the crisis of global capitalism. By the 1950s, a whole field of discussion about "mass culture" had grown up. But James, in contrast with these mostly hostile commentaries, was fascinated by the way these forms sought to acknowledge social conflicts and mirror reality. Where other Marxists looked upon popular entertainment as contributing to the stabilization of the crisis, James discerned an immense force of aspiration and rage in mass culture.

For instance, the sudden popularity of gangster films and the Dick Tracy comic strip during the Depression impressed him as expressions of desperate individualism—charged with a desire for violence against the official society. The vast audience for radio serials ("soap operas") revealed the deep need, especially among women, for some kind of reflection and affirmation of day-to-day existence. And the Hollywood star system— "whereby," James wrote, "a certain selected few individuals symbolize in their film existence *and their private and public existence* the revolt against the general conditions"[56]—likewise endorsed, and displaced, that striving for individual freedom and expression that was ingrained in American culture but was increasingly frustrated by industrial society.

Works designed for entertainment had to satisfy a diverse mass audience. Furthermore, they were created in more or less industrial conditions, by large business enterprises (e.g., the studios, the networks). The popular culture James wrote about was very much a *product* of capitalism. In this respect, he concurred (unknowingly) with Adorno and Horkheimer with regard to the commodification of culture. And, too, like their *Dialectic of Enlightenment*, James's *Notes on American Civilization* recognized a degree of commonality between these cultural "products" and the totalitarian state. At one point, he even treats the show trial as a debased and manipulative form of mass-culture drama. In either case—in the popular arts of commodified leisure, or in modern dictatorship—a decisive force of repression operates: the conflict between labor and capital must be denied or dispersed. The workers' efforts to control production and to develop their own individual abilities must be subordinated to capital's demand for heightened productivity.

In a lecture delivered in Paris in 1954, "Popular Culture and the Cultural Tradition," James reiterated a thesis argued in *American Civilization*: "It was the depression of 1929 which opened the split in the national consciousness in the United States," and thereby began a decline in the quality of popular arts. Griffith and Chaplin had been the epic and lyric poets, respectively, of the common person. In their films, they could take on such matters as labor conflict, unemployment, and race (albeit in a thoroughly reactionary fashion, as in Griffith's *Birth of a Nation*). "The mass popular audience of Griffith and the early Chaplin lived in an atmosphere of social freedom and absence of traditional restraints characteristic of the growth of the United States," said James. The Depression heightened social tensions, effectively splitting the audience, so that certain topics became dangerous:

> Today . . . so tense is the relation between the different classes, and so highly organized their representative institutions, that immense areas of social experience have no opportunity to be presented on screen. In this respect Aeschylus and Shakespeare had infinitely greater freedom than any modern film director.[57]

James's intention was not to become an aesthetician. Nor was he especially concerned with advocating any particular form of art. Rather, his interest lay in the possibility that the mass media and popular culture might serve as a form of communication (however distorted) within the class. He saw such exchange as a decisive aspect of class independence. "What happens in a revolution," he wrote in 1962, "is that the class for the first time finds itself free to think its own thoughts and give some concrete form to its own experience accumulated over the generations."[58] And Marxist activity, James thought, should seek to foster such communication.

In this respect it is important to take notice of a project discussed by James and some friends near the end of World War II. A biography of Richard Wright by Constance Webb (to whom James was married at one time) recalls the plans that James, Wright, Ralph Ellison, and others made to start a magazine. Wright proposed the name *American Pages* and drew up the prospectus. Webb describes the intended range of the publication:

There would be no "preaching" in the articles or feature stories but an attempt to depict what . . . a lack of balanced living gave rise to in all Americans: mob violence, casual cruelty, adolescent posturing, crime, race hate, gang life, drunkenness, crazy fads, restlessness, cheap movie adoration, cheap pathos, cheap morals, cheap art, cheap journalism, cheap aspirations, and inescapable loneliness.

More specifically, there would be fiction, articles, essays, poetry, cartoons, profiles of individuals who lived "the American way" such as Frank Sinatra, Gene Krupa, Frances Farmer; surveys on race tensions, popularly written, excerpts from novels which revealed the American scene, studies of crime and criminals, black and white.

What would be the primary assumption of such a publication? It was to be that the Negro problem was the problem of all minorities, and the problems of antisocial individuals were but phases of one overall national cultural problem, a lag in consciousness, a primitive expression of personalities caught in an industrial society whose demands were far beyond the emotional capacities of the people to contain or resolve them.[59]

American Pages only reached the stage of the prospectus. But the Johnson-Forest Tendency, after leaving the Trotskyist movement, launched a similar project. Its newspaper, *Correspondence*, encouraged workers, housewives, students, and others to write about what concerned them in their lives and in society at large. Members of the group would listen to discussions and remarks from people around them and then write them up as short articles. A related effort was the organization's series of pamphlets and books: *Indignant Heart*, a black auto worker's life story; *A Woman's Place*, reflections of working women on their role in society and the home; *Artie Cuts Out*, the narrative of a student rebellion; and *Punching Out*, an anecdotal and analytical treatment of factory life and union bureaucracy.

These projects—all encouraged by James and consistent with his emphasis on developing the means for "the class . . . to think its own thoughts and give some concrete form to its own experience accumulated over the generations"—were designed as interventions in the sphere of popular culture. The pamphlets were small enough to fit in a shirt pocket. The books (Charles Denby's *Indignant Heart*, or the later political statement *Facing Reality*) were published in the format of mass-market paperbacks and were priced cheaply. This was, in effect, an attempt to slip into the mass-culture mainstream.[60]

A passage from *Correspondence* displayed the group's attitude and showed where it directed its attention:

[F]rom the stories that we get every day from the shops, we can see a new form of struggle emerging. It never seems to be carried to its complete end, yet its existence is continuous. The real essence of this struggle and its ultimate goal is: a better life, a new society, the emergence of the individual as a human being. Each scrap with the boss, each manifestation with things as they are, all tend to smash down the old and help the new emerge. . . . This is the struggle to establish here and now a new culture, a workers' culture. . . . It is this that we must be extremely sensitive to. We must watch with an eagle eye every change or indication of the things that these changes reflect.[61]

The whole effort somewhat resembled a premature form of New Left cultural practice from the 1960s. Likewise, such post-Trotskyist political documents as *State Capitalism and World Revolution* and *Facing Reality* bore similarities to later New Left thinking. (Not by accident, either: the young Marx's writings were a decisive influence on both.) But in the 1950s, an intransigent commitment to a revolutionary perspective must have coexisted, uneasily, with a grim awareness that the economy and the politics of the day denied the short-term prospects for change. Someone who knew James during his American years referred to his "fuck you" theory of history—"every time a worker says 'fuck you' a revolution is about to begin."[62] Only much later would such an uncompromising optimism appear heroic, even prophetic. In the meantime, James was driven out of the country.

Rediscovering his writings now, one notices how often James views things "from a theoretical height," to borrow a phrase of Trotsky's that James repeats throughout his tribute. And he had a clear appreciation of how much his own vantage owed to the collective work of the parties and groups to which he belonged. By means of their associated labor, he could survey "a new field, a new prairie, a new landscape" seldom explored by other Marxists in the United States. But James did not dwell entirely in the upper regions. The writings from this period—from his years as "an underground man"—also suggest that James tried to track the progress, deep below the visible terrain, of what Marx once called "the old mole": the force of social revolution, which disappears from sight for years at a time, then pops up, out from his undermining burrows, when and where least expected.

SCOTT MCLEMEE

Notes

1. Letter to Arnold Ruge, May 1943, in Karl Marx, *Early Writings*, trans. Rodney Livingstone and Gregor Benton (New York: Vintage Books, 1975), p. 206.

2. "Introduction to *Dialectics of Nature,*" Karl Marx and Frederich Engels, *Selected Works in One Volume* (London: Lawrence and Wishart, 1968), p. 339.
3. Paul Buhle, *C. L. R. James: The Artist as Revolutionary* (London and New York: Verso, 1988).
4. "The Revolutionary Answer" is James's most anthologized piece. It was reprinted in the Socialist Workers party's *Documents on the Negro Struggle* (New York: Pioneer Publishers, 1962); Paul Buhle, ed., *The C. L. R. James Anthology* (Cambridge, MA: Radical America, 1970); *The Future in the Present: Selected Writings* (London: Allison & Busby, 1977); Tony Bogues, ed., *Marxism and Black Liberation* (Cleveland: Hera Press, 1980); and Anna Grimshaw, ed., *The C. L. R. James Reader* (Oxford: Blackwell, 1992). In the early 1970s, Paul Buhle suggested publishing an edited version of "Trotsky's Place in History" in *Radical America,* but it did not appear. My thanks to Buhle for sending me copies of his letters and James's replies.
5. The most comprehensive bibliography at present is that appended to *The C. L. R. James Reader.* The editor describes it as "a revised and updated version" of the "careful original compilation" that first appeared in *At the Rendezvous of Victory* (London: Allison & Busby, 1984). Both versions are riddled with errors and omissions, many of them substantial, and some inexplicable. The term "revision" to describe the *Reader* bibliography is somewhat misleading. The main difference seems to be the addition of items published later, not the correction of mistakes from the original.

   For instance, the first and probably most widely circulated anthology of James's writings, published by *Radical America* in 1970, does not receive an entry or a description of contents. Only a fraction of the material from *New International* and *Fourth International* is covered. Several important theoretical writings published in internal discussion bulletins are overlooked, while the listing for one such document, "Production for the Sake of Production" (1943), attributes it to the wrong organization.
6. James's participation in Marxist organizations in the United States has caused some confusion. Names, dates, and points of arrival and departure are often garbled. For instance, it is widely repeated that James and his group left the Socialist Workers party in 1950, although the correct date is 1951. Two otherwise fine studies, Ivar Oxaal's *Black Intellectuals Come to Power: The Rise of Creole Nationalism in Trinidad and Tobago* (Cambridge, MA: Schenkman Publishing Company, 1968) and Cedric Robinson's *Black Marxism: The Making of the Black Radical Tradition* (London: Zed Press, 1983), contain numerous mistakes concerning James's organizational affiliations. No date given in either source should be taken as valid except insofar as it corresponds to information in Paul Le Blanc's Introduction to the present volume, which may be regarded as a definitive source.

   For an account of various problems and misleading indications in secondary sources, see Scott McLemee, "To Set the Record Straight," forthcoming in *The C. L. R. James Journal.*
7. That work is summarized in Kent Worcester, *C. L. R. James: A Political Biography* (Oxford: Blackwell, 1993). See also his *C. L. R. James and the American Century: 1938–1953* (Puerto Rico: Inter-American University of Puerto Rico, CISCLA Working Paper No. 12, 1984); *West Indian Politics and Cricket: C. L. R. James and Trinidad, 1958–63* (Puerto Rico: Inter-American University of Puerto Rico, CISCLA Working Paper No. 20, 1985); "C. L. R. James,

Marxism, and America," *Research and Society*, Vol. 4 (1991); and "C. L. R. James and the Gospel of American Modernity," *Socialism and Democracy*, Nos. 16–17, 1992.

8. Anna Grimshaw and Keith Hart, eds., *American Civilization* (Oxford: Blackwell, forthcoming).

9. A section of the play (Act 2, Scene 1) was published in the British cultural journal *Life and Letters Today*, Vol. 14, No. 3 (1936). For a discussion of this fragment, James's view of Robeson, and the place of *Toussaint-Louverture* in James's career, see Selwyn Cudjoe, ed., *C. L. R. James: His Intellectual Legacies* (Amherst: University of Massachusetts Press, 1993). In *The C. L. R. James Reader*, Anna Grimshaw reproduces a play titled *The Black Jacobins*. The chronological structure of the anthology suggests that this is a version of the 1936 play. But in fact James did not actually write it; it was adapted from his historical book *The Black Jacobins*, by other hands. Unfortunately, Grimshaw does not indicate this, and presents it as if it were the same play Robeson had appeared in.

10. *World Revolution 1917–1936: The Rise and Fall of the Communist International* (London: Martin Secker and Warburg Ltd., 1937), pp. 36–37. This book has recently been reprinted in May 1993 by Humanities Press in its Revolutionary Studies series.

11. *C. L. R. James and British Trotskyism: An Interview* (London: Socialist Platform, 1987), p. 11.

12. *Mariners, Renegades, and Castaways* (London: Allison & Busby, 1985), p. 167.

13. Buhle, *C. L. R. James: The Artist as Revolutionary*, p. 66.

14. The characterization of James as "underground man" appears in "Johnsonism: A Political Appraisal" (April 1956), a memorandum signed "O'Brian" (later identified as Peter Mallory), found in the Raya Dunayevskaya Collection at the Wayne State University Archives in Detroit. I am quoting from a microfilm edition of the Dunayevskaya archives. Unfortunately, I have not been able to locate a copy of Nkrumah's *Autobiography* to give an exact citation.

15. Eventually Shachtman did get his passport. James left Shachtman's group, the Workers party, in 1947; two years later, it changed its name to the Independent Socialist League. During the early 1950s, the ISL fought a legal battle that resulted in its name being removed from the attorney general's list of subversive organizations.

16. Quoted in Cary Fraser, "United States Policy towards the British Caribbean, 1945–1964," unpublished dissertation (University of Geneva, 1990), p. 238. Fraser cited by Kent Worcester, introduction to the third edition of C. L. R. James, *Modern Politics*, ed. Scott McLemee (Humanities Press, forthcoming).

17. Robert Hill, "In England, 1932–38," in Paul Buhle, ed., *C. L. R. James: His Life and His Work* (London: Allison & Busby, 1986).

18. The meeting at Dwight Macdonald's in December 1939 is noted in Elizabeth Pollet, ed., *Portrait of Delmore: Journals and Notes of Delmore Schwartz 1939–1959* (New York: Farrar Straus Giroux, 1986), p. 7. Schwartz refers to "C. W. L. James, the Negro." Information in the editor's note makes clear that C. L. R. James is meant.

An important source treating the cultural and political milieu of American Trotskyism is Alan Wald, *The New York Intellectuals: The Rise and Decline of the Anti-Stalinist Left from the 1930s to the 1980s* (Chapel Hill, NC: University of North Carolina Press, 1987). For a discussion of the relation of James's work to the group Wald discusses, see my essay, "C. L. R. James and the New York

Intellectuals; Or, Cultural Politics at the End of Ideology," in Paul Buhle, ed., "C. L. R. James's America," a special issue of *The C. L. R. James Journal* (forthcoming).

19. For instance, see *State Capitalism and World Revolution* (Chicago: Charles H. Kerr, 1986). Written in collaboration with Raya Dunayevskaya and Grace Lee, this document first appeared in 1950 as an internal discussion bulletin of the Socialist Workers party.

20. Hill, "In England, 1932–38," p. 69.

21. The group was known simply as "the minority" throughout most of the period it existed in the Workers party. The tendency's first public appearance under the name "Johnson-Forest" seems to have been during the "interim period" of 1947, between leaving the WP and joining the SWP. Inside the SWP, they were called "the Johnsonites," although James appears to have abandoned the pen name until 1950, when *State Capitalism and World Revolution* was circulated as a document signed by Johnson and Forest (although Grace Lee had contributed the final section on philosophy). After leaving the Trotskyist movement entirely in 1951, the group became Correspondence Committees. Within the radical milieu they were still sometimes called "the Johnsonites."

22. A good survey of James's philosophical orientation is provided by Alrick Cambridge, "C. L. R. James: Freedom through History and Dialectics," in Alistair Hennessy, ed., *Intellectuals in the Twentieth-Century Caribbean, Volume I: Spectre of the New Class: The Commonwealth Caribbean* (London: Macmillan Caribbean, 1992), pp. 163–78. With regard to James's philosophical and theoretical work in the Johnson-Forest Tendency, see Scott McLemee, "Western Marxism or Hegelian Leninism? Reading James and Lukács," in Selwyn Cudjoe, ed., *C. L. R. James: His Intellectual Legacies* (Amherst: University of Massachusetts Press, 1993).

23. See the letters in the Raya Dunayevskaya Collection at Wayne State University. My thanks to Paul Buhle for providing me with a photocopy of these dense, elliptical missives on Hegel, Marx, and Lenin. A detailed analysis of this correspondence, in connection with other theoretical writings of the Johnson-Forest Tendency, is essayed in Scott McLemee, *Revolution in the New World: C. L. R. James on Politics, Culture, and the Dialectics of Liberation* (in preparation).

24. *Perspectives and Proposals* (Detroit: Facing Reality, 1966), p. 33. This mimeographed document consists of three lectures given in London in August 1963.

25. Letter to Constance Webb, 1945; quoted by Anna Grimshaw, *The C. L. R. James Reader*, p. 10.

26. *The Invading Socialist Society* (Detroit: Bewick Editions, 1972; 1st ed., 1947), was signed by C. L. R. James, Raya Dunayevskaya (F. Forest), and Grace Lee (Ria Stone); *State Capitalism and World Revolution* (Chicago: Charles H. Kerr, 1986; 1st ed., 1950), written in collaboration with Dunayevskaya and Lee; *Facing Reality* (Detroit: Correspondence, 1958), signed by James, Lee, and Cornelius Castoriadis (Pierre Chaulieu). On the title page of *Negro Americans Take the Lead: A Statement on the Crisis in American Civilization* (Detroit: Facing Reality, 1964), authorship is given as "Facing Reality Publishing Company," while at the end of the document appears the name of Martin Glaberman. The bibliography in *The C. L. R. James Reader* attributes the pamphlet, inaccurately, to James. According to Glaberman, the text was prepared by the Facing Reality group from notes based on a discussion with James in London in 1963. In this case, authorship was truly collective. *The Gathering Forces* (Detroit: Facing Reality,

1967) was a collaborative statement written by James, Glaberman, William Gorman, and George Rawick. Circulated in draft and unsigned, the document solicited comments and contributions from its audience.

27. In *Bibliographie des Bulletins Intérieurs du Secrétariat International de la Quatrième Internationale, Période de 1947 à 1951* (Paris: Centre d'Etudes et de Recherches sur les Mouvements Trotskyste et Revolutionnaires Internationaux, 1982), the following documents are listed: "La question négre: La résolution suivante fut présentée par la minorité Johnson-Forest du Workers Party des Etats-Unis à son Congrès de 1944," in Vol. 2, No. 17, August 1947; "La tendance économiste dans la IVme Internationale—par Ria Stone," Numero Special, January 1948; and "La Situation Politique Mondiale et la IV Internationale" (described as "Document Soumais au Congrès Mondial par les Camarades de la Tendance Johnson-Forest [Minorité du SWP]," 1948).

28. Letter to Constance Webb, 1945. Quoted in Buhle, *C. L. R. James: The Artist as Revolutionary*, p. 85.

29. "The American People in 'One World,'" this volume, p. 176.

30. "Revolution and the Negro," this volume, p. 77.

31. For an analysis of the development of James's sense of history over the years 1930 to 1960, see Scott McLemee, "Cosmopolitan History and Revolutionary Democracy: Social Dialectics and Rhetorical Form in *Modern Politics*," the afterword to C. L. R. James, *Modern Politics: A Course of Lectures*, ed. Scott McLemee (Atlantic Highlands, NJ: Humanities Press, forthcoming).

32. "Native Son and Revolution," the present volume, p. 89.

33. What actually happened, following the 1955 split between James and Dunayevskaya, was that Dunayevskaya rushed the group's work into print as *Marxism and Freedom: From 1776 until Today* (New York: Bookman Associates, 1958). Although drawing heavily on the contributions of others in the Johnson-Forest Tendency—especially the work of James, Grace Lee, and William Gorman—Dunayevskaya never credits her former associates. Over the years, Dunayevskaya repeatedly claimed that her "translations" from Marx's 1844 manuscripts (actually, a translation at second hand, from a Russian version of the German text) in an appendix to *Marxism and Freedom* were the first such published in English. This was a clear and knowing distortion, since the Johnson-Forest group had published Grace Lee's translations some ten years before. (Dunayevskaya's subsequent accounts of Johnson-Forest history range from the self-aggrandizing to the stylistically incomprehensible; I hope eventually to publish a study of her career that will include an account of the financial dispute which was the real basis of the 1955 split.) Despite being the result of an intellectual and political expropriation of collective labor for the benefit of an individual, *Marxism and Freedom* remains an important work for understanding Johnson-Forest theory.

34. *Education, Propaganda, Agitation* (Detroit: Facing Reality, n.d.), p. 26. For some reason, the date of the original publication of this document is usually indicated to be 1943; internal evidence suggests it was written no later than 1944, and in a later Johnson-Forest text the date for it is given as October 1944.

35. From "Marxism and the Intellectuals" (1962) in *Spheres of Existence: Selected Writings* (Westport, CT: Lawrence Hill and Co., 1980), p. 127.

36. Leon Trotsky, "Perspectives of American Marxism: Open Letter to V. F. Calverton," dated November 4, 1932, in *Writings of Leon Trotsky, 1932* (New York: Pathfinder Press, 1973). For a good study of Calverton, an important but

neglected figure in the intellectual history of American radicalism, see Leonard Wilcox, *V. F. Calverton: Radical in the American Grain* (Philadelphia: Temple University Press, 1992).

37. See Note 34, above. This text first circulated in 1944 as an internal discussion document within the Workers party. It is devoted to internal organizational matters in the party, especially James's criticism of the press—*Labor Action, New International*, and the books and pamphlets distributed by the group. But it is also one of the most important sources for understanding James's sense of his own political practice while in the United States. Because it is seldom discussed in the literature on James or this period, I have quoted extensively from it in the present essay.

38. *Education, Propaganda, Agitation*, pp. 17–18.

39. Ibid., p. 16.

40. Ibid., pp. 16–17.

41. Ibid., p. 17.

42. Ibid., p. 18.

43. Ibid., p. 17.

44. Ibid., p. 25.

45. "Stalinism and Negro History," this volume, p. 189.

46. James makes the analogy between the Klan and Fascist organizations in "Popular Culture and the Cultural Tradition" (1954), a lecture published in *Third Text*, No. 10, 1990, and reprinted in *The C. L. R. James Reader*.

47. William Gorman, "Civil War and the Labor Party," *Internal Bulletin of the Johnson-Forest Tendency*, No. 12, September 29, 1947.

48. *Notes on Dialectics: Hegel and Marxism*, 2nd ed. (Detroit: Friends of Facing Reality Publications, 1971), pp. 144–45. Nearly all of the contents of this mimeographed edition are reproduced in *Notes on Dialectics: Hegel, Marx, Lenin* (Westport, CT: Lawrence Hill and Co., 1980)—but James's "complaint" about the work he felt compelled to do was left out of the later edition.

49. Letter to Constance Webb, in *The C. L. R. James Reader*, p. 147.

50. It seems to have been one of only two items published under his own signature during these years, the other being a letter in *Les Temps modernes* in 1949.

51. I am indebted to William Cain for sending me his unpublished manuscript which surveys and evaluates James's literary criticism.

52. See Oxaal, *Black Intellectuals Come to Power*, p. 189: "During an interview with the writer in 1962 Mr. James referred to this book as 'my masterpiece.'" James makes the same claim for *State Capitalism and World Revolution* as his major writing from the American years in a set of political letters written at about the same time as the interview with Oxaal. See *Letters on Organization* (Detroit: Facing Reality, n.d.).

53. Anna Grimshaw, "Popular Democracy and the Creative Imagination: The Writings of C. L. R. James, 1950–1963," *Third Text*, No. 10, 1990, p. 12.

54. Anna Grimshaw and Keith Hart, *C. L. R. James and the Struggle for Happiness* (New York: The C. L. R. James Institute, 1991), p. 42.

55. "Native Son and Revolution," this volume, p. 91.

56. "Notes on American Civilization" (1950), unpublished typescript. Emphasis in the original.

57. "Popular Culture and the Cultural Tradition," *The C. L. R. James Reader*, p. 254.

58. "Marxism and the Intellectuals," *Spheres of Existence*, p. 117.

59. Constance Webb, *Richard Wright: A Biography* (New York: G. P. Putnam's Sons, 1968), p. 220.
60. According to Martin Glaberman, the book design was modeled on the drugstore paperbacks or "pocket books" of the early 1950s. Glaberman indicates this was done very deliberately. Telephone conversation, August 1992.
61. From an editorial in *Correspondence*, reprinted in *The Correspondence Booklet* (Detroit: Correspondence Publishing Company, 1954), p. 38.
62. Remark attributed to B. J. Widick by George Rawick, interview with Kent Worcester, December 1981.

Index

Abolitionist (anti-slavery) movement, 69, 81, 83, 84, 172, 183, 190–207, 214
Abraham Lincoln Brigade, 86
Adamic, Louis, 73
Adorno, Theodor, 55, 229
Aeschylus, 53
Africa, 1, 5, 6, 36, 43–44, 45, 46, 47, 63, 72, 77, 84–85, 86, 87, 131–40, 164, 166, 169, 170, 175, 184, 191, 210, 212, 215, 219
African Americans, 1, 5, 6, 10, 17, 19, 23, 28–29, 31–32, 43, 46, 47, 48, 49, 53, 54, 55, 61, 62–64, 68, 69, 70, 71, 77, 81, 82–84, 86–87, 88–91, 148, 172, 173, 177, 179–87, 188–207, 211, 216, 219, 220, 221, 225, 231
African Survey (Hailey), 132–37, 138
Alexander, Robert J., 28
Allen, James, 189
Allen, Naomi, 28, 29
Allen, Robert L., 27
Althusser, Louis, 55
American Anti-Slavery Society, 193, 201
American Civil War (1861–1865), 64, 82–84, 93, 105, 106, 147–48, 168, 172–73, 177, 183–84, 188–89, 191, 192, 199, 202, 203, 204, 206, 207, 221, 224, 225
American Civilization (James), 211, 214, 226, 227, 228, 229–30
American Dilemma, The (Myrdal), 179
American Federation of Labor, 60, 101, 152
American Magazine, The (periodical), 154
American Pages (magazine), 215, 230–31
"American People in 'One World,' The" (James), 8, 166–78, 218, 224
American Revolution (1775–1783), 81,

105, 106, 133, 145, 167, 169–70, 172, 173, 177, 184, 193, 221
"American Scholar, The" (Emerson), 209
American Slave Revolts (Aptheker), 194, 198
American Worker, The (Romano and Stone [Lee]), 15, 35, 216
Ammunition (newspaper), 159
Amyot, 119
Anarchism, 35, 56
Anderson, Perry, 2–3, 28, 55–56, 73
André (of Haiti), 81
Anti-Dühring (Engels), 60, 66, 74
Appeal to the Colored Citizens of the World (Walker), 191, 192, 193, 195
Aptheker, Herbert, 183, 189–90, 192–94, 196, 197–200, 202, 203, 204, 205, 206–8, 219
Aristotle, 53, 112
Artie Cuts Out (pamphlet), 231
Asia, 6, 119, 161, 164, 175, 183. See also Burma; China; India; Japan; Korea; Malaya; Turkey
At the Rendezvous of Victory (James), 1, 27, 233
Athenians, 119
Atlantic Charter, 159
Attucks, Crispus, 81
Aurelius, Marcus, 142
Australia, 153
Austria, 94, 95
Austro-Marxists, 94
Autographs for Freedom (Griffiths), 203

Babeuf, François-Noël (Gracchus), 120
Baldwin, Stanley, 92
Balzac, Honoré de, 92
Bank of England, 132
Barbusse, Henri, 98
Barnave, Antoine, 80
Barnes, Leonard, 85
Barrett, Tom, 28

239

About Haymarket Books

Haymarket Books is a radical, independent, nonprofit book publisher based in Chicago.

Our mission is to publish books that contribute to struggles for social and economic justice. We strive to make our books a vibrant and organic part of social movements and the education and development of a critical, engaged, international left.

We take inspiration and courage from our namesakes, the Haymarket martyrs, who gave their lives fighting for a better world. Their 1886 struggle for the eight-hour day—which gave us May Day, the international workers' holiday—reminds workers around the world that ordinary people can organize and struggle for their own liberation. These struggles continue today across the globe—struggles against oppression, exploitation, poverty, and war.

Since our founding in 2001, Haymarket Books has published more than five hundred titles. Radically independent, we seek to drive a wedge into the risk-averse world of corporate book publishing. Our authors include Noam Chomsky, Arundhati Roy, Rebecca Solnit, Angela Y. Davis, Howard Zinn, Amy Goodman, Wallace Shawn, Mike Davis, Winona LaDuke, Ilan Pappé, Richard Wolff, Dave Zirin, Keeanga-Yamahtta Taylor, Nick Turse, Dahr Jamail, David Barsamian, Elizabeth Laird, Amira Hass, Mark Steel, Avi Lewis, Naomi Klein, and Neil Davidson. We are also the trade publishers of the acclaimed Historical Materialism Book Series and of Dispatch Books.

Printed in the USA
CPSIA information can be obtained
at www.ICGtesting.com
JSHW022344081023
49670JS00001B/1

9 781608 468645